DAMIAN and MONGOOSE

To Raymond,

In honor of those who protect our country's secrets and bring its traitors to justice.

Danny L. Williams

Damian and Mongoose: How a U.S. Army Counterespionage Agent Infiltrated an International Spy Ring

Published by Wheatmark®

610 East Delano Street, Suite 104, Tucson, Arizona 85705 U.S.A.

www.wheatmark.com

ISBN: 978-1-60494-516-4

LCCN: 2011923132

Dedicated to Shirley,
whose respect, devotion, and understanding
inspired a successful operation and this book.

Table of Contents

DAMIAN and
MONGOOSE

How a U.S. Army Counterespionage Agent
Infiltrated an International Spy Ring

Danny L. Williams

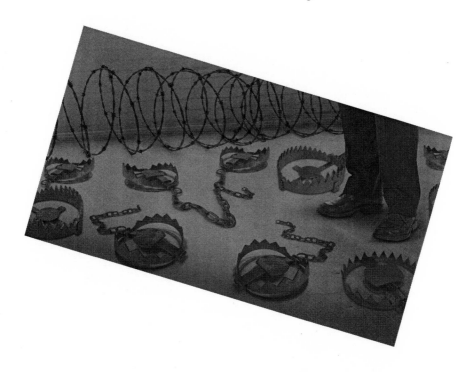

1

DANGEROUS ALLIANCE

"Danny, if I find you're a threat to my family, I'll put a bullet between your eyes. Family is everything."

"I understand that, Clyde. If I were in your position, I would say the same thing—and mean it."

"You would; wouldn't you?" He smiled as he studied me.

"I'd like to think you just came around to visit an old friend, but as soon as I realized I was under investigation, I sat down and thought, *I wonder when Danny will show up.* Are you here on your own, or did they send you?"

"Who the hell are 'they,' Clyde?"

"You're counterintelligence. You tell me." He leaned forward and gave me a hint. "Who got Al Capone?"

"Elliot Ness?"

"The Treasury Department."

"What makes you think you're under investigation by the Treasury Department?"

"Someone told me they investigated my American Express bank account back to forever. Then I got word that my Holland accounts were investigated, then my Swiss accounts."

"I don't see how that's possible. No one can just open your bank accounts."

"Oh, yes they can—if they want to prove I'm evading taxes."

"What did the guy say they were looking for?"

"Not a guy, but I know exactly what they found in my American Express account: two hundred dollars. Then I got a message: 'Your phone is bad.' I also know I'm under surveillance. They don't know I take late walks."

Clyde Conrad had never threatened to kill me before, but I knew he was serious. He had often made it clear in the twelve years we'd been friends and fellow soldiers that he had extracurricular activities he intended to protect, any way necessary, even from a good friend.

Although we had maintained a friendship out of respect for each other's military professionalism and commitment to duty, he had always been more than a little suspicious of me because I didn't share his amoral views and I refused his and other soldiers' offers to join their illegal activities.

While other soldiers were more open with their offers to join their drug dealing, black-marketing, and loan-sharking, Clyde had been more secretive and confined his eventual offer to me to a "chance to make some extra money." He gave no details, at least none I could believe.

I'd remained slightly skeptical and often accused him of half-truths about most of his comments concerning his private life, but I'd never given him cause to make any personal threats during our three years working together in the infantry or my past nine years as a counterintelligence agent. I had made it clear that I didn't give a damn about his or anyone else's illegal affairs.

This situation was different. Now that he seemed so sure he was under investigation, he'd be less likely to believe that I still had no intention of interfering with his private life. His heightened fear of me had become obvious, several hours earlier, as I pulled into his driveway in Bosenheim, Germany.

It was 22 April, 1987, when I found Clyde Conrad and his wife, Gitta, sitting together on a two-foot-tall block fence that encompassed a backyard garden behind their two-story duplex. As I stepped out of my car, Gitta rose and approached me with a big smile, saying, "I don't believe it," as she looked back at Clyde.

He still didn't look up. As Gitta met me with a hug, I watched him slowly put his cigarette out on the ground and take a deep breath.

Gitta repeated to me, "I don't believe it." Then she turned back to Clyde and said, "Guess who? It's Danny."

Glancing back at me, she said, loudly enough for Clyde to hear, "He's going blind in his old age." Her expression suggested she was embarrassed at his taking so long to acknowledge me.

Clyde stood up and started slowly toward us with discomfort written all over his face.

At five feet seven, he had always been slim and in good

3

physical condition. Thirty-nine years old now, with considerable grey hair and an extra thirty pounds, he looked closer to fifty-nine. Avoiding his *I wonder what you're doing here* stare, the kind he'd given me almost every time our paths had crossed, I turned toward a tall teenager standing on their back porch and smiled as I asked Gitta, "That can't be Jeurgen?"

"That's Jeurgen," she answered proudly.

"Not the monster?"

"He was a monster, wasn't he? You wouldn't know him now. He's turned out to be a real sweet guy."

Jeurgen stepped off the porch and joined his dad, who was still walking toward me with his head down. After shaking hands with both of them and reminding Jeurgen who I was, I addressed Clyde.

"I phoned about an hour ago and got no answer. Bad Kreuznach (BK) information gave me your number after Specialist Kane at 8ID (Eighth Infantry Division) Headquarters told me you were retired and gave me directions to Bosenheim. He couldn't find your address, but he remembered the name of your town. I asked a German lady who was walking past the swimming pool on the street beside your house if she knew where the Conrads lived. She told me to ask the people sitting over here behind this house."

Clyde knew I was apologizing for dropping in on them. He clenched his jaw and looked down for a second, analyzing my explanation the way he did with most people, then slowly he lifted his head and said, "We were probably digging in the garden when you called."

Gitta smiled and said, "Let's sit on the front porch and talk a while, then have lunch later."

"I'd love to. Thanks, Gitta"

4

DANGEROUS ALLIANCE

We spent a couple of hours catching up on the five years since we'd seen each other. When Gitta asked what I was doing in Bad Kreuznach, I answered, "I'm assigned to B Company, 527th Military Intelligence Battalion (527th MI) in Stuttgart, but I'm on temporary duty (TDY) to coordinate with units in Rheinland-Pfalz and Hesse concerning my unit's wartime deployment.

"I'm sorry I can't tell you more, but most of it is classified. I was selected for this TDY by the battalion commander of 527th MI, located in K-town (Kaiserslautern), because I'm B Company's new operations NCOIC (noncommissioned officer in charge) and have an infantry background in the BK area, but mostly because I'm in Germany without Shirley. She still teaches school, and she's staying with friends in Sierra Vista, Arizona, until school is out at the end of May.

"I'll be traveling quite a bit, coordinating with units in K-town, BK, Mainz, Frankfurt, Giessen, Baumholder, and A Company, 527th MI, in Holland. BK is right in the middle of all that, and I wanted to spend some time with you guys because I thought Clyde still worked at 8ID. I was happy to hear you lived so close to BK—"

Gitta interrupted me by calling out, "Look who's here," to someone on my right. When I looked, I saw Hanelore, Gitta's oldest daughter, rounding the bushes that covered the front of the house.

Hanelore raised her head as she started up the steps on the side of the porch. She appeared startled, then frowned. As I stood up to greet her, she demanded, "What are you doing here?"

"I'm assigned to Germany again, and since I'm on temporary duty in the area, I thought I'd look you guys up."

She reached the porch and turned to face me. With her eyes narrowed, she asked, "But what are you doing here?"

I felt all eyes on me. I pondered her question for a second, then responded with, "Oh! I'm assigned to B Company, 527th MI, in Stuttgart, but I'm working on their war plan and coordinating with units in this area."

Clyde lowered his head as he listened, but he finally raised it and invited his stepdaughter to sit down and have a beer. From his tone and the set of his jaw, I interpreted his invitation as an order, which she obeyed.

She hadn't changed much. She was about five feet eight inches, in her mid-twenties, very pretty, with a great figure. She was one of those girls Shirley often described as "a tall woman with a long neck, whose hair does all the right things." She said she had a cold and had just come from her doctor, who had prescribed a few days off work.

In response to my queries, she talked about her job as a producer with a German television station. She had studied that field in California during Clyde's assignment there and later followed Clyde and Gitta back to Germany when he was reassigned to 8ID.

I sensed a lingering tenseness in her voice, so I said, "You're still as great looking as ever."

My compliment seemed to relax her, and she started talking about a boyfriend who had cheated on her while she was in school in California. She ended her story with, "He kept a girl in his apartment right over there in front of my parents' house. He'll be sorry when he figures out what he's missing."

Clyde quickly interjected, "I told her to forget it and consider it just meaningless sex." I glanced from Gitta to Hanelore, but neither responded. Clyde continued, "Gitta and I have talked about this before. She asked me what I would do if I found out she had slept with some other guy. I said I would just forget about it. What would you do, Danny?"

I looked at Hanelore again as I answered, "Well, there is more than one way to love someone. Sometimes you just have to let go. Shirley has always said, 'If you cheat on me, you'll find your things on the porch.'"

Hanelore nodded but made no comment. Clyde frowned in disappointment at my answer, so I distracted him by describing the extensive traveling I'd done for the Army the past couple of years to Korea, Japan, Hawaii, Germany, and coast to coast in the States. After several minutes, Clyde interrupted with a comment to Gitta.

"Don't you just love to hear him talk? Danny is the only guy I know who doesn't let his religion keep him from enjoying life."

A lady friend of Gitta's dropped by. Gitta introduced me, then the ladies went into the kitchen, and Gitta started lunch. Clyde asked me to take a walk with him.

He lit a cigarette, then stared at the ground quite a while, deep in thought, as we walked around the soccer field located between his duplex and the apartment complex Hanelore had pointed out. That pensive mood usually signaled he was getting ready to warn me, without being too accusatory, that he still knew how to protect his personal interests. I started the conversation, knowing he would interrupt me when he was ready. He always had.

"Clyde—" I waited to see if he was irritated at my interruption of his thoughts, then I smiled. "You really put me on the spot with that question about what I would do if Shirley cheated on me. You know that was a no-win situation. If I'd said I would just forgive and forget, Gitta would think I was implying I'd want Shirley to just forgive me for the same thing."

"I know that. I like to put you on the spot just to see what you'll say." He looked up and smiled.

"Thanks," I said sarcastically. "I also thought I should support Hanelore's decision to let that guy go."

"She's a dog."

"I hope you're not talking about her looks!"

"She's a dog! You want me to fix you up with her?"

"No! Thanks again, Clyde," I said as a rebuke. I was angry at the implication that he had that kind of power over his stepdaughter.

I changed the subject and asked, "How long have you lived the good life of retirement?"

"About a year." He didn't volunteer any further details, and he became silent again as we continued to walk.

"I looked for your name on the master sergeant (MSG) list," I said sadly. "I was sorry I didn't see it."

"Yeah, some specialist at MILPO (military personnel office) screwed up my record. It didn't even have my picture when it went before the board. When I saw Danny Williams on the list, I said to the guys in G-3 (General Staff, Training/Operations), 'The Army finally promoted someone who actually deserves it.'"

"Thanks. When I didn't see your name, I remembered you once told me you didn't want to get promoted because they would ship you back to the States and you didn't want to leave Germany again."

His eyes widened as he responded, "You got that right! They had me on orders to go to Drill Sergeant School at Fort Binning about two years before my retirement. No matter what I told my assignments branch, they wouldn't change it. I finally told General Partin I didn't want to go. He picked up the phone and called a friend in MILPO and said, 'I have Sergeant First Class Conrad here, and I want you to take him off levy and stabilize his tour here.' Now that's power!"

"General Partin must have been a good friend. Was he commander of 8ID?"

"Yeah. We went out on a terrain walk together when he first got here. He was discussing some preparation with the G-3 for possible enemy approaches. I said, 'General, you might want to look at this terrain map before you make that decision. You can see what would happen to that approach if it rains here.' He kept me by his side for the rest of the walk and told the G-3 later, 'I will not go on a terrain walk unless Sergeant Conrad is there.' He's going places. He'll make Army Chief of Staff."

"Sounds like you made yourself pretty indispensable. By the way, shortly before receiving my orders to Stuttgart, I completed my BS degree—"

Clyde interjected, "I had more than enough hours to get a degree before I retired. I decided all I really needed was the knowledge."

"I'm sure you're right. My original orders were to K-town and my household goods are being shipped there and will have to be redirected. At the last minute, I received new orders to Stuttgart."

"I don't know why you do that, Danny. Don't you just get tired of the incompetence?"

"I guess that's always been the difference between us, Clyde. We're both professionals, we both do our jobs better than anyone wants them done, and we've both had our share of incompetent bosses, but I've always kept on trying to persuade 'em, while you never had much tolerance for them."

"Fuck 'em! It never makes any difference!"

"Yeah, you've always said that. Sometimes I think that too. Take this job, for instance. I could have trained a specialist to do this job while I got started as operations NCO for B Company in Stuttgart. I'm here because the commander of 527th MI Battalion was one of the commanders I worked for while I was at Fort Huachuca, Arizona. He insisted I do this job myself because I always get the job done right.

"The only thing hard about this job is going to be getting all his detachment commanders to provide me with the coordination they've done in this area. I'll bet you they haven't done any."

He listened intently, as if he'd been waiting for a better explanation for my assignment to BK. He pondered a few seconds, then said with contempt, "It's all worthless. There are only so many things you can do for contingency war plans, and everybody knows what they are."

"Probably, but while I'm this close to Idar Oberstein, I may pick up some gemstones. I started collecting gems and jewelry during those trips to Korea in my last assignment."

"I'm sure you can't match Gitta's collection of jewelry," he said with an arrogant tone.

"Oh, I don't doubt that. I have to admit, I may have gone over the limit getting some of them through customs, but I was actually following the advice of a customs officer who told me to stuff them in my pocket instead of mailing them to Shirley."

"You shouldn't get into something like that. There's no money in it."

His tone had changed quickly, and I recognized a sales pitch coming. I attempted to cut him off. "Yeah, I know, and I'm out of it. I don't even know why I did it in the first place."

"I can tell you why. It's because of your religion. It teaches that nothing a man does has any effect on his relation with God." His remark surprised me, but I made no reply. Gitta was calling us for lunch.

After lunch, he took me on a tour through his duplex. He showed me his two Apple computers and the education programs he had devised to help Jeurgen, who attended a German school. I explained that I had a computer just like his two in my room in Stuttgart, as well as some Apple education programs Shirley had used in her classroom. He expressed an interest in the programs.

After the tour, I sat down in his living room to listen to Jeurgen play a few popular songs on his keyboard. He was very talented and was taking lessons from a local music teacher. Clyde changed clothes, then insisted I join him for a walk through Bosenheim.

He quietly smoked another cigarette for several minutes, looking at the ground as we walked along the cobblestone road that led us into the middle of Bosenheim. About two blocks from his back door, without looking up, he finally spoke.

"Danny," he said with a warning in his voice, "I appreciate you coming by and paying us a visit, but you might not want to be around me much while you're here. I've been a bad boy."

"Ask me if I'm surprised. I've always known you lived on the dark side."

"Yeah, but I mean a really bad boy. I have a lot of friends and a lot of connections."

11

He chose his words carefully, haltingly, and his pauses were agonizingly long, but I let him take his time because I had seen from the beginning he was more uneasy than usual about my visit.

"I've put buyers in touch with bank robbers who needed to get rid of some money. I've arranged buyers for stolen art. You read about that theft of some art gallery not long ago?"

"No, I don't think so. I haven't been in country but a few weeks."

"Several artists had placed their collections there to be counted and registered for an art show. The art disappeared before it was registered. I have some of that on my wall right now."

I listened with my usual skepticism as he continued bouncing from one subject to another while we walked. He smoked constantly and kept his eyes focused on the ground, only raising his head slightly to catch my reaction to each revelation.

"I once met with a Swedish lawyer and some of my other contacts. I was there on some other business, but the lawyer was trying to line up a deal to obtain arms for the Middle East. I bowed out of that one."

"Why?"

"I wasn't interested in getting into that sort of thing. I once flushed several liters of strychnine. You know what strychnine is used for?"

"Of course."

"There was enough there to do-in a few thousand people. I know where some vials are stashed to be picked up by terrorists. That's something you might be interested in. I could give you directions." He smiled as he waited for my response.

"How do you know about them, and how do you know they're still there?" I didn't conceal my disbelief.

12

"Because I saw the map, and I know they're still there because they haven't been picked up. You ought to look into that."

"Maybe, Clyde. I'll give it some thought; although, I would have to figure out some alternate source I could attribute the information to before I did something like that."

"Good! I've met with defense ministers of foreign countries."

He interrupted himself because we were entering a *Gasthaus*. As he was opening the door, I had just enough time to ask one question.

"Met with defense ministers for what, Clyde?"

"Various things."

The owners of the Gasthaus, which had one booth, a few tables, and a short bar, were remodeling. They asked us to return later that evening. He took me to another one just around the corner. I declined his offer of a beer because I'd already had two at his house and had taken some cold medicine earlier that morning, but he ignored me and ordered each of us a beer.

I figured Clyde wanted me drinking while he told me more than he had ever told me about his private life, so I drank. I expected him to continue the subject of his meeting with defense ministers of foreign countries, but after our beers were served, he started a new subject.

"I reached a point in life when I made a decision. No matter how hard you try, nothing matters. So I sat down one day and invented a way to make money."

He leaned back in the booth and thought a few seconds, then he seemed to start a background story. "On one of my assignments, I MAPTOEd the entire office. You know what MAPTOE is?"

"Yes. It's the organization on paper of work flow for a unit with a table of organization and equipment. I took the fifth corps (V Corps) course when I was stationed in Mainz."

"Right. I organized everything, designed job books with SOPs (standard operating procedures) for each position in my unit. Anyone who took over a position could just look in their books and find out what their responsibilities were, what points of contact or shortcuts went with the job. I went back to that unit sometime later and asked the guy who took over from me how the books were working out. He said he threw them out during the last inspection because they weren't needed. Can you believe that? What a dick! So I devised a way to make my efforts count for me, a way to make myself some money."

It was clear to me he did not remember having told me that same story about the MAPTOE books, with the same contempt, around 1976, while we worked together in G-3, 8ID. I wondered if he had been on the verge eleven years earlier of telling me that he had invented a way to make money.

It was over a year later that he offered me a chance to make some extra money, but he never explained the details. He seemed to be trying to decide even now how much he wanted to tell me.

"I sat down and figured out what someone would buy. I invented a product, then offered someone a deal to sell it for me."

I chuckled as I reminded him. "Yeah, you offered me a deal once, but I didn't take you up on it."

He gave me a quick glance, studying my expression, then said, "That's immaterial. I had my invented product translated and then sold it to the embassy for one hundred thousand Marks. I did it more than once, but I finally quit because they didn't want to pay enough."

"How the hell could one hundred thousand Marks not be enough?"

"I wanted more."

As we laughed, I reflected on the way he answered my questions without revealing much information. He'd always done that. I'd learned this same technique years before from my cookware sales manager, a good friend who called this way of answering questions direct evasiveness. Clyde was good at it, and he definitely wanted to sell me something, but since he was more con artist than salesman, I knew he would tell me only half-truths.

He made a vague reference to something he called abstract thinking, which centered around the art of analyzing people and their systems until he figured out a way to exploit them. He said these were concepts that set him apart from other people. Still generalizing, he emphasized that the product he had sold the embassy was his own invention based on those abstract concepts.

After a couple of hours and four beers apiece, Clyde stood up. I wasn't sure why he was anxious to leave, but I was glad. I had a splitting headache. Even with food, I usually got a headache after more than two beers. I would have gotten a headache from his cigarette smoke even with no beers. I vowed to remember my Excedrin next time. I could hardly believe it when he took me back to the Gasthaus we had visited earlier. I knew then I was in for one hell of a night.

He never returned to the subject of defense ministers, but after we settled in for more beers at the remodeled Gasthaus, he got to what was really on his mind and issued his threat to kill me if he decided I was part of the investigation he was sure he had

discovered. But there were more surprises yet to come as he saw
to it my glass stayed full.

"You know, Danny," he said with a slight smirk, "I've always
recognized you as one of two people I should fear."

"Well, I've always had the good sense to recognize you as
someone to respect."

"Yeah, I know you like the word 'respect,' but there must be at
least one other person you fear?"

"You're talking about Zolton Szabo."

He smiled, leaned forward, and lowered his voice as he continued. "You remember that time, about ten years ago, you and
Z almost got into it in the field? He ordered you down off the
command track (tracked, armored personnel carrier). I remember
what you said to him.

"You said, 'I don't want any part of you, and I don't think you
want any part of me, but you're going to have to come up here to
find out.' I watched and waited 'til Z left. I knew then you had
sense enough to know who to fear, and so did Z."

"Well, I never liked that little RIFed (reduction in force) captain
much. Is he still around?"

He leaned forward and lowered his voice again as he answered.
"He's a colonel in the GRU (Russian military intelligence). And
that wife of his is a Hungarian agent."

"He's a what?"

"He's a colonel in the GRU!"

"And he's still in the Army?"

"No. He retired before I did. He lives in Austria now. Z did me
some dirt, and I've taken care of him. I took the contract out myself."

"Damn, Clyde. I wish you'd mentioned that little tidbit about Z before we spent all this time together!" I leaned back and glanced around to see that no one else had entered the Gasthaus in case he was right about surveillance. I looked down and asked myself aloud, "What am I doing here?"

"You may be right. That remains to be seen." Then he asked me again, "Were you sent, or did you come on your own?"

"Clyde," I asked, shaking my head, "Why the hell would they send me? The Treasury Department is not going to tell Army CI what they're doing."

"Because of your past association with me."

I lowered my head again and reflected on his statement. "Yes, I'm sure you're right. Someone would be asking me questions even if I hadn't come to see you. Why not just pay the back taxes? How much would you owe?"

"About a million dollars."

"Oh, I see! Well, not only have I come on my own, but frankly, I don't give a damn what you think, and I'm finding a lot of what you've been telling me hard to believe!"

He leaned back and surprised me again with an expectant tone. "Danny, if there was one thing you wanted, one name, what would it be?"

"What kind of name? You mean criminal, terrorist, agent? What?"

"Yeah! Anything!" He had a sparkle in his eye as he waited for my response.

"I can't think of anything I want from you unless you can think of a way to tell me something and give me another plausible source for the information."

"Eva Svensen. S-V-E-N-S-E-N." He looked away as he spelled it, but he watched my reaction out of the corner of his eye.

"Who is Eva Svensen?"

"She's someone who makes sure that the very important in any circles have safe passage between countries."

"What particular circles do you mean?"

"Only the important ones. They show up, give her a signal, and she takes care of them."

"If you have all this information, I don't see your problem. Even the Treasury Department would have to step aside if you let someone know you had this information."

"I can't let myself be questioned. It can never happen. When I realized the government was investigating me, and I knew my friends knew too, I thought about it. I wondered if maybe I could let the government talk to me and just clam up, but I realized that would never work.

"I knew who would get the contract on me, so I met with him and made a deal with him for half. I agreed to make it easy for him if he split the money with me."

"Wait a minute, Clyde! Are you telling me that because you're under investigation, your friends have put a contract out on you?"

"Partly that. That's why I can't be talked to. I know those guys have their ways. Suspicion is one thing, but there is no evidence except what comes out of my mouth. They wouldn't pick me up unless they intended to make me talk.

"My family is the only leverage my friends would have, so I can't take a chance. Family is everything! So I just decided to look the guy up and make a deal to make sure it wouldn't happen when my family was around."

I was becoming even more skeptical than usual, so I asked,

"Why would it be worth half the money to the guy with the contract for you to make it easy for him?"

"Now he knows I know, and I'll be ready for him. But for my family's sake, I will be wherever he wants me, when he wants me."

"And how will you know if he pays the money?"

"It's already deposited, and my lawyers will see to it that my family is taken care of."

"Do you expect me to believe you've given up and are just sitting around waiting to be taken out?"

"Family is everything. You come around in a couple of months, and it will all be over."

"I'm not going to accept that!"

"You've got no choice!"

He became silent for a few seconds, and I tried to decide what I really thought about his revelations.

I wouldn't accept this under any circumstances, Clyde. This doesn't sound like you, unless there are other reasons your friends have put out a contract on you. Or do you really think it's CI investigating you, and you're still so sure I'm part of the investigation you expect me to tell CI that there's no point in arresting you because you would not allow yourself to be taken and you're about to be eliminated anyhow.

Or could you be buying time to skip the country? Damn you, Clyde! That statement about no evidence except what comes out of your mouth could only apply to espionage.

The owner of the Gasthaus walked up to the table, and Clyde introduced us and invited her to sit down. She talked a few minutes about the renovations, then she left.

I was finishing my tenth beer of the day when Clyde suggested we start home. I had never drunk that much beer, but since he wouldn't allow me to have an empty glass and I don't like warm beer, the number quickly mounted.

I welcomed the cool breeze as we walked in the dark along the cobblestone alley toward his house. I was startled when he asked, "What kind of training have you had for self-defense?"

"Actually, I never cared for most of the martial arts training I could get from the Army, so I took some training on my own in hapkido. It's a Korean self-defense system designed to quickly neutralize an attack."

"Show me what you would do if someone tried to take you out."

Now I was wary. He had a very cocky grin on his face as he glanced up at me from his position to my left. I thought, *Whoa, Clyde! Don't do this!* As he turned his face forward, I dropped one step behind him and slightly to my left and stole a quick glance around the area.

I assumed Clyde was right about being under surveillance, and I wondered if we could be seen very well in the dark. I hoped he wouldn't try anything for another few yards, where we would round a corner, which would place us out of plain sight, between a large cathedral on the right and a high stone fence on the left. I remembered it from earlier in the evening.

"I'm serious," he said as a warning. "We're talking about professionals here. You'll never know what hit you."

I was still slightly behind him. He halted abruptly just before we reached the corner, pivoted, and swung his right arm backward, stopping his swing with the edge of his hand on the right side of my neck. I stiffened up and stood still in the dark, hoping we

20

hadn't attracted anyone's attention. I saw no movement in our vicinity.

He removed his arm and said, "Under normal circumstances, that would have finished you. Come on, show me what you would do!"

We continued walking, but I knew he was probably right. Delivered with sufficient follow-through, that blow could have downed me if he'd had a lot less beer. I stole another glance behind me, at the same time expecting him to try again. Just as we rounded the corner, he stopped again and raised his right arm slightly.

I took a quick step forward and placed my right foot next to his and my right shoulder behind his right arm to block his swing. With my thumb and fingers in the shape of a C, I quickly brought my right hand under his right arm and stopped at his windpipe, a tiger's claw strike in hapkido. Then, with a firm grip on his windpipe, I took a step back with my left foot and swung him backward in a quarter-circle against the wall of the cathedral, keeping my left hand behind his head to shield it from the brick wall. Still holding on, I leaned close to his ear and said, "If you knock my hand away, I'm taking part of your throat with me."

I let go of him as quickly as I had grabbed him and said apologetically, "Clyde, let's not talk like this."

At first his eyes widened, but he quickly regained his composure and said, "We'd better get home. Gitta will be worried."

We walked silently for several seconds as we neared his house. Then, I said, "I still can't just stand by and watch a friend let himself be taken out."

He looked up to see where we were and cautioned me, "We'd better stop talking. We're too close to the house."

21

Gitta was on the back porch as we approached, and she looked mad as she said to Clyde, "Why didn't you tell me you were going to stay out all night."

Clyde didn't say anything. I knew he wouldn't. He never argued with anyone in public. I offered an apology. "It was my fault, Gitta. We were catching up on years gone by, and the time just got away from us. I'm really sorry."

"That's okay, but Clyde should have said something!"

Clyde said softly, "Gitta, Danny can't drive tonight."

In a more pleasant tone, she answered, "You can stay in the bedroom in the cellar, Danny. I have the keys right here."

Clyde took the keys from Gitta and showed me to the bedroom. After pointing out the toilet in a large room across the hall, he went upstairs for some aspirin I requested, then he retired for the night.

I spent most of what was left of the night hugging the commode. My headache kept me awake until first light, then I slept until almost noon. I heard Clyde open the door to look in on me sometime that morning, but knowing I was in no shape to get up, I didn't acknowledge him, and he went back upstairs.

When I finally got up, I declined lunch and apologized to Gitta for overstaying my welcome. At the rear of my car, Clyde stopped me with a serious comment.

"Danny, for your own good, this should be the last time you see me. Come around after a couple of months, and it will all be over."

I knew he was capable of giving an order that left no room for doubt. This didn't seem like one of those. I took a chance. "Clyde," I said hesitantly, "I'm not going to find that easy to accept. I don't want to get in your way concerning your plans, but I came here hoping to spend some time with an old friend, and you're telling me this is it. I don't know how I'm going to take that."

He didn't respond, just looked down at the ground. I decided he wasn't insisting, and after offering my itinerary for the next few days, I explained, "Right now, I've got to worry about mixing all that alcohol with the medicine I've been taking for this cold. I'll be lucky if I make it back to my hotel, let alone get any work done today." With that parting comment, I drove away.

I slept all afternoon and night, but early the next morning. I changed to a less expensive hotel about three blocks down the street. It was a nice three-story hotel with a restaurant that included a deck overlooking the Nahe River.

Then, I drove to K-town to pick up gas coupons for the BMW I'd been assigned by B Company. I also picked up all the phone numbers and rosters of military and CI units in the BK area. After returning to my hotel for lunch, I visited A Company's Frankfurt and Mainz counterintelligence detachments.

They were surprised to see me and even more surprised to hear that they and their resident officers (ROs) were to be chopped to B Company during wartime. They were cooperative, but they indicated they needed considerable time to coordinate with their headquarters in Holland and study Battalion's draft war plan, which they hadn't seen yet.

They requested that, in the meantime, I contact their ROs directly and provide each of them any assistance I could in converting and finalizing their war plans and coordinating with local German agencies and United States combat units. I assured them I would.

DAMIAN and MONGOOSE

On Friday, I started direct coordination right away to convince the commanders of those CI elements in central Germany that our battalion commander would rather have good plans than hurried ones. Recognizing their desire for plenty of time to respond, I suggested they take as long as they needed but anticipate a conference at battalion headquarters among the concerned parties within the next couple of months.

The situation seemed perfect for me. It left my schedule completely unstructured and assured me some time to visit with Clyde. I wasn't certain he would even let me visit him again, but I wanted to try.

After coordination with an RO in Baumholder, I ate dinner in a German restaurant there, which I had enjoyed in a previous assignment to Germany, and arrived at my hotel very late on Friday. Late that afternoon, I left all my wartime-planning paperwork in a BK unit's classified safe for the weekend.

I was tired, but I leaned against the headboard and thought over my long conversation with Clyde. I didn't know how much of his story I could believe, especially the part about the contract on his life.

I wasn't sure who he really thought was investigating him, but I knew why he would be expecting me to be a part of that investigation. He probably believed I was responsible for the investigation, assuming I had reported his previous offer to join him in his illegal activities. In fact, I had thought very little about Clyde's offer over the past ten years.

Early the following morning, while unpacking the trunk of my car, I discovered an excuse to visit Clyde again. About 10:30 AM, I tried to call him from a pay phone. When I got no answer, I checked again with the German information operator and found I had previously written down an extra number. When Gitta answered, I apologized again for keeping Clyde out so late on Wednesday night. She accepted my apology and called Clyde to the phone.

"Hello, Danny, he said with no surprise in his voice."

"Clyde," I said apologetically, "I know you didn't expect to hear from me so soon, but I discovered some of Shirley's education computer disks were still in the luggage I brought with me from Stuttgart. I also found a magazine for ordering more educational disks from Apple, and I'd like to show it to you."

"I want to see that."

"How about letting me buy your lunch today?"

"I'll come down to your hotel at 12:00 PM."

He hung up before I could tell him I had changed hotels. A little before twelve, I walked three blocks to my first hotel and stood on the corner. When he arrived and parked his car along the street, I handed him the magazine, saying, "I'm glad if this will be of any help to Jeurgen, but I really just wanted to talk to you about a few things."

"I know that. I don't want to eat; why don't we walk a while." We were standing in the hotel's sidewalk cafe, but the way he took off across the street told me he didn't like staying in one place very long.

He looked the magazine over for some time as we walked, then he said, "I would like to keep this." I described the computer programs on math and English that I had found in my luggage, and he said he already had those programs.

We crossed the bridge behind my hotel to the west side of the Nahe River, then turned north along the trail bordered by

25

forty-foot cliffs on our left and the rushing river on our right. We strolled about two hundred yards before crossing back across the Nahe on another bridge to the hot springs behind the Kurhaus, a large hotel/spa located a long block down the street from my hotel.

It was a fairly clear, mild day, and people were strolling along the bank of the river behind the Kurhaus and through the garden in front. We'd been talking about Jeurgen's education in the German school. Then, as we walked around to the front of the Kurhaus and started down a garden path, I told him there were several things I wanted to discuss with him.

"I spent some time Friday at my battalion headquarters in K-town, and I got no indication that anyone wants to talk to me. That doesn't surprise me, since the government doesn't like to tell the military its business and may never let the military know anything." When he didn't respond, I continued. "Also, I'm sorry you were disappointed in me about the gems I have dealt with."

"I checked into that. I contacted someone who has some jewelry—"

"That's the point I want to make," I interrupted. "Now that I'm in Germany and have lost my contacts, I'm taking your advice and leaving that alone."

"Good! You should." He led me into a tobacco shop and purchased some cigarettes.

As we left the shop, I said, "While I'm at it, I did want to correct something you said on Wednesday. You said you figure I got into the illegal end of gem collecting because of my religion. It was not because of but in spite of it."

"I don't think it's in spite of your religion, Danny. I think

I understand you better than you understand yourself. You remember those Bible lessons on tape you left with me when you left BK? I listened to every one of those. I know what your religion teaches. It teaches that what you do in life doesn't matter. You're still going to heaven when you die."

I laughed. I had completely forgotten that Clyde had asked me to leave him a set of those tapes in 1978, and I was surprised that he had listened to them but certainly not surprised that he had distorted what he heard.

"Clyde, while what you say is true, I'd be more inclined to consider my decisions a weakness on my part. It was something I chose to do because I wanted to."

He continued his previous subject, completely ignoring my earlier refusal. "I talked to a woman about some jewelry she has. She said she would sell one hundred seventy thousand Marks worth of Cartier jewelry for ten thousand Marks."

"I've decided I'm not going to get started in that again."

"I'm glad to hear that."

"Besides, I've decided what I want to do to occupy my mind while I wait for the local CI Commanders to catch up. I want to help you think of a solution to your problems."

"Why?" His head snapped toward me with his usual suspicion but with a lot more anger than I'd seen before, so I raised my eyebrows and looked straight ahead. I hoped an answer would come to me.

After a few seconds, I said, "Because I believe in heroes."

That startled him, and he asked, "What's your definition of a hero?"

Instead of answering, I quickly addressed another issue because

27

I didn't have a definition. "There was another thing I wanted to talk to you about. If you're right about an investigation and surveillance, the government might not ever approach me. It would be better for me if they did. If they don't, it could mean they are investigating me too. If they do question me, what do I say?"

"Say nothing!"

"Okay, so all we've done is talk about old times, shoot the bull, and talk about getting some educational computer programs for Jeurgen, right?" I could see from his expression that wasn't right, that he had meant just clam up. He made his disappointment in my response obvious as he answered.

"Yes. Danny?" He had not intended to agree with me, so he assumed a more persuasive tone. "Don't you have any skeletons in the closet?"

"Clyde, all my skeletons have been out and looked at. Actually, they were only suspicions that proved untrue, but that didn't make any difference. There are still people who believe them even now. An investigation can do only as much harm to me as I will allow it by caring what people think."

"You think just because you're innocent that will be enough?"

"I have to believe that."

"You know, maybe just the fact that you believe that will actually save you."

I didn't understand his statement entirely, but I had finally figured out an answer to his earlier question. "Let me tell you my definition of a hero. A hero is someone who bucks all the odds and wins."

I waited while he thought that over for a few seconds, hoping he would accept that as the reason I wanted to keep coming back and keep asking questions, trying to get a better feel for his situation in hopes of helping my friend figure out a way to extricate himself from his plight with his associates. After a long pause, he responded with some admiration.

"That's not a bad definition."

"I have to ask you one more question—on the subject of skeletons in the closet. Please don't take this wrong, but I have to protect myself. Did you ever mention to anyone that you once made an offer to me to get involved in one of your deals?"

"Absolutely not! I have always made it a point never to let any of my contacts meet each other."

"Not even inadvertently? I know you realize there has to be a reason if, in fact, you are being investigated. Maybe these so-called friends of yours have done some talking."

"I've learned that when I get into trouble, it's usually because of mistakes I make myself."

"Is that really the way you have it figured?"

"Yes. Speaking of friendship, I thought about that. I wondered about you not reporting that, and I figured it's a matter of survival!"

He held his head back, narrowed his eyes, and glared a warning. I knew he was implying, *I mean your survival in the future as well.*

His threat was obvious, and I made my recognition of it obvious. I'd always known he was ruthless, and I respected that enough that I didn't take his warning lightly. I also knew he appreciated that kind of respect.

"I don't know exactly why it never occurred to me to report your proposal. I admit I didn't believe most of what you were telling me back then, but you could be right about survival being the reason, although I did consider us friends."

DAMIAN and MONGOOSE

"Let me give you my definition of a friend. When a friend calls and says, 'I need you,' you come! That's the bottom line."

"I've always believed that too. I have another rule: Never interfere with a friend's private life unless he chooses to involve you. I do have a hard time with that, but I try. Another thing I wanted to talk to you about is the question you asked me about what I would want if I could get it from you."

"Yeah!" He had a smirk on his face and that *I've got you now* gleam in his eye again. I proceeded cautiously.

"I still can't think of anything I want personally, and I can't think of another source I could use to explain my knowledge, but as I thought over your question, I concluded that the one thing commanders want to know most these days is the immediate threat to their organizations. They want to know about terrorists. I don't know what you know, and I don't know if I could use it, but you asked, and that's all I could think of."

He stroked his chin as he thought how to answer my request, finally asking, with considerable surprise in his voice, "Is that what you want to know?"

"That's been the primary focus of most of the commanders I've worked for since the Red Army Faction bombed my CI field office while I was in Giessen. But, like I've already told you, the problem I face is having to come up with a plausible source for any information you give me. Don't you have any enemies?"

"I thought of that," he said with a grin. "I really did. I thought of one guy that did me some dirt. I talked to some friends about what to do to him so he would go slowly. You know what they said? Sugar water! You put it into a syringe and shoot it into the spine and it causes the fluid to expand and crush the vertebrae. Isn't that a great way for someone to get it? With pain?"

He obviously didn't want to use a name, but I was sure he'd already forgotten he'd named Szabo as someone who did him some dirt. Or was this yet another enemy? I wasn't sure when I said, "So make that guy the source."

"I thought about that, but I decided we had a personal argument to settle, and it didn't have anything to do with business."

"So why give me any names? Why Eva Svensen?"

"She deserves it. You want a source? Try Sable. I can't remember her last name. Maybe I'll think of it. She's a sharp Swedish lawyer. There aren't likely to be any other Sables listed among the lawyers of Sweden."

"That's fine, but why would she be a source for names of terrorists?"

"For money. Olafsen! That's her name. She might be willing to give up some names."

"Where am I supposed to have gotten her name?"

"Wait two months and it won't matter."

His answer made me wonder. *Damn, Clyde! I'm beginning to almost believe this contract business.* Then I asked, "What about Szabo as an alternate source"?

"Don't worry about Szabo. That's taken care of. He gets his right after I get mine. Otherwise, I would be in a bad position."

A thought came to me: *Are you saying Z knows things about you that would put your family in danger when you're gone? Does that mean your associates are the same as GRU, Colonel Szabo's?*

"What about his wife in Austria?"

31

Clyde jerked his head toward me as he narrowed his eyes. He was angry again.

Whoa! That's the same look you gave me when you asked why I wanted to help you. You don't remember telling me about her, do you? Now you figure I know that from somewhere else. "You said Z lives in Austria. I thought he had divorced his wife when I was still in BK, so I assumed he has another one in Austria."

"Oh. The girl in Austria is okay. His wife is bad business. Z has a home in Austria, and he has a villa in Spain, next door to that actor."

"What actor?"

"That German actor"

He mumbled a name. I didn't understand it, but he was looking around like he didn't want to continue that subject, so I didn't ask him to repeat it. We had reached the hotel where we had started. He suggested we have some coffee at their outside café, then he took a seat with his back to the wall, with a clear view of the street and the rest of the tables. I was grateful he hadn't ordered beer. After the waitress brought coffee, he started explaining what he would do if he were in my profession.

"If I was in your position, Danny, I would design a decision matrix. All you have to do is make a list of the soldiers in your area who have a passport. If they don't have a passport, eliminate them. Narrow that down to the ones who travel to neutral or East-block countries. Find out which ones rent cars to travel, which ones have watches. Choose your own discriminators. There are lots more. And if they don't have a watch, eliminate them. If you do this in your own area, you will know who is working either as an agent or a courier."

"That sounds reasonable. How do you know that?"

"It's a matter of logic based on known MO or plausible MO." He ended the subject abruptly and motioned for the waitress, whom I paid.

We had finished our coffee rather quickly, and Clyde didn't want to stay there any longer. We started walking again the same route as before, but he seemed a little agitated, as if he had said more than he intended.

I wondered if his decision matrix could be connected to the invented product he had sold some embassy. This was beginning to sound more like espionage by the minute, but because he was uncomfortable, I decided to change the subject. I asked him to explain how his family could possibly not know he was in trouble.

"Being aware that I'm in trouble and knowing the details are two different things. For a couple of months, I've been avoiding the phone. I tell Gitta to say I'm not home. I know she is aware that something is wrong, but that's all she knows."

By his tone, I knew that subject was closed. So I dropped it, lowered my head, and said, "I know you want me to believe how serious this situation is, and I'm going to treat it that way, but I only believe less than half of anything you tell me." He started to interrupt me, but I quickly continued," Because you like to jack people around."

His serious expression changed, and he smiled when he replied, "I love to do that! I do! I used to think that knowledge was power, but I've come to appreciate the fact that too much knowledge can get you in trouble. It's the fact that I have so much knowledge that makes me a threat to my friends, and that's why I can't be talked to."

"I know you've already described yourself as rotten—"

"I am," he interjected.

33

"And I don't doubt that, but let me ask you something. Do you draw any lines as far as what you will do for money?"

"Draw any lines? Funny you should put it that way. Once, as we looked at the Berlin wall, Jeurgen said, 'So those are the bad guys.' I told him, 'You shouldn't call them the bad guys, son. They are different; we are different, not right or wrong. They are just different.'"

"Didn't you make a choice?"

"What do you mean?"

"Didn't you make a choice as to what political system you wanted to rear your son in?"

"Circumstances chose that for me."

So that's it, Clyde? You don't draw any lines because there is no right or wrong? You're apolitical as well as amoral? Is this your way of saying that your activities have included espionage?

"Danny—" His eyes rolled upward as he tried to decide what he was willing to tell me. "I sat down and took excerpts from unclassified sources. And along with my decision matrix, I put together a letter. I had someone translate it into a language I've never been able to master. Then I had that person approach someone and ask one hundred thousand Marks for it. They paid it, and I got fifty thousand and the other guy got fifty thousand."

He was talking as if either he didn't remember telling me about the invented product he had sold the embassy or it wasn't the same scheme. I was convinced, though, that his insistence his sources were unclassified most likely meant they were classified. Although doubtful that he would tell me the truth, I asked, "Who in the world would want to pay one hundred thousand Marks for unclassified information?"

"Bonn."

I wanted to ask whether "Bonn" referred to the German government or the American Embassy there, but he screwed up his face as if he might have revealed too much already, so I asked, "For example?"

He answered quickly. "For example, if you watch the guard at any East-block border crossing, you will see a guard in a different uniform come out and check certain people's passports. When you see that guard come out, you know that guy he checked is working. And if you check to see who crosses a neutral border at one crossing and then a few hours later returns through another crossing about one hundred kilometers away, you know who your couriers are."

The details suggested this was more than mere speculation. It was certainly more than I expected him to reveal, so I tried a backdoor approach to identify Bonn.

"Clyde, the Germans already know that."

His response startled me. "That's classified, Danny. Don't tell me anything classified."

"I'm not going to tell you anything classified. I was going to say, when I was stationed in Giessen, we made certain observations along the Czech and East German borders, and occasionally the Germans told us to leave it alone; they were aware of it. So why would anyone want to pay you for what they can see for themselves? When did they buy this stuff?"

He looked down at the ground a few seconds, then said, "Six months ago."

I doubt that. You waited too long to answer. Was that because you don't want me to know the time or because I have the government wrong and you don't want to correct me?

"That's what I mean, Clyde. Years ago they made it clear they watch these same things. So why would someone pay you for it six months ago?"

"Confirmation!"

"Well that's certainly plausible. Then what did you do, Clyde?"

"We did it again."

That parallels the story about the invented product you sold the embassy. But which embassy? You wouldn't call German a language you've never been able to master, but why would you use a foreign language with the American Embassy?

We were nearing Clyde's car, and he had to be getting home. I reminded him I would be doing a lot of traveling and would probably make a trip to A Company headquarters in Holland.

In his car, he hung the Apple magazine out his window and pointed to a couple of educational programs he'd like me to order for him. I said I'd get Shirley to order them and telephone him when the programs arrived.

"Or maybe I'll mail them." As he was driving away, I called after him, "I haven't decided which, but I don't think I'm ready to give up on you."

He didn't respond, but I already knew I had no choice. In the last few days, my best friend in the Army had made our destinies inseparable.

I telephoned Shirley in Arizona, and we talked about Clyde's retirement, his family and home in Bosenheim, and Jeurgen's attendance at a German school. I arranged for her to order the educational CDs Clyde wanted and mail them to me at my hotel.

The next morning, I drove south on Mannheimer Strasse to the edge of BK, then east along a heavily wooded country road about a mile to Alzey. After driving through the ancient arch, I turned left down a side street and parked. I walked a couple of blocks back to the Alzey Museum I had passed and climbed the wide stairs to the front door, which I found locked.

While I read the schedule on the wall, an American walked up beside me. We discovered together that the museum wouldn't open for another hour. He left, and I finished reading some of the history of Alzey before walking to a Gasthaus across the parking lot in front of the museum.

Upon entering, I observed one patron at the bar, one couple at a table, and the American sitting alone at a booth by the windows. I approached his booth, and he asked me to join him for a beer. As soon as the waitress left with our order, he started a conversation.

"Did you meet with your friend?"

"Yes. I did."

"Do you have anything significant to report?"

"I have roughly fourteen hours of significant information to report."

He was startled and a bit annoyed when he said, "After we finish our beers, I will leave. You wait five minutes, then meet me in room six in the hotel on the road coming into Alzey. It's on the left leaving town just after the arch."

I followed his instructions and joined counterespionage agent, Grant Poster, from USAI, in his hotel room. I knew USAI was actually a misnomer used by members of the section known as FCA (Foreign Counterintelligence Activity), formerly SOD (Special Operations Division), under the command of INSCOM (Intelligence and Security Command).

DAMIAN and MONGOOSE

USAI was INSCOM. I assumed the acronym was intended to stand for U.S. Army Intelligence and was used to maintain a semblance of anonymity. We both took seats by the window across from the door.

Grant was slightly shorter than my six feet and at least fifteen pounds heavier than my one hundred seventy-five. His brown hair was long, and he was dressed as he had been the only other time I'd met him. He wore the baggy slacks and short jacket typical of an agent on a surveillance team in Germany.

I began by stating that I had met with Clyde twice and would try to distinguish his comments during the first meeting from those made at the second meeting when that would make sense. I told him Clyde often repeated himself, was very careful choosing his words, and was purposely ambiguous.

"I don't know how long it will take for me to give you all the information I have, but so that I don't forget to tell you something, I'd like to start from the beginning and tell the story chronologically. That's the only way I can remember it all. If you'd like, I can give you a brief outline of the main topics to let you know what to expect."

He thought that over before responding, "That might be a good idea."

My intention, after he had the outline, was to relay my conversations with Clyde verbatim when possible. I wanted Grant to have some understanding of the psychology Clyde and I had used.

"Clyde told me he has a number of contacts. To include bank-robbers, he helped launder their stolen money. He knows people who stole some art from a gallery, which he helped sell and some of which he has. He knows a lady with Cartier jewelry worth several thousand Marks, which she would be willing to sell cheap.

"He knows he is under investigation, he says by the Treasury Department. He knows he is under surveillance and his phone is tapped. He was expecting me to show up.

"He gave me a couple of names of lawyers who are involved with terrorists and other criminals. He said retired SFC Zolton Szabo, who was our NCOIC of G-3 Training, 8ID, when Clyde and I worked there, is a colonel in the GRU and his wife is a Hungarian agent—"

"Wait a minute!" Grant had stood and was walking toward me, his eyes flashing, slightly in shock. He almost stumbled over the corner of the bed as he rounded it and pointed his finger at me. "Sit right there and get your thoughts together. I'll be with you in a few minutes."

He hesitated a second as if he wasn't sure he wanted me in the room, then he hurried to his telephone. I didn't hear much of the conversation except his reference to "source twenty-seven," which I assumed was the identity they had given me. He returned to his seat, and he wasn't smiling when he ordered me, "Start from the beginning, Danny."

As I progressed through the story, I became very frustrated with interruptions like, "Were those his exact words?" I would explain that in some cases I was putting together bits of information Clyde had given in fragmented statements during the two meetings. I assured him I would identify actual quotes.

I did that, but it didn't help. He continued to ask for additional information about Clyde's friends and my previous knowledge of his friends, descriptions of personal items in Clyde's house, and a description of Hanelore's car. The little-to-no information I could provide on those subjects threw me out of sequence. When I finished, I wasn't sure I had remembered to tell him everything.

Grant said he would type a statement from his notes, then let me correct and swear to it later. Then he asked me a question I was expecting. "Danny, why did you decide to call Clyde and meet him a second time?"

"Well, for one thing, I was told when to meet with you, whether I had met with Clyde or not. I was not told how many times to meet with him. For another thing, nothing he told me was time sensitive, requiring me to move our meeting time.

"I was also afraid to wait too long before seeing him again after he had warned me not to come around. I didn't believe he really meant it, but I needed to be able to tell you if he was going to let me. As it turns out, he is expecting me to call him again."

Without responding to my answer, he quickly stated, "I will arrange a time for our next meeting. It may be some time. In the mean time, I don't want you to call him or initiate another meeting with him until I talk with you. If he calls you, stall him. Is there something you can be doing 'til I get back to you?"

"Certainly. He won't expect a call from me until the mail arrives from Shirley. That could take a week or more. I'll be doing a lot of traveling to 527th MI detachments and resident offices. I also need to return to Stuttgart to look at some apartments I've located. I have to decide on one before Shirley arrives in a month or so."

"That's great. You've really done good, Danny. I'm sure you know that."

"I hope so." I was expecting a patronizing expression from him, but I thought I saw a genuine sense of satisfaction and excitement

40

in his eyes. Still, I was concerned Grant's opinion of me would be influenced by our superiors who had already demonstrated their lack of confidence in my counterespionage investigative ability.

They considered me a controlled source rather than an undercover CI agent. I knew my relationship with them was going to be at least as perilous as my relationship with Clyde.

On my return to my hotel, I tried to anticipate the pitfalls inherent in working for superiors who considered me too close a friend to their suspect and who suspected I might be as guilty as he. I started thinking about the circumstances the past several months that had brought me into this operation.

2

DESTINY

In mid-1986, I received a telephone call at my operation security desk from Lane Romski, with U.S. Army Intelligence (USAI), who arranged to interview me at the CI field office on Fort Huachuca concerning someone I once worked with. My boss had overheard his secretary announce Romski's name to me, and in his office after the call, he informed me that he knew Romski worked for FCA (Foreign Counterintelligence Activity).

At the CI field office, on post, I gave Romski my identification. While he looked it over, I analyzed him. He was dressed in civilian clothes, but I gave him the respect of a superior. Whether he was an intelligence officer, warrant officer, NCO, or civilian, his title would be mister because he was intelligence but not in uniform.

In conversations in the military, statements or questions are often prefaced by a title. The custom is used to recognize authority as well as to command it. A superior can address the last name, without the title, and a subordinate only the title, as in Sir or Captain. Even if the right to use first names in private has been earned, the courtesy of addressing that name before a comment or question is often still extended.

Romski was at least an inch taller than I and fairly thin. He had one of those boyish haircuts, purposely too long to appear military. I'd met a few agents from his unit. Like them, he was self assured, courteous, and cocky. He didn't waste any time.

"Master Sergeant Williams, do you know Clyde Conrad?"

"Clyde Conrad?"

"Didn't you work with Sergeant Conrad at eight infantry division in Germany?"

"Of course. It just never occurred to me that CI would have any interest in Clyde Conrad."

If Romski realized I had already assumed this was an espionage investigation instead of a routine background investigation, he gave no indication and simply continued the interview. "What can you tell me about Clyde Conrad, Sergeant Williams?"

"Probably just about anything you want to know."

Romski's head snapped forward, and he looked me in the eyes. Until then, he had been turned a little sideways, looking at his notes and asking questions like a robot, clearly not expecting to learn much. As his eyes narrowed, he seemed skeptical.

That didn't surprise me. If he had been interviewing people about Clyde Conrad's personal life, I suspected he wasn't learning much. The Clyde I knew was usually a very private person, but I figured Romski thought he knew something that suggested

Clyde's involvement in espionage or he wouldn't be there. I reflected on the implications. *Damn, Clyde! You've brought this on yourself with those shady schemes of yours.*

I tried to characterize my knowledge of Clyde so Romski could focus on what he was most interested in pursuing. I hoped to at least provide another perspective from which he might view Clyde's activities.

"Clyde Conrad is probably the closest friend I have in the Army. My wife and I are personal friends of his wife and children. I consider him the most professional soldier I know. I also consider him the most loyal. I've always liked Clyde Conrad, although I haven't always approved of him."

"What do you mean by that, Sergeant Williams?"

"Well, actually, there were a number of things over the years I've known Clyde that led me to believe he was engaged in some sort of illegal activity, although I don't know for a fact that he was. I assure you, I never suspected anything of any CI interest."

"When was the last time you were in contact with Clyde Conrad?"

There was a slight panic in his voice. I had to think a few seconds, but I knew my answer might raise more suspicion. I finally figured out how long ago it had been. "I last saw Clyde about four years ago, around 1982, while I was stationed in Giessen, Germany."

"Have you corresponded with him since then, by phone or by mail?"

"No, Sir."

"If you're such good friends, why haven't you kept in touch?"

Now you're in your interrogator mode. I tried to hide my indignation that he was impugning my integrity, but it still showed when I launched into my answer.

DESTINY

"Let me put it this way, Mr. Romski: Clyde and I have a very strong respect for each other as professional soldiers, and we've worked very well together. Our friendship has never depended on keeping in touch by mail or by phone for chitchat. Every time we've found ourselves in the same area, we've just started where we left off. We enjoy each other's company, sharing our military experiences."

He had settled down some when he asked his next question. "What was the occasion in 1982 when you saw him last?"

"He came up from Bad Kreuznach to my quarters in Giessen to collect some things of his that I had agreed to ship for him with my household goods when I left Monterey, California, in 1980." *Whoa! There's that panic in your eyes again. I'd better explain that.*

"When I was leaving my intermediate Polish language course for Giessen, Clyde still had a few months left in his basic German course in Monterey. He knew he was going to be over his weight allowance, and I wasn't, so I volunteered to ship some of his things back to Germany with me and hold them until he got back to Bad Kreuznach, where his next assignment was going to be."

"What kind of things?" His eyebrows were still raised.

"Mostly clothes, heavy coats and jackets, and several of Gitta's fur coats. There were also several of Jeurgen's toys."

"You call her Gitta?" He said that without looking at me, as if he had detected a discrepancy in my claim to know Clyde well.

"I've always called her Gitta. That's what Clyde calls her. In fact, that's what she calls herself. I'm not sure of the spelling of her name, nor the pronunciation, but I've seen it written somewhere. I think it's Brigit."

Romski appeared surprised that I actually knew her German

name. He narrowed his eyes and continued as if he hadn't been listening to my previous explanation. "Where was he stationed when you made this arrangement?"

"At the time I left Monterey in early 1980, he was assigned to the Defense Language Institute at the Presidio of Monterey and living at Fort Ord. He had been assigned to the only infantry unit at Fort Ord about a year before, when I first learned he was in the States."

"How did you know he was at Fort Ord?"

"Actually, I found out by accident. My wife and I stopped at the Fort Ord gas station and saw Clyde filling up his van on the other side of the pump. He had his whole family with him. They were going on a picnic. They had only been there a few weeks and were living on post. We exchanged phone numbers and addresses. Some time later I called him, and my wife and I went to their quarters for a visit."

If you keep interrogating me at every sentence, Romski, by the time I get back to the shady side of Clyde, you'll think I've been avoiding telling you.

"Mr. Romski, may I make a suggestion? It will probably take all afternoon to tell you everything I know about Clyde Conrad. Why don't I tell you some of the things I know that have led me to suspect he might be into something illegal? Judge for yourself. Then, you can tell me any other areas you're interested in, and I'll give you everything I know."

"Okay. Why don't you do that."

"In approximately 1977, while Clyde and I were on an 8ID FTX (field training exercise), Clyde offered me a chance to make some extra money by carrying briefcases full of money across German borders to deposit in different foreign bank accounts."

DESTINY

Romski slammed his chair down, leaned forward, and asked, with his eyes wide, "How much money was he talking about?"

"If you mean in the briefcase, he didn't say. If you mean how much I was going to make, he said three thousand dollars a month."

Romski seemed stunned and just sat there staring at me. An involuntary thought popped into my head. *Are you going to let me explain, Mr. Romski, or are you going to read me my rights?*

Romski settled down in his chair. I was sure he was going to tell me to continue. Instead, he softened his tone for his next question. That tone and his knowing expression revealed that he expected an affirmative answer, when he asked, "Did you take him up on his offer?"

I tried to answer in a manner that would convince Romski I was being completely candid. I launched into the story nonstop.

"No, I did not. As a matter of fact, he didn't actually make me an offer. What he said was, 'Danny, are you basically an honest person?' To which I replied, 'Yes, Clyde, I am basically an honest person, but you know that. Why do you ask?' He said, 'I thought so. I was just going to make you an offer, but it doesn't matter.' I said, 'I'm not interested in any of your shady deals. I've always suspected you were into some, but if I'd said I wasn't an honest person, what would you have offered me?'

"I really expected him, if he even answered that, to give me some cock-and-bull story. Then, I would challenge him and maybe learn something from his expressions. I was curious.

"Clyde hesitated for some time before asking me, 'You and your wife travel a lot, don't you?' I said, 'I guess so. We've seen a lot of Europe.' Then he said, 'So, you wouldn't have any trouble carrying something across the border?' I asked, 'Like what, and across what borders?' He said, 'Country borders, and like a briefcase full of money.' I asked, 'For what purpose?' He said, 'To put in various bank accounts.' I asked, 'Whose bank accounts?' He said, 'Mine, and you might have to open some bank accounts of your own.'

"Oh, and he said I might have to carry some merchandise across the border as well, but he never explained what kind of merchandise."

Romski interrupted. "Did he say how much money?"

You've already asked me that. "No, actually, I asked him how much money and where it would come from. Then he told me I couldn't ask any questions. I laughed because I was sure he was cooking that story up just to put me off."

"Did he say what countries?"

"No, Sir."

"What else did he say?"

"Well, I asked him something like, 'Just out of curiosity, how much would I make on this little scheme?' He said, 'Three thousand dollars a month.' And—"

"Were those his exact words?"

"Mr. Romski, I can't swear he didn't say, 'around three thousand a month,' but I laughed at him, and he just smiled."

"What do you think it was?"

"Well, actually, Clyde asked me that. I kept asking him, but he just said, 'You're very smart. What do you think it is?'

"I thought about some things I had learned from him over the previous year and a half. I remembered he had told me that his wife's family was in manufacturing. I had heard of firms who sold their surplus merchandise retail when they had only a wholesale license. I suggested they would have to hide that money in foreign banks."

"Okay, that's what you thought then. What do you think now?"

"I think the same thing. Espionage never entered my mind. Even though I can see how this may sound like a classic pitch, I still don't believe that's what it was.

"I offered Clyde a couple of other suggestions. I'd heard about guys who bought whole train carloads of unclaimed freight and didn't claim all the income when they sold it. I also knew he had an apartment on the side that he might be using the way a guy I knew in Mainz had. He might be renting it out to soldiers to take their girlfriends for the night."

"He had an apartment on the side? Where?"

"I don't know where. In fact, I don't know for sure that he had an apartment. One day he took me out to one of the suburbs of BK. I don't remember the name. He said he was meeting a German real estate lady who was going to show him a house he was thinking of buying.

"When she didn't show up, I asked him where he had met her. He said she had rented him an apartment he kept on the side. I asked him why he kept an apartment on the side, and he said, 'Every married guy keeps an apartment on the side. You never know when you might need it.'

"But, during this incident in the field, I wasn't learning much that I could believe, so I finally said, 'Clyde, just tell me what you're into.' He said, 'It isn't drugs and it's nothing against the United States.' That was the end of the conversation.

"I took his last statement to mean he wasn't black-marketing

American goods. We never talked about it again, except one time when he invited me to lunch and I said, 'Don't bother trying to con me into your illegal schemes.'"

"Why didn't you—? Obviously you never reported it, Sergeant Williams, but other than the fact he was your friend, why didn't you report it?"

So, there it is. Make sure you build a case against me for failure to report. Well, you asked, damn it, but you probably won't accept it.

"In the first place, there was nothing to report, except statements he could deny. In the second place, there was no one who wanted to hear it. Most everyone around me in the military was into drugs, black-market activity, loan sharking, pimping, and gang-banging, both black gangs and white gangs, in the field and in garrison. The CI and the CID (Criminal Intelligence Division) agents I knew spent most of their off duty time in high-stakes poker games and as dealers at the military clubs on Monte Carlo nights."

Mr. Romski didn't seem impressed, and although I hadn't given much thought to my reason for not reporting Clyde's offer until he asked, I was thinking now. Actually, my whole military career up to that point was the reason I didn't report the incident. I knew he wouldn't want to hear all that, but I couldn't keep it from flashing through my mind.

I enlisted in the Army in April of 1973, expecting to be sent to Viet Nam, but the war was over and the troops were being returned by the time I finished basic and advanced infantry training at Fort Polk, Louisiana. I was sent to Frankfurt, Germany, then to Mainz, where I was assigned to B Company, Second Battalion, Twenty

DESTINY

Eighth Infantry, (2/28th), a combat company consisting mostly of returning Viet Nam veterans.

I expected a highly structured atmosphere of discipline and esprit de corps and a code of ethics like I had experienced in the Corps of Cadets at Texas A&M College. I'd seen a little of that in basic training. What I found instead, in 2/28th, at Lee Barracks, well named, "The Animal Farm," was a combination of all the garbage I had lived through from age nine to fourteen.

I'd been reared in Houston in a government project where I fought gangs, a foster-home where I fought an arrogant foster-brother and his friends, and a welfare agency where I fought everyone. I fought physical battles not only to protect myself and my younger siblings, but often just to avoid being sucked into criminal activity.

With gangs, I learned to run when possible and, when cornered, to fight the leader and leave him with the message that if his gang didn't mess with me or my family, I wouldn't mess with him. I stood up to my first foster-brother when I had to, but because I always won, I often hid out at a neighbor's home to avoid the ridicule from my foster-mother. After fulfilling my promise to my caseworker that I'd try it for one year, I ran away from that foster-home.

I spent four years at the welfare agency, where I minded my own business, worked hard to succeed at everything available to me, tried to stay out of trouble, and never backed down when I had to fight, even when I didn't win. At my second foster-home, at age fourteen, I figured out what my new family wanted from me and adjusted to it.

Now, here I was at age thirty-three, having to fall back on all those earlier defense mechanisms on my first assignment in the Army. Fortunately, I had also learned a few nonphysical, defensive skills, which included the ability to read people. I quickly learned that skill needed some improvement.

A few months after my assignment to 2/28th, I was sitting at my typewriter in the company training room. I hadn't noticed the new Training NCO close the door of our small office and stand in front of my desk until he made an announcement.

"Williams, there's something you should know."

Sergeant (SGT) Chan's statement surprised me. He seldom spoke to me, and then only to give me orders, but this time his tone sounded unusually friendly. I looked up to see him pacing as he continued.

"I don't know why I'm telling you. I'm not sure about you myself, but there's a contract out on you."

I was dismayed, and I couldn't avoid the image that suddenly flashed through my mind of a B Company soldier I'd learned about earlier, lying in his bunk, near dead, with a gash in his head from an intrenching shovel. That image gave way to anger at the emotional pain Shirley would suffer if anyone even tried something like that with me, whether they were successful or not.

My anger quickly turned inward at my realization that I had failed to live up to a basic Sun Tsu precept to know your enemy. I didn't even know if Chan was my enemy. I wondered about that. *Is this a friendly warning or are you just delivering the message to get my reaction?*

Chan continued. "I don't know what you can do about it, Williams, but I thought you should know. You have the first sergeant to blame for this. Your first day in the company, after you had left his desk and he finished reading your file, he said, 'This son-of-a-bitch is a captain or better and CID or I'll eat my hat.' Every squad leader in the company was in the orderly room and heard that.'" Chan hesitated a few seconds then asked, "What are you going to do about it?"

"Well, I'm going to do what I always do, Sergeant Chan: my job. Right now, I'm going to finish typing this week's training schedule and get it run off at Battalion before the deadline. After that, I have several lesson plans to research and type for squad leaders. I'm sure you're right though; there isn't much else I can do about it."

He looked at his watch then responded, "True. I'm gone for the afternoon, Williams. I'm taking my family to a doctor's appointment. I'll be here in the morning."

As he walked out the door, I wondered if he was on his way to report my reaction. I wasn't sure about him either, but I was sure what I was going to do about his warning. I leaned back in my chair and said a short prayer.

I thanked my Heavenly Father for His promise to make even my enemies to be at peace with me. I asked for wisdom in dealing with this threat and the strength to wait for Him to handle the problem instead of making it a personal challenge, as was my inclination. I thanked Him for my sense of destiny and my confidence that He had led me to an infantry company of soldiers fully capable of teaching me the soldier skills and military leadership I had joined the Army to learn.

I finished the training schedule, walked to the motor pool where the rest of B Company was preparing for our next FTX and secured the commander's signature on the schedule. I left the motor pool and started the long trek to Battalion headquarters to run off copies for the company first sergeant and the platoon sergeants.

Walking along the road that encircled the parade field, I started thinking of ways I could defend myself from someone sneaking up on me at night. An experience from early childhood popped into my head. I was nine and living in a government project.

My mother was attending school to become a hair stylist and had hired the girl next door to sit with me, my brother, and two younger sisters. An hour after Mother left, the girl told me we were on our own, then she went home. I started looking for my two-year-old sister and found her standing outside at the front door crying.

I looked to my left and saw our sitter's fifteen-year-old brother, the leader of a neighborhood gang, standing at his front door about to throw another rock at my sister. I rushed him so hard I knocked him off his feet and had him subdued with several punches to his face, when a fist-sized rock came out of nowhere and cut a gash in his head. I looked up to see my six-year-old brother, David, about to throw another rock at the gang leader, so I jumped up and pushed him and my sister into the house.

I had locked the front door and gathered everyone into the kitchen when I heard the living room window screen crash to the floor behind me. I turned and stood at the kitchen entrance as the gang leader climbed through an open window and took one step onto the couch with a butcher knife in his hand.

I focused on the knife and was about to rush him and grab that hand as soon as his first foot touched the floor, then swing him headfirst into the front door. Before he stepped down, his eyes opened wide with fear, and he turned and scrambled back through the window.

DESTINY

At the same time, I felt my brother brush by me carrying two butcher knives. I caught him at the couch and calmed him, and we secured the house and waited for Mother.

It wasn't unusual for my past experiences to come to mind when I faced serious challenges, although it was sometimes difficult to tie the lesson learned to the situation at hand. This time I knew exactly what the lesson was.

My brother and I both had the right solution: make your first move quick, unexpected, and decisive. I was confident those principles would apply to my current situation and certain the details would come to me, if and when the need materialized.

As I continued the walk to Battalion Headquarters, I couldn't help wondering how I'd missed the fact that the whole company suspected me of being a CID plant and that their suspicion had escalated to a contract on my life. I knew many of my fellow soldiers considered me a possible threat because I didn't use drugs, refused offers to get involved with selling drugs, and wouldn't sell them my unused cigarette and liquor rations. I also hadn't been intimidated by gangs running protection rackets in the barracks.

They'd made it very clear, since they weren't all that secretive about most of their activities, that they couldn't trust me unless I participated. Several past incidents came to mind, and a situation at my first FTX a few months earlier started to take on new meaning.

My first night in Grafenwoehr, I found myself looking up from the barracks floor at my squad leader, Sergeant McNeal, standing over me. He had awakened me by tipping me out of my bunk for the second time that night. As he had before, he stood there with all the lights on in the barracks and several soldiers and squad leaders looking on, waiting for me to jump up from the floor and throw a punch so he could bring me up on charges.

I'd avoided his trap the first time by turning my bunk upright and going back to sleep. This time, I righted my bunk, rolled up my sleeping bag, and carried it out the barracks door into the snow. I rounded the corner of the barracks with Sergeant McNeal and another squad leader close behind. McNeal yelled at me.

"Where the hell do you think you're going, Private Williams?"

I spun around and stood at attention as I answered, "I'm going to find a place to get some sleep, Squad Leader."

When he caught up with me, he glared at me through drug-blurred eyes and slurred his response. "I'll tell you what you're gonna do, Private Williams. You're gonna stop jumpin' for the man, trying to make my men look bad, or I'm gonna have you out of my squad."

"Sergeant McNeal, if you're telling me I have to learn to loaf instead of doing my job, I'm too old at thirty-three to change my ways."

He again slurred his words and rocked back and forth as he declared, "We'll see about that. Starting tomorrow morning, I'll see that you get every dirty job in the company, while we're in the field and when we get back to Mainz. You'll soon be begging to get out of this company and the Army." He ordered me back into the barracks, and beginning with KP the next morning, made good his threat.

Since returning to Mainz from Grafenwoehr, I'd been reporting every morning at 0530 to clean the four-stall basement latrine and pass Sergeant McNeal's white glove inspections. I intended to keep passing his inspections, learn every military skill these tough guys could teach, and still stay clear of their illegal activities.

I'd hoped letting my work speak for me would eventually earn me some respect, but with them pegging me for CID, I knew now I had a greater challenge to meet. I faced their threat head-on during the company's next FTX, shortly after Sergeant Chan's warning.

I was lying on the bottom of a double bunk on the second floor of an old, wooden, two-story troop barracks in Baumholder, following a long day of range firing. The bare bulbs swinging on cords from the ceiling cast a very dim light for reading Louis L'Amour's latest novel as I leaned against the head of my bunk.

In Mainz, I'd been adjusting the position of my bunk at night to protect myself from being approached from the rear, but that wasn't necessary here. There were two rows of double bunks, one along each wall, with seven-foot-tall, double wooden lockers pressed against the head of each bunk and a four-foot corridor down the center of the barracks between the rows of lockers.

Our newest private, drunk as a skunk in his bunk behind me across the corridor, started yelling for his mother and had to be carried to the infirmary to have his stomach pumped.

An hour later, my Platoon Sergeant, Staff Sergeant (SSG) Ruffy, almost as drunk, stormed up the stairs and through the door to our floor screaming at Sergeant Gonzalez. "Alright, damn it. I've had all the lying I'm gonna take. Get your ass out here. I'm gonna beat the shit out of you and settle this once and for all."

Gonzalez had told Ruffy earlier that he had given the First Sergeant (1SG) the drunk private's wallet, which had fallen to the

57

ground when the private slipped and landed on his back in the frozen snow coming into the barracks. Now Ruffy was really mad because 1SG Easton denied any knowledge of the wallet.

Several senior noncommissioned officers (NCOs) were trying hard to hold SSG Ruffy back while friends had no trouble holding Gonzalez, who wisely wanted no part of Ruffy. 1SG Easton showed up with Field-First Hildegard, and each grabbed one of Ruffy's arms. At the same time, two other NCOs grabbed his legs. They had him squirming and cursing in midair, about four feet off the floor, with his head free and bobbing about three feet from my bunk.

In the dim light, no one else seemed to notice Private Bushaven slithering around the head of my bunk carrying a steel helmet. He began maneuvering for a clear shot at Ruffy's head. Just as he started to take a roundhouse swing at Ruffy, I reached up and jerked the helmet from his hand and slid it under my bunk. When he spun around and glared at me, I growled a warning.

"You get back to your bunk or I'll give you what you were about to give SSG Ruffy."

He did, and the ruckus subsided as quickly as it had started. Field-First Hildegard had received the wallet from Gonzalez and failed to inform First Sergeant Easton it was in his desk.

As everyone returned to their own bunks, I caught the eye of SGT Jimmy Thompson standing behind his bunk at the far end of the barracks, where he had been observing everything. I got the impression he'd been watching me, but I dismissed the idea and returned to my book. A few minutes later, SGT Thompson startled me by sitting down at the foot of my bunk and issuing a command.

"Williams, I want to know what you said to Bushaven."

SGT Thompson was a conundrum to me. He was an excellent

NCO, who had the respect of everyone in the company. I'd heard a few things about him: no one messed with him; he had been involved with drugs; and he was loyal to SSG Ruffy, who had saved him from jail on a drug possession charge. I'd learned most of that from SSG Ruffy, my current Platoon Sergeant and the former Training NCO before SGT Chan took over.

I considered Ruffy a tough, smart, and highly trained NCO, second only to 1SG Easton. Ruffy was a recovered heroin addict, who saw leadership qualities in SGT Thompson in spite of his own drug involvement and his association with the roughest characters in B Company. I wasn't interested in stirring up SGT Thompson's anger against Bushaven, so I took a chance with an NCO who wasn't in my direct chain-of-command.

"What I told Bushaven is none of your business, SGT Thompson."

"I know, but I want to know what you said to him."

"You'll have to ask Bushaven."

"I don't want to ask Bushaven. I want you to tell me."

He wasn't angry, and he seemed to respect the position I was taking, but he wasn't going to give up, and I was beginning to recognize an opportunity. I offered him a deal.

"Alright, I'll tell you on one condition: When I've told you, you listen to something else I have to tell you."

"Okay. What did you say?"

I wasn't sure how much he had observed, so I told him what Bushaven had tried to do, what I did, and what I said to him. Then I showed him the helmet. He stared at it for several seconds with fire in his eyes until I shoved the helmet back and interrupted his thoughts.

"Now, let me tell you something else. I do the best job I can, SGT Thompson, and I don't mess with anyone. I'm not interested in drugs. I don't even care if you all choose to kill yourselves with them. I'm not interested in any of the criminal activity I've observed in this company, but I know about the contract on me.

"If anyone is that afraid of me, they will have to do better than they did with an intrenching tool to the head of that other soldier, because I don't sleep that soundly. And I won't be like that captain they beat up and tossed out the second floor window. I'll not only give names; I'll tell where to find their bodies."

"Why are you telling me this, Williams?"

"SGT Thompson, I doubt if anything goes on in this company you don't at least know about. Who else would I tell?"

He thought for a moment, then, looking me straight in the eyes, said, "Williams, I understand you read the Bible."

"That's true, and I try to apply the principles of the Bible to my life."

"You want to know what my bible is? I'll show you." He reached into his back pocket and pulled out a small booklet with a picture of Angela Davis on the cover and said, "This is my bible. Before I came into the Army, I was a street enforcer, and until I see the black man achieve equality in the Army, I'll stay an enforcer."

"Maybe, SGT Thompson, but I can't believe equality is really what you want, not with whites or blacks. You're smarter and more capable than many of the soldiers and NCOs around you, so I know you don't want to be equal with them, and you sure as hell don't want them just handed the rank you busted your butt for.

"I suspect the same thing SSG Ruffy thinks. Guys like you can

60

do anything you put your mind to, and the only one who can hold you back is you."

He smiled, then he said, "I know how I feel, Williams. Don't try to confuse me with logic." He got up and walked away, still smiling.

I never had another occasion to talk to SGT Thompson. I wasn't sure, and I didn't care if his influence wasn't actually as strong as I had thought. The solution to my problem wasn't in his hands or mine. I had taken the opportunity to let my enemies know I was perfectly willing to make whoever took the contract on me pay a heavy price. Although I had no intention of burying bodies, I believed Thompson understood I was capable of defending myself. A couple of things he had said suggested to me he would at least deliver my message.

The fact that I read my Bible was known only to my two roommates, who didn't run with that crowd. So Thompson had to have asked them about me. Also, his statement that he intended to stay an enforcer sounded as much like a threat as a confession.

What I had said about him was what I believed, the same as SSG Ruffy did, but I also believed he was smart. I hoped it would not occur to him that a CID plant might have said the same things I had said.

A short time after we returned from that FTX and Shirley had arrived from Arizona, we were on a train to Wiesbaden to have dinner with SGT Chan and his wife and four children. Chan sat in a seat across from us. During a lull in chit-chat, he blurted out a new revelation.

"By the way, Danny, I've been meaning to tell you. I don't know what you did, but that contract on you has been lifted."

As I glared at him, Shirley's green eyes widened, and she snapped her head in my direction and asked, "What contract?"

"I'll tell you about it later, honey."

"Tell me what?" Her fiery personality matched her red hair.

"It's been taken care of, babe. I promise I'll tell you all about it later."

Al Chan was stunned as he asked incredulously, "You didn't tell her?"

"I'll tell her later, Al."

SGT Chan apologized in the office the next day, then said, "I can't believe you never told her." I explained that I didn't see any reason to worry Shirley about something I couldn't change.

Al Chan and I soon became good friends. He confided to me that he paid his rent with cases of rationed Johnny Walker and he occasionally used drugs. He eventually even made me a back-handed offer.

"Danny, I can't believe you let Shirley's and your cigarette and liquor rations go to waste every month. Do you know how much you could make selling to German cab drivers? I sometimes get seventy-five Marks for Johnnie Walker Red."

"Not interested, Al."

He never brought it up again. He seemed to respect my principles, but he always seemed to be not sure of me.

The same suspicion was still shared by others. Even my commander, CPT Goodyear, stopping at my desk to assign me yet another extra duty, walked away shaking his head and saying, "I just don't know about you, Williams." Several incidents proved some not-so-friendly soldiers were not happy the contract on me had been lifted.

DESTINY

One afternoon on my way out of the barracks, I glanced at the Charge of Quarters duty roster and realized that, in the last few minutes, my name had replaced that of SGT McNeal for duty that evening. He showed up the next morning to see if I had pulled the all-night duty. Apparently angry that I wasn't AWOL, he found me in the commander's office cleaning off the desk.

While two of his friends stood in the office doorway, he walked up behind me and slapped a handcuff on my right wrist. Before he could attach the other cuff to the arm of the commander's chair, I had both his arms behind him and forced him headfirst out the open window. I held him suspended there about 10 feet from the ground and said I would drop him on his head if he didn't hand me the key to the cuffs.

When he did, I pulled him back and threw the cuffs at him, and he and his friends left the room. I hadn't worried about his friends, because I had noticed their reluctance to come into the room, and their expressions told me they didn't approve of SGT McNeal's actions.

The next day, the supply sergeant in charge of duty assignments ordered me to write out a complaint against SGT McNeal for tampering with his duty roster, a court-martial offence. I talked him out of it, saying, "One day I will outrank SGT McNeal. If he or any of his friends find themselves under my command, they will have no excuse not to obey any order I give." There were other incidents, but none involved SGT McNeal.

I continued to consider most of my fellow soldiers heroes who had just risked their lives for my country and weren't getting their due respect. I even made a few friends. I think 1SG Easton became a friend, in spite of his own illegal activities. He provided me the kind of concentrated training I had expected to get on a tour in Viet Nam. He also convinced me I could learn most everything else I needed by studying army regulations and field manuals.

After my promotion to Buck Sergeant and graduation from Seventh Army NCO Academy in Bad Toelz, he appointed me to a Staff Sergeant position as Section Sergeant of the TOW Anti-tank Section. Soon after, on the 1SG's recommendation, the battalion commander appointed me Battalion Training NCO.

In my third year, I was transferred to 8ID Headquarters in Bad Kreuznach at the request of my former company commander, now *Major* Goodyear, who had become the training officer for 8ID. I expected this assignment to be the last in my four-year enlistment and to complete my training for my country's next war.

Fortunately, the skills in escape and evasion I had sharpened at the Animal Farm prepared me for my assignment as 8ID Training NCO, working alongside SSG Clyde Lee Conrad. Not only did SSG Conrad become my greatest test of those evasion skills, he also became my friend and military mentor.

I didn't relay all this military history to Mr. Romski, but I did give him a few more examples of the generally accepted behavior of the soldiers around me in Headquarters, 8ID.

"Even the NCOIC of G-3, Training, SFC Zolton Szabo, a REFed Captain, when he was caught stealing thousands of dollars of gasoline rations, got off with an eight hundred dollar fine and loss of his security clearance, but he didn't lose a single stripe. Clyde told me it was because so many of the officers on the court-martial board owed Szabo favors. Clyde seemed to be the only one in the unit who knew about Szabo's problems."

Romski's next question indicated that, although he may have accepted my reasons for not reporting Clyde's offer, his interpretation of that offer hadn't changed. "But do you think it's possible that Clyde could have been talking about espionage?"

"Of course it's possible, since I never found out what it really was, but from what I think I know about Clyde, I still believe it's highly unlikely."

"Do you think Clyde is capable of committing espionage?"

"Well, since you put it like that, I suppose Clyde is capable of anything if you're asking if he would be good at it. I've always considered him basically amoral, but I still believe he is loyal. Can I tell you a few more things that have led me to believe he is involved in some other kind of illegal activity?"

"Sure."

"Several months before the incident in the field, I told Clyde I was really interested in buying a Minox camera I had seen in a camera store in downtown BK. He told me to give him the model number and he could get it really cheap . . . ."

"He said that?"

Damn! I should have known how this would sound. To you, the name Minox can only refer to espionage. It's just a camera to me.

"He not only said that; he got me one. I'd been looking at one for months. The owner of the camera store had told me they took great pictures and that a lot of Germans took them on vacation so they wouldn't have to carry a camera on their shoulder like a tourist. I've taken hundreds of sightseeing pictures with it. I've always been a miniature enthusiast."

You're not buying this, are you, Romski. You're still hung-up on Minox, the spy camera.

"I tried to get Clyde to let me pay for it. He finally said he didn't pay anything for it, so I forced him to take fifty dollars."

"Do you know where he got the Minox camera?"

"Not really, although I had some suspicions. A few months later I saw a portable recorder Clyde kept in his desk . . . ."

"He kept a tape recorder in his desk?"

Damn, everything sounds like espionage to you. "Actually, several soldiers in G-3 had tape recorders. Most were ordered through supply, but that took forever. Clyde and I were on the annual general inspection team for 8ID. I wanted one to keep notes in when we traveled around Germany on inspections, to help me write my reports later. Several inspectors carried one for the same reason. I assumed that was what Clyde did with his.

"When I asked him where he got his, he said he got it from the same guy he got the camera from. He said he would get me one but it would take a while because the guy was only in the area every month or two, and he never knew exactly when the guy would be there."

"Did he say who the guy was?"

"No, but that's what I'm trying to tell you. I asked Clyde if I could take his tape recorder back to my desk and try it out before I decided if I wanted one like it. I don't remember what brand it is, but I have it at home. He said I could take it, but he followed me to my office.

Seeing a cassette in the recorder, I pressed the play button to make sure he didn't have anything on it before I recorded over it. I heard some laughter and several people talking. I could hear Clyde and Gitta. I also heard what I believed to be either one or both of Gitta's daughters, Hanelore and Sabine.

66

"I heard another voice that sounded like Zolton Szabo, but before I could be sure, Clyde realized I was playing his tape and grabbed the recorder from me. He immediately started explaining that the family had been clowning around when he first got the recorder and that he didn't know he had left anything on the tape. He said it was a very private conversation, and he started erasing it. That made me think the voice I heard may have been Szabo, or maybe even—"

"Why wouldn't he want you to hear Szabo?"

"Well, the point is he didn't want me to hear the tape. He had already made it clear he didn't want me to know who supplied the recorder. I assumed the guy I heard may have been the one he got his merchandise from, since he said the family had been clowning around when he first got the recorder.

"I took that to mean the recorder was being delivered the day he made the recording. Either Clyde thought I would recognize the voice, meaning it was likely Szabo, or the guy was some member of the family who might identify himself on the tape.

"I said to Clyde, 'That still sounds like Szabo to me. Is he the guy you're getting this stuff from?' He said, 'Szabo doesn't have anything to do with it; it was just a private family conversation.'

"The man on the tape had Szabo's Hungarian accent. I knew Clyde and Szabo socialized, but it could have been a member of the family. Clyde had mentioned a number of times that Gitta's family was always giving her and the kids expensive gifts and money.

"Gitta also explained once that she got a lot of clothing, furniture, and other household things with a special discount through German department stores, like Kaufoff and Hertie, because she took orders for their catalogue items from several of the soldiers' wives in the BK housing area. They had a lot of nice things, but there always seemed to be a logical explanation for them.

"Couldn't those explanations have been invented just for your benefit, Sergeant Williams?"

"Certainly, at least some of them. Although I knew exactly how he got several of the expensive things he owned. They had a very expensive piece of hand-carved furniture for which I know he only paid four hundred Marks. I was the one who found the deal for him at an antique auction house in BK.

"Szabo also sold him some things real cheap when he was arrested and thought he would have to pay a large fine. He sold his Thunderbird and his camper trailer to Clyde. Clyde sold the T Bird for three times what he paid for it to an SFC in Operations, who later crashed it and killed himself. He kept the camper at his lot on the *Rhein* River."

"What kind of lot on the river?"

"Germans rented small lots along the Rhein, where they kept fishing gear in a small cabin or camper trailer. Shirley and I attended a couple of picnics there with Clyde and his family. He didn't try to keep it a secret. I knew an Army chaplain in Mainz who had one as well.

"I sold him my two Volkswagen Super Beetles for the price of one when I left BK for Arizona because I didn't have time to wait for a fair price. He told me in California he sold one of them for what he had paid me for both and gave the other to Hanelore. Shirley never forgave him for such a lousy deal."

"There wasn't anything illegal about that was there?"

"No, and I didn't have any problem with it."

I'm not talking about illegal activity; I'm explaining some of his apparent affluence.

"What can you tell me about Szabo's problems?"

"Only what Clyde told me. Szabo covered his gas ration card each month with combat acetate, which is practically invisible and makes ink easily erasable. When the cashier at the post exchange (PX) marked Xs on the card for the gas coupons he purchased at our military discount, Szabo would erase the Xs.

He would buy more coupons during that month at PXs around the country and keep erasing the Xs. Then he would sell the coupons to a German service station owner, who would be reimbursed by the government at the market price for gas. The owner didn't have to give up any gas, and he split the profit with Szabo.

Szabo finally got caught when he went to the same PX on the same day and the cashier recognized him. I believe that was the Air Force Base Exchange in Wiesbaden."

I told Romski all I knew about Clyde's collection of gold coins, his tours in Viet Nam and Baumholder, and his family in the States. His next question angered me.

"Sergeant Williams, why do you think you remember all these things so vividly?"

I hesitated, then answered indignantly, "Because they happened."

"Is there anything else you think we should know?"

"I'm sure your investigation will reveal that Clyde is not involved in espionage, but I realize you will have to know what he is involved in before you can be sure. I can only think of one way you can learn the truth about his affairs."

"What is the one way you think we can do that?"

"I could ask him."

"Why would he tell you?"

I would just find a way, but I'm sure you wouldn't understand that.

"Because we're friends."

"I believe that's all I have for you, Sergeant Williams. If you think of anything else, call me."

Romski gave me his telephone number, and I made a parting remark. "Mr. Romski, although I believe Clyde is loyal, I assure you, if you find you need my help in learning the truth about him, I would consider it my duty to report only the truth."

"Sergeant Williams, are you saying, if we were to investigate Clyde, you would be willing to help?"

What else would I be saying? Oh, that's your way of denying that you are even investigating him. "That's exactly what I'm saying."

"Why would you do that."

"Mr. Romski, the principle I've taught my own agents, as well as agents at the Intelligent Center and School, is that it's often harder to prove a suspect innocent than it is to prove him guilty. Even though an investigation might lead to Clyde's activity having to be reported to another agency, I believe his career and his family would suffer less than they would from the lingering suspicion of espionage that will result from a CE investigation, even if no proof of guilt is found unless the truth is revealed."

Several months after that interview, I received assignment instructions for Korea, with assurance of a 1SG position. Before getting the actual orders, I received a telephone call at home from Mr. Romski. He wanted me to meet him in Tucson the following day. I considered the possible reasons for this meeting.

Have they decided to charge me with failure to report Clyde's offer?

DESTINY

Have they been unable to verify anything I told them and suspect me of lying? Have they decided to ask me to help them learn the truth about Clyde?

I know they are going to give me a PE (polygraph examination), because Romski said, "Don't drink any alcohol or take any medication before you come to Tucson." In any case, a PE would be standard procedure.

I'd met several polygraph examiners and was yet to be favorably impressed. Although this exam was grueling, intended primarily to determine my veracity concerning the information I had given them about Clyde and about myself, the examiner was a true professional.

Following his evaluation of the results, I met with Romski, who told me I had passed the PE and asked me if I was willing to help them with their investigation of Clyde Conrad. I volunteered. He told me he would take care of changing my assignment from Korea to Germany. He gave me a name and number at my assignment branch to call for my new orders and said he would arrange another meeting with me in Arizona within a few weeks.

When I called my assignment branch as directed, I discovered they had not made the change in my assignment arranged by FCA, but they started the process right then, and within a week, I received orders to 527th MI Battalion in Kaiserslautern.

I later received instruction to meet Romski at the Stake Out Restaurant in Sonoita, one of the most famous restaurants in Southern Arizona. It was the last meeting place I would have chosen.

My coworkers and my supervisor often frequented the Stake Out Restaurant. I knew if I ended up having to introduce Romski to any of them that evening, the excuses I'd been offering for the sudden change in my assignment and earlier reporting date, as well as my insistence that my original interview with Romski had been a routine background interview, would be worthless. Fortunately, I saw no one from my unit that evening.

At the meeting, Romski insisted I not answer the welcome letter I had already received from the Command Sergeant Major (CSM) of 527th because everything had been taken care of. Romski said he would contact me in Germany and arrange for me to meet the agent in charge of me in Germany, who would give me further instructions.

On the day I was to depart Fort Huachuca, I stopped by my old office at Information Systems Command to say farewell to my coworkers. I discovered I had just received new orders changing my assignment to B Company, 527th MI in Stuttgart. That meant I would have to make new arrangements when I reached Frankfurt.

At the Frankfurt Airport, I telephoned the 527th CSM in K-town to give him an opportunity to tell me if he wanted to see me before I reported to Stuttgart. "Hello, Sergeant Major Bradley. This is Master Sergeant Williams from Fort Huachuca. I'm at the Frankfurt Airport. I wanted to touch base with you before reporting to B Company."

"I'm glad to hear from you, Sergeant Williams. Didn't 1SG Frey meet you at the airport?"

"No, Sergeant Major. I haven't talked to anyone at B Company yet. I didn't get my assignment orders to Stuttgart until the day I left Fort Huachuca." I was holding my breath, hoping he would say something to indicate someone had told him why I hadn't answered his welcome letter. When he didn't reply, I continued.

"I got the B Company 1SG's telephone number from your secretary, Sergeant Major. I'll get in touch with someone in Stuttgart. It won't be a problem."

"Well, we're really glad to have you, Sergeant Williams. Lieutenant Colonel (LTC) Cameron has nothing but great things to say about you. I want you to make an appointment with me in a couple of weeks, after you get settled in, but let me tell you my plan for you. You are going to be the Operations NCO of B Company. Then, after eighteen months, I'm going to switch you with 1SG Frey, and you will be Company First Sergeant for your last eighteen months."

That sounds fantastic, Sergeant Major. Thanks. I'll get back to you soon."

Actually, I was flabbergasted, considering Romski's warning at our Sonoita meeting that "Your assignment will be for the convenience of this operation, with no consideration for your career." I wondered what this new arrangement could mean.

Could it be these guys have seen the light and decided to play this the natural, military way instead of the cloak-and-dagger way? I hope so. Clyde is a soldier. Things have to be strictly military to even start to fool him.

I thanked CSM Bradley and phoned B Company. Mr. Beard, the Company Operations Officer, answered and apologized for not knowing I was arriving and having anyone at the airport to meet me. He asked me to find a place to stay overnight in Frankfurt so he could pick me up the next morning.

He said I would remember him as soon as we met, because I had been his instructor in Special Operations when he was training to become a MICCEP (Military Intelligence Civilian Career Excepted

Program) Officer. He had some things he wanted to talk over with me on the way back to Stuttgart.

I called the home of an officer friend stationed in Frankfurt. His gracious wife offered to put me up for the night, and he took me to the Frankfurt CI Field Office the next morning, where Mr. Beard picked me up.

I did remember him from his Special Operations Course. Most of the trip to Stuttgart we talked about my duties as B Company Operations NCO. Then, Mr. Beard became very serious.

"I really need an Operations NCO, and I'm planning to meet with LTC Cameron as soon as possible to put a stop to this special assignment he has for you. I'm tired of these guys coming out of the States and taking my people away from me and not even telling me what's going on."

Well, this is SNAFU! My own people are going to kill this operation before it gets off the ground.

"I'm sure you know all about this assignment he has for you, Sergeant Williams, but I have some important DCE (Defensive Counterespionage) cases at B Company, and I've already got people out there that I have no control over."

No, Mr. Beard. I don't know. I've only talked to CSM Bradley, and he didn't say anything about any special assignment. I might be able to guess, since I worked with LTC Cameron in the States before he took command of 527th. We worked together providing CI support to a few dozen special access programs (SAPs). Some were in Germany. I suppose, since I've already been read-on to them, it might be something like that, but nobody told me."

"Well, I know what he says it is, Sergeant Williams. He says he wants to send you around Germany to become familiar with the

Battalion before you take over as Operations NCO, but I'm not buying it."

Whoa! I wouldn't buy that either. Neither will my buddy in BK.

"It's those damn guys from the States, running operations with my people! I'm sorry, Sergeant Williams. I'm going to have to put a stop to it."

"Hey, Mr. Beard, you're the boss."

He was clearly angry, and I wanted to calm him as much as possible. He seemed satisfied with my attitude as he dropped me off at a hotel about four blocks from B Company Headquarters.

I spent the next couple of weeks processing into my unit, getting my US Army Europe (USAEUR) and international driver's licenses. I began looking for an apartment, read a ton of DCE messages, and familiarized myself with a dozen or so ongoing DCE cases.

Mr. Beard spent a lot of that time on the telephone trying to arrange an audience with LTC Cameron to talk him out of the special project he had for me. I learned that LTC Cameron had instead scheduled a meeting with Major Daniels, B Company Commander.

Within a couple of weeks, I received word that Mr. Romski was in town and wanted to meet with me in Frankfurt at the PX complex. I was again concerned we were likely to run into people who knew me.

Mr. Romski spent thirty minutes explaining that I would meet with LTC Cameron to learn about the job he had for me to put me in the BK area. I was told to make certain that I did not discuss anything operational with LTC Cameron. Later, I would have a meeting with my CI contact in Germany, Grant Poster, to learn their operational plan. Then Romski leaned back in his chair and asked me a question I had not anticipated.

DAMIAN and MONGOOSE

"Danny, what do you think Clyde will say when you look him up after all these years?"

Does that mean you've figured out what he will say and you want to know if I'm prepared for it? Or does that just mean you wonder if we will still be friends after all these years? Are you even ready for my answer?

"I'm not sure what you mean, Mr. Romski."

"What will his reaction be, Danny? What will he say when you first approach him?"

"Actually, Mr. Romski, I think I know exactly what he will say, but I'm not sure you really want to hear it."

Romski didn't respond. He just sat there in awkward silence, a typical interrogator technique used by the guys from his unit to draw conversation from me.

Maybe you are ready for this. Maybe the purpose of this meeting is to make sure I really know what I'm up against.

"Well, Mr. Romski, probably Clyde will say, 'Are you here on your own, or were you sent?'"

Romski's chair slammed down and he started to shift from side to side. He appeared to be looking for his partner somewhere in the room. Finally, he leaned forward with his forehead all screwed up and asked, a bit angrily, "Why in the world would he say that?"

Whoa! I've misjudged you! You guys are living in a dream world! No, damn it! It's more than that. You suspect I've called Clyde and warned him. I see that's the only way you can imagine he could be expecting me.

"Because he knows he's under investigation."

"Now how the hell would he know that, Danny?" The implication in Romski's tone was obvious, and my response was involuntarily indignant.

DESTINY

"How long have you been investigating him?"

"I'm not going to tell you that!"

"Well, if it's been more than two weeks, he knows it."

We were glaring at each other, but Romski made an effort to be less accusatory with his next question. "Why do you think he knows it?"

Because, the way you guys throw your weight around, who wouldn't know? Back off, Williams. Think!

"Because he has a lot of friends, and he prides himself in knowing what is going on around him before most people know it. Maybe I'm wrong. Maybe he hasn't a clue that he's under investigation. But, in his case, you'd have to be especially careful."

"Well, I understand your concerns. If I thought there was any possibility whatsoever that you could be right, we would close this operation down right now."

"And I'm sure I'm wrong."

Even as I was telling that little white lie, Romski was saying, "But, I don't think you have to worry about that, Danny."

I see you calmed down when you thought I was angry. You've done that before, Romski. You're a peacemaker. I'll have to remember that.

He dropped that subject abruptly and ended our meeting. I assumed I was to proceed as planned. He seemed less worried as we parted company. I had plenty to think about on my trip back to Stuttgart.

I may have gotten out of that by the skin of my teeth. Now I almost hope Romski believes that Clyde doesn't know he's under investigation, although it's fortunate I don't believe it. Someone has to worry about that. Even if I were mistaken, I'd have to assume he knew and prepare for it.

77

DAMIAN and MONGOOSE

I've seen too many of their investigations. They flash their Bs and Cs (badge and credentials) and throw down a Secrecy Affirmation Statement for every interviewee to sign, then assume fear of them will keep their investigation secure. I've seen too damn many cases go to hell because some agent made that assumption.

It's not that hard to get information about a suspect without ever giving his or her name. I always asked general enough questions to make the person interviewed bring up the name and end up telling me things I didn't even ask about my suspect, without realizing I was interested.

Why couldn't I teach that? Even when I taught Special Operations, only a few agents seemed to understand it, and even they were afraid such devious techniques would rob them of that CI mystique and the power they could wield with their Bs and Cs.

Will Romski be able to talk the guys back at headquarters into going on with the operation after he conveys my answer to his question? Hopefully, they will chalk-up my suggestion to my incredible arrogance.

A couple of nights after returning to Stuttgart, I sat in my hotel room trying to imagine agent Poster's plan for my being in BK. My meeting with LTC Cameron was already scheduled for the next morning, but I didn't know when I would meet with Poster. I usually prepared myself for any kind of meeting or conference, but I'd been lax lately and had been hit with some real surprises.

I knew Clyde wouldn't question my reason for being in Germany. In CI jargon, my cover for status was my position as Operations NCO for B Company, 527TH MI. Thus far, I had no legitimate reason for being in Bad Kreuznach or my cover for action. Clyde would never buy familiarizing myself with the Battalion area of operation, and Romski hadn't mentioned it.

I couldn't decide what Poster might have coordinated with LTC

Cameron, so I closed my eyes to let the right side of my brain take over. I let all the known facts and reasonable suppositions flow freely in hopes that an idea would pop into my head of just what their plan might be. After fifteen minutes, it did! Like a bolt of lightning on a moonless night, the only possible conclusion seemed to light up the room!

They don't have a plan! They left the cover for action to LTC Cameron, and they are going to play the rest by ear. They don't believe you can decide what to do until you actually get there, then you just pull a plan out of your ass.

I knew that wouldn't work with Clyde. I didn't like it either. I believed you could anticipate people and circumstances. In my opinion, forethought was vital to the success of this operation. There were already security problems developing within my own unit, because they hadn't been logically anticipated.

I knew my superiors weren't interested in my opinion, but somehow I had to create an atmosphere in which my portion of this operation would have some chance of succeeding, and I had to do it without stepping on their toes. I had to plan something before LTC Cameron briefed my B Company Commander, whose meeting was just after mine.

I needed something that would work on Clyde and at the same time pacify Mr. Beard, but first I'd have to sell it to LTC Cameron. Ideas started flashing in my mind, and by the time I reached K-town the next day, I was ready.

As soon as I walked into Battalion Headquarters, I went to the CSM's office. I spent only a few minutes. He greeted me and said he wanted to talk to me immediately after my briefing by LTC Cameron. He explained that the Colonel was anxious to see me.

DAMIAN and MONGOOSE

When the Colonel saw me in his outer office, he grabbed his hat and told his secretary he couldn't be reached for a while. He shook my hand vigorously and led me out of the building. I made a mental note to ask the Colonel not to show me so much attention in the future. We walked to his private auto and took a drive through the Kaiserslautern countryside. He started the conversation immediately.

"Tell me the truth, Danny. How long is this going to take?"

"Sir, they've told me they will give it sixty days. If nothing comes of it by then, they will shut it down. I expect things to go much faster. I'd say within a week you will know the score."

"Who is running this operation, Danny? I want to know."

"Sir, I really haven't met anyone here except the one guy who recruited me in the States, and they have warmed me not to discuss operational matters with anyone."

"I know that! I want to know who is running this thing! I'm not going to let this drag out! I need you for operations at B Company!"

"Sir, I've been told that Grant Poster will be my contact here...."

"I know him, Danny. He used to be in the Battalion."

"And, I don't know whether Mr. Romski will stay here or go back to the States, but that's all I know, really. Believe me, Sir, I won't let this drag out."

"I don't know Romski, but I appreciate that, Danny."

Realizing that the Colonel's primary concern was the same as Mr. Beard's, I knew I had to assure him I could fulfill my responsibilities as B company Operations NCO and still accomplish this special mission. However, I also had to prepare him for the possibility this mission might turn out to be worthy of more time and resources than he'd been led to believe. We had been in similar operations together, so I was certain he would follow my train of thought.

LTC Cameron was one of the few officers I knew who genuinely respected the opinions of their senior NCOs. Even fewer had his patience with such a self-confident, enthusiastic, and talkative NCO. He had demonstrated that patience and respect in previous challenges we had met, but I knew he liked to get to the point, so I talked as rapidly as I could.

"Sir, you know they will be giving me polygraph exams periodically, and the first thing they will ask me is whether I have discussed the case with anyone. To keep from getting into that, I would like to discuss something with you that I think is vital to the security of this operation and that you alone control."

"Okay, Danny. Whatever you need."

"Well, Sir, it has to do with my reason for being in BK. I hope you realize that we are targeting a really professional soldier. For that reason, he will never buy my floating around his area familiarizing with the Battalion."

But, that's not the only problem. Mr. Beard isn't buying that either, and he's pressuring Major Daniels to petition you to get someone else. The point is, Mr. Beard has made it pretty clear throughout B Company Headquarters that he believes I am on some investigation run by 'those damn guys from the States.'

"I don't know for sure that the target has other friends in Military Intelligence, but he has friends everywhere. The less speculation and discussion by anyone about my involvement in any kind of CE operation while I'm in BK, the better the chance of success, but I have a plan that may correct all that if you're willing."

"What does your contact have in mind, Danny? They left this in my hands and didn't express any preference whatever."

"I've guessed as much, Sir. They haven't said anything to me except that you would tell me what your job is for me in BK. Believe me, they don't have a plan, and they are not aware of the importance of a cover for action, possibly because they are under-estimating the target.

"During the years you and I worked together back in the States, you know what my expertise was, my experience in implement-ing cover stories. Let me tell you what I've learned in the past weeks and what I think may solve all these problems."

"Go ahead."

"As you know, your Battalion S-3 has tasked B Company to develop a war time GDP (General Deployment Plan). According to Battalion's draft GDP, B Company will gain the Mainz and K-town Detachments from A Company during war time, and they cover the 8ID rear-area of operation.

"I'm the only agent in B Company Headquarters with infantry experience in this part of Germany and quite a bit of experience with the GDPs of 8ID units. It would make sense for Major Daniels to send me to coordinate with the ROs (Resident Offices) under your Mainz and K-town CI Detachments and to identify all the 8ID units in the area B Company will support in war time.

"That makes BK the center of B Company's new war time area of operation. If this new GDP is as high a priority as I've been told, I can actually accomplish that mission while I'm there and have a legitimate reason for being TDY in the area. I can perform this operation without attracting attention.

"Also, if you would tell Major Daniels when you meet with him this afternoon that this mission to BK, while it will produce information to help write the B Company GDP, is actually a cover for counterintelligence support to some of Fifth Corps' SAPs (special-access programs), programs you and I worked with before, he will have something with which to appease Mr. Beard.

"You understand, this probably won't fool Major Daniels because he once worked at Special Operations Division before it became FCA. However, he will get the message and can use that story to make Mr. Beard believe he's been taken into the Major's confidence.

"One more slight problem, Sir. I've discovered the term, 'special-access-programs,' has an entirely different meaning to most CI agents, especially Mr. Beard. They immediately think it refers to a counterespionage operation.

"You will need to emphasize to Major Daniels that these SAPs belong to some combat units in the area and the program managers of these military SAPs insist on classifying my CI support to them. It isn't perfect, but I think it's the only thing that may restore the security that has been lost and stands a chance against a professional soldier like our target. What do you think?"

"I have no problem with it. The people you will need to coordinate with on GDP are 21st Support Command. There Headquarters is here in K-town. But, you will have to promise me one thing, Danny. Under no circumstance are you to allow any of these Commands you coordinate with to assume there will be any direct support to their units during wartime."

"Oh, I understand completely. B Company will answer to 527th and provide only strategic counterintelligence support during war time. I promise.

"I have one other request, Sir. I'd appreciate it if you could make your meetings with me a little less dramatic."

The Colonel laughed and assured me he would. Before we completed our drive through the Kaiserslautern countryside, he gave me the name of the one other officer at Battalion Headquarters I could contact if I had an emergency related to the undercover operation and couldn't reach my USAI contact. Soon after I returned to Stuttgart, I received word that my contact, Grant Poster, was ready to meet with me.

After spending a night in a Wiesbaden hotel, I met Poster in another hotel between there and Frankfurt. I waited patiently for even the mention of an approach plan, but Poster didn't seem to want to discuss that.

Although he seemed capable, he was a little hesitant. We hadn't even sat down since I entered the room. I couldn't decide if he was new at this game or just wary of me. We agreed to call each other by our first names, then Grant asked me how I intended to find Clyde.

Realizing he had no plan for me, I told him about LTC Cameron's GDP coordination mission for me. I said I would just walk into 8ID, G-3 to discuss GDPs and ensure that my previous assignment there came up in conversation. I'd wait for Clyde's name to be mentioned and ask someone where to find him.

Romski had told me nothing about Clyde, what section he worked in or where he lived. I'd decided they weren't confident I could act natural and be convincing if they gave me any information. I didn't mind that. I liked the challenge. But Grant asked me something that set my mind reeling.

"What do you think Clyde's reaction is going to be when you look him up after all these years?"

I'm dammed if I'll fall for that again! Surely Romski told you what I think.

I cringed when I answered, "Grant, when I was asked that by Romski, I simply gave him my gut feeling. He has convinced me there is no chance I was right.

"What did you think?"

Is this a test? "Well, at the time, I said that Clyde might ask, 'Are you here on your own, or were you sent?'"

Grant took a step back and nearly fell against the wall. He was totally surprised. I continued quickly. "But I said that because Clyde has a lot of friends and prides himself in staying informed about what's going on around him."

My explanation didn't help. Grant did not recover quickly. I was wondering why Romski hadn't conveyed my impressions to the guy down in the trenches with me.

Has Romski withheld my opinion from everyone, or just Grant? Is this his way of keeping Grant under control as well as me? I hope Grant can take it. I know I can.

Grant regained his composure, then he said something that reminded me they were all trained in the same school. "You realize, Danny, if they thought you were right, they would never let you do this."

"Of course! And, I'm convinced that I was wrong."

"Do you think he will repeat his offer to you, Danny?"

"I've been giving that some thought. If the occasion arises naturally, I thought I might mention to Clyde that I've collected a little jewelry the last few years. In fact, I have. I've been mulling over how I might imply that I've grown accustomed to having some kind of venture on the side, especially since the Army has sent me TDY so much over the years."

"That might work, Danny, but you realize you can't ask him if he has a deal for you?"

"Certainly. I would like to ask you a question though, Grant."

"Please do."

"What exactly do you want me to find out for you?"

"Well, what we would really like for you to find out, if you can, is where he is working and who his friends are."

"What do you mean, where he is working?"

"Danny, you do know he's retired?"

"No. I didn't. I thought he was still working at 8ID Headquarters."

"So, how do you think you will find him?"

"When I find out from 8ID, G-3, that my old buddy, Clyde, is retired and still living in the area, I'll call him. I still have his phone number in my notebook back at the hotel."

"How will you get his number if it's changed?"

"I'll look in the phonebook or call German information."

"Okay, I have some instructions for you concerning where and when we will meet next, whether you contact Clyde or not. Your TDY will start on 21 April. We will meet on 27 April in Alzey. Do you know where Alzey is?"

"Yes, I know where it is."

He recommended a hotel I should stay in, just outside of BK, because Clyde sometimes ate there. I thought that was danger-ously obvious.

I also listened to his instructions concerning the location in Alzey where someone would walk up beside me and tell me in a very low voice to proceed to another place where I could sit and report to him. I had taught the procedure and arranged many practical exercises almost identical to his scenario, but he seemed to have left out an important aspect of this clandestine procedure: integrating the location into my routine activity. But this was their operation. I returned to Stuttgart and obtained my TDY orders.

On 21 April, I signed for a BMW from B Company and drove to BK. Since that day was a German holiday, the only hotel open for business was the most expensive one in town, located just down the street from the Kurhaus. I paid a visit to G-3 8ID and learned where Clyde Conrad lived before I even checked into my hotel room. The next morning, I was on my way to Bosenheim.

COVER FOR ACTION

Following my two visits with Clyde and my debriefing by Grant Poster in Alzey, I spent the next week doing exactly what I told Clyde I was going to do: I drove to Stuttgart to look at apartments and worked the Company B war plan in and around BK, Mainz, Frankfurt, Giessen, Baumholder, and K-town. I had CI units everywhere agreeing to coordinate with United States and German combat and support units who would occupy the rear-area in war time.

I even visited the US Embassy in Frankfurt to revive some coordination I had started six years earlier, while stationed in Giessen. I knew I had to convince everyone in 527th and everyone in the BK area that I had a legitimate mission not associated with any FCA special activity. I left early in the morning and stayed late, knowing Clyde might check on me to see if I was really working. Even if he didn't see me, he had friends everywhere he could ask about my activities.

I was still waiting for Grant to give me permission to meet with Clyde again. Whether our superiors decided to continue using me or proceed in another direction, protecting the investigation from Clyde, who was still very suspicious, as well as from my own unit, to prevent loose talk, was clearly my duty.

No one had directed me to take on this responsibility, or even acknowledged my efforts, but I knew its importance, and I knew how to do it. I had taught it from the platform using the same books they should be using, and I had done it successfully in previous operations.

The only thing I had no control over was the failure of my FCA contacts or their partners to recognize the need for a cover story to explain their presence in the area. Everyone else in CI knew these agents considered themselves the invisible element of CI.

Their attitude reminded me of the infamous Colonel Flag, on the TV show *M*A*S*H*, who took pride in saying, "Don't pretend you see me, because I know I'm not here."

When Grant Poster notified me to meet him on 3 May at the Mainz CI Detachment, I realized my concept of security was always going to clash with that of FCA.

I had spent several hours at the Mainz Detachment, convincing people in my Battalion that my only purpose for being in the area was to work on war plans. Now, I found myself signing in at the Military Police Station on the first floor and proceeding to the CI Detachment on the second floor for a clandestine meeting late in the evening with a former 527th agent known to be working for FCA.

DESTINY

Speculation as to the purpose of my meeting by a detachment agent who might check-in that evening to catch-up on work would be hard to counter the next time I visited them. Of course, that's exactly what almost happened that evening.

The minute I entered the debriefing room, Grant heard a noise in another office. He made me hide behind a door while he persuaded the agent who had come in off leave not to interrupt his meeting in the next room. As I waited behind the door for Grant's return, I was still concerned the agent might hear our conversation, then recognize my voice the next time I visited his office.

I was already irritated about having been told I was there, a whole week after my meetings with Clyde, to write a sworn statement in longhand. I was expecting a typed statement from Grant's notes, which I would correct and then sign. Although Grant didn't say so, I surmised before the evening was over that the handwritten statement wasn't his idea.

At 0200 hours, after I'd completed the twenty-nine-page statement, Grant apologized for making me write it and assured me he would make other arrangements in the future because I shouldn't have to work so hard. I wanted to suggest that I pick a safe location of my own to type an agent report of all my meetings with Clyde, but I decided instead to convey my commitment to their mission.

"If there is some operational requirement for these procedures and these hours, in support of the investigation, don't worry about me. I'd rather do this kind of work than sleep or eat! Believe me, Grant, I'll tell you when I'm too tired to do the work."

I executed the statement, and Grant arranged our next clandestine meeting place. I explained that I had called Shirley and learned the Apple CDs had been sent. Since they hadn't arrived yet, I had contrived another excuse for calling Clyde and meeting with him. Grant agreed to my idea and officially gave me permission to meet with Clyde again.

I had met a jeweler near the Kurhaus, who was one of the leading opal dealers of Europe. I showed him some samples of lepidolite which I had acquired from my jeweler friend in Arizona, who had access to several tons. The opal dealer thought my gems might be worth investing in for jewelry and asked me to have them analyzed by the School of Gemology in Idar Oberstein. I called Clyde and asked him to go to the school with me and translate. He agreed.

Grant had instructed me, during my debriefing, that his superiors wanted to know what Clyde's family knew about his activities. He also said it was very important to get Clyde to make statements clarifying his personal activities. I realized that was the one thing Clyde was careful to avoid, but I tried to follow Grant's instructions on our trip to Idar Oberstein and several late-night walks with Clyde around BK during the next couple of weeks. A pattern quickly developed.

On our drive to the School of Gemology, I said, "Clyde, correct me if I'm wrong, but you seem torn between saving our friendship and admitting that you are selling information to foreign governments."

He not only didn't answer me, he didn't look at me. I could see a slight smile, then a tenseness in his jaw, as he let several moments pass with no verbal response. I kept my eyes on the road as more awkward moments passed. Finally, realizing that silence would be his only response, I changed the subject.

"I'm still in the process of reconciling myself to your activities.

However, I'm not ready to accept your departing the scene without a fight."

He seemed to relax slightly, but he continued to resist every attempt to get him to make specific statements about himself or the nature of his activity. He did seem to want to discuss general concepts and schemes that illustrated those concepts, but he wouldn't discuss details or his personal involvement in those schemes. A typical warning told me he intended to stick to that scenario.

"Danny, I have a lot of experience with people. There is no way you can work against me without my knowing it. I've already laid several traps for you, verbal tests, and you didn't pass."

"Clyde, you've made your suspicion of me very clear. I can't help that."

"Just a warning. There is one thing I recommend: Don't come to the house again. It would just be better for both of us."

"Why tell me your family knows nothing of your activities and then tell me not to come to the house? Are you afraid I might say something stupid in front of them or they might say something stupid in front of me?"

"That's not it at all." He was extremely agitated, but I pressed him further.

"The reason I ask, Clyde, is something Hanelore said to me the moment she saw me at the house. She asked me, 'What are you doing here?'"

"No! No, no. That was just— She was just asking why you were in BK."

"Yeah, right." My sarcasm was softened by a smile, but Clyde looked very serious for a moment before introducing a new subject.

DAMIAN and MONGOOSE

"I have a doctor friend who's in the same business. He's received very special training for very special projects. He's considered a weapons expert, and he's won some shooting awards in his country. I asked him once why he was in this business when he already has plenty of money. He said, 'For the excitement.'"

I recognized the warning, but I didn't acknowledge it. I changed the subject. "Have your friends accepted the fact that you have resigned yourself to your fate?"

"I contacted everyone who has worked with me when I realized I was under investigation. I told them, 'Shut down!' I said, 'After I'm gone, do whatever you want.' I closed my accounts, destroyed all the material, and wiped information from my computers.

"A controller always carries a red badge when he comes to a neutral country to meet with workers. I have identified certain controllers who always use the same hotel."

Clyde liked to throw things out to get my reaction. I knew "controller" could only refer to an agent handler and "red badge" to a Diplomatic Passport, and he would expect me to know. So, I simply asked him how he identified their hotels.

"I asked them. They told me their favorite hotel and their favorite restaurants. I sat down and I thought, *All I have to do is set up a video camera and take pictures of the American soldiers who come in and out of that hotel during the weekends those controllers are there. Then, I know who's working.* I went to a friend to get him to man the video camera."

"What friend?"

"A friend. I figured I could sell the pictures to the Embassy, but someone went to them. So, I never got a chance to do it. They have a machine they place on a person's head that twists the head with a jerk when they don't like the answer to a question."

"Who has this machine?"

"The people this guy reports to. They had an inquest, and this guy told them about the video camera. Then a friend was summoned. When he left the inquest, he went to a safe phone and called me. He had said exactly what I told him to say."

"Is this the real reason you've been targeted for a contract, Clyde?"

"Partly. Another friend told me everything that was said at the meeting."

I wasn't sure whether the meeting was the same as the inquest, but it seemed clear the someone who went to the controllers was the friend he had asked to man the video. I had realized the moment he started this story, he was providing some insight into the real reason for the contract on his life.

He told stories the way I do, starting with an illustration then making the point it's intended to explain. Clyde, however, often left me to figure out the point of his illustrations. This time, he made his point very clear.

"I'm just waiting for a call to tell me where to be to have my accident."

"Do you really believe there's no other way than to let someone kill you?"

"It's inevitable. You know, you ought to look into those stashes of strychnine. One is in a pub in England hidden under a rug in a dark hallway. The other is in an ink bottle buried under a tree on the main road leading into London. I'll bring you a map and show you where they are.

"I went to my doctor friend, who was going to put together a case for me with all the equipment and medications I would need for various situations, like truth serum."

"I hope you realize, I'm not getting any clear picture of just what you do for a living."

"Danny," he said impatiently. "What I'm doing is sharing some of the concepts I call, 'abstract thinking.' I've tried to explain them to my associates, but none of them ever quite grasped them or appreciated them. All they ever said was, 'How much can I make? How much can I make?'"

Clyde's very general revelations continued, scattered between discussions about the educational CDs which had not yet arrived and numerous unfriendly visits Clyde had made to Jeurgen's school to complain about their poor instruction. Each meeting I had with Clyde was followed by a clandestine rendezvous with Grant for a complete debriefing.

My cat-and-mouse exchanges with Clyde were not as frustrating to me as they became for Grant and his superiors. Grant conveyed their antagonism during a debriefing.

"Danny, the Justice Department is concerned about your continual interruptions of Clyde. They want you to let him talk. They want him to admit his actual activities, tell us who he is working for, and tell us how long he's been doing it. No one is impressed with his abstract thinking. They are concerned you are allowing yourself to again be deceived by Clyde.

"You don't seem to realize that most of what he is telling you is a figment of his imagination. His inflated view of his own importance is no doubt being exploited by his foreign intelligence handlers. We're certain he has sold secrets to a foreign government, and he might have introduced other soldiers to them, but any suggestion that he has any influence over anyone is a fabrication, or an exaggeration, even though he might believe some of his own claims. In fact, do you think he could be jacking us around?"

"Of course he could, Grant, but you know, even though he contradicts details when he repeats many of his stories, and he will purposely continue to do that for his own protection, he has been consistent in the basic facts." Grant had previously agreed with that observation, but he had apparently been unable to sell that to his superiors.

They couldn't seem to recognize that Clyde often supplied pieces to the puzzle with images on both sides, with only one side being genuine. I was certain they were forcing these pieces into their own erroneous picture.

Still more dangerous was the fact that Clyde's continued suspicion of me eluded them completely, not just his suspicion that I might already be part of the investigation, but that my principles would lead me to report what he was telling me before he could persuade me to join him, if in fact his associates could be persuaded to trust him again.

Since our superiors thought he wouldn't have told me anything, to include his fabrications, unless he completely trusted me, Grant insisted, "The Justice department is convinced he will supply the smoking gun and incriminate himself if you will just let him do all the talking."

I insisted, "Clyde is just waiting for his talkative friend to just stop talking at some point and begin eliciting information from him in ways he will recognize."

DAMIAN and MONGOOSE

Grant seemed to understand that too, but it only frustrated him more. He had his instructions. Those included specific questions I was to ask in order to speed up Clyde's self-incrimination. At one of my debriefings, he minced no words.

3

SECURITY

"Danny, the Justice Department wants to know when Clyde started in espionage, what information he has provided, who is getting the information, why he thinks his family wouldn't be investigated if something happened to him, and the names of some of his friends."

"Of course, but you understand, I have to make sure the atmosphere and the context of the conversation is right for those specific questions."

"Danny, why can't you just follow my instructions instead of making excuses for not asking Clyde the questions I've directed?"

"I'm not saying I won't try to work those questions in, but those aren't the subjects Clyde is going to want to talk about at our next meeting."

"How could you possibly know what he is going to talk about at your next meeting?"

"Remember how he ended the last meeting? I had challenged some of his claims because he was so vague about the details. He went home and immediately started thinking about my doubts and deciding what he is willing to tell me in order to dispel those doubts.

"I might be able to work your questions into the conversation later in the evening, but because he's been reluctant to provide answers to those questions, I have to work in a plausible reason for asking those things. I can't let them sound like I've been directed to ask about them."

Grant didn't respond, and he made no comment at my next debriefing when I reported that Clyde had started our conversation with the very subject I had anticipated and sidestepped as usual my numerous attempts to obtain the information they had requested. Hoping to convince Grant I could eventually get the information my way, I asked, "What is the most important information you need?"

He said he would get back to me on that. He did, and his answer was, "We want all we can get."

It was becoming increasingly clear they had rejected almost everything Clyde had given me over the past month but were still convinced he would eventually hang himself for them. They only wanted him to hand them their smoking gun. Anything else was a figment of his imagination. Concern over their lack of complete control over my conversations with Clyde had reached its peak.

Since Grant sometimes mirrored their anger, I wasn't surprised when he told me I would be attending a meeting in the States. I asked him what plausible reason he had established for my trip to the States. He answered, "There's no need for a reason; Clyde won't be asking you about it." He also had no explanation for me to give if I should run into someone from my battalion at the airport.

He took my BMW keys when we reached the Frankfurt airport. I hoped he was going to hide my car somewhere it wasn't likely to be seen and require an explanation, either to someone in the Battalion or to Clyde, who had bragged about his collection of license plate numbers from cars driven by CI. Just before I entered the boarding lounge, Grant took me aside and confirmed my general assessment of him.

"Danny, I want to say one thing before you go. Don't roll over for them. Just tell them what you've been telling me, and don't roll over for them."

With no further discussion, I started for the airport security gate, assured that I needed no more preparation for this meeting in the States. It was enough that the guy in the trenches with me understood what I was doing, in spite of the instructions from his superiors he had to follow. I believed saving the mission was his motive for this warning, and I accepted the burden he had placed on me.

Predictably, as soon as I reached the boarding lounge, I encountered two agents from 527th MI Bn, one from A Company's Headquarters in Holland and one from Battalion Headquarters in K-town.

The A Company Operations Officer from Holland approached me and engaged me in friendly conversation, while his companion leaned against the windows about twenty feet away and waved.

Mr. Stalwart shook my hand and greeted me. "Hello, Danny. How are things?"

"Things are going great. I'm making progress with my coordination with your units on B Company's GDP. How are you guys?"

"We've been selected to represent the Battalion at the annual MICCEP Conference. Where are you going?"

I couldn't afford to invent a story that my superiors might not approve, or one that might be repeated within the Battalion. These particular gentlemen, as officers in the Military Intelligence Career Accepted Program, had excellent reputations. MICCEPs were Special Agents whose career positions were primarily confined to counterintelligence supervision.

I enlisted their cooperation. "Mr. Stalwart, I'd like to ask a favor of you. I'd like you to forget you've seen me at the airport and convince Mr. Gallant to do the same. You can check directly with LTC Cameron when you return from your trip if you have any problem with my request."

"That won't be necessary, Danny. We are perfectly willing to forget we have seen you."

"Thanks. I appreciate that."

The afternoon of my arrival in the States, I was joined in my hotel room by a gentleman employed by the FBI. We sat opposite each other in hotel chairs. He relayed his qualifications in behavioral science, then made a pronouncement.

"I am very familiar with the case you're working and the kind of personality you are dealing with in Clyde Conrad. I've seen a lot of these personalities in previous cases and can see a lot of the same symptoms of the classic alcoholic in Clyde."

Then, he began to characterize Clyde in terms I'd been hearing from Grant. "Clyde is paranoid and suffers from delusions of grandeur. He may even believe many of the stories he is telling you. It should be helpful for you to know that so you won't be completely taken-in by him because he is your friend. He is extremely remorseful and is desperately seeking someone to whom he can confess. He no doubt wants to turn himself in.

"He knows in his heart that you were sent, but he wants to believe that you are his friend. I've derived my conclusions from several of the facts I've gleaned from the investigative reports."

For once, I listened without interruption, but not without an overwhelming sense of exasperation. When he paused, waiting for my reaction, I asked him if he was interested in my assessment of Clyde. He was. I put both feet on the floor, leaned forward slightly with my hands clasped in my lap, and looked straight into his eyes.

"I believe Clyde drinks because he likes to, certainly, but also because he wants to make sure I'm drinking. That's his personal lie-detector. Since I can't vouch for the truthfulness of any of his stories, I will have to accept your word that they have all been investigated and proven false. Although, I think it's best if I don't know that for sure so that I won't inadvertently reveal to Clyde some knowledge I can't explain.

"Clyde is not confessing; he's bragging. He's sharing his experiences with someone who appreciates what he calls abstract thinking. Whether he has actually done all the things he's describing remains to be seen. Maybe he has only thought of some of them. He has no remorse because he doesn't believe he has done anything wrong. He is totally amoral.

"I believe you are completely right about his knowing I was

sent but wanting to believe that I wasn't. I am his friend, and he is mine, but Clyde is a user. Right now there's a certain kind of friend he wants me to be, one who will compromise any and all principles and do whatever Clyde wants me to do."

This behavior specialist was what my superiors would call a good listener, who displays no verbal agreement or disagreement. However, I sensed some serious concerns in his expressions over my strong opinions of Clyde and my inability to see Clyde as an expert saw him. My perceptions were based on more than sentience. His body language warned me that I should back-up my opinions with some systematic logic, even though it meant bringing up a subject I had purposely not mentioned in my reports to Grant.

"I want to explain to you why Clyde is not completely convinced that I was sent. I've been allowing him to formulate in his mind and describe to me the person I would have to be, the person he would believe I can be, in order for him to be convinced I wasn't sent, will not pose any danger to him in the future, and might even join him. I am reluctantly, but steadily assuming that role.

"He has listened to some Bible tapes which I left with him years ago. From those tapes, he has concluded that my faith teaches that nothing I do in life, after I have believed in Jesus Christ, has any effect on my going to heaven when I die—"

"He's right!"

I knew immediately he had interrupted involuntarily and wasn't planning any theological discussion, but I sensed I needed to let him know I agreed with him. I answered, "Of course he's right, but the point is, he has distorted that truth in order to justify whatever he is doing."

I watched him nod his agreement, then I continued. "He is confident that distortion will motivate me to abandon my principles. I'm not planning to give in too easily, but I will let him convince himself I am that friend he wants me to be.

"He prides himself in his ability to read people, exploit their beliefs, and con anyone. It's arrogance, not remorse, that's driving Clyde."

He tilted his head back and tightened his jaw, apparently still very concerned about my assessment of Clyde. Then, he looked at his watch and seemed to be about to end the interview, but he thought of one more question. "Do you think he would turn himself in?"

"Never! And he will not say a word if he is arrested."

He frowned, took a deep breath, and stood to leave. His parting statement neither confirmed nor refuted my suspicion that he hadn't changed his opinion. "In that case, Danny, I think we need to discuss this a little bit more tomorrow."

The following morning, he completely surprised me. After a friendly greeting we took our seats, and he began with a stern expression.

"Well, I can see you have given a great deal of thought to your assessment of Clyde. You may be right. You certainly would know Clyde better than anyone else. But, I have to tell you, for your sake, I will recommend that your involvement in the operation be terminated."

"Why?" I was incredulous.

"Because, based on your strong sense of values and Christian background, you will not be able to continue lying to your friend. I'm sure you think you can, but when you finally realize that he is a traitor to his country, and you will, it will be much harder on you than you think."

"In that case, I'd like to explain something else to you. I believe, as strongly as I believe in the principles you have mentioned, that it would be immoral for me to not do my best possible job as a counterespionage agent, even when I discover beyond doubt that my friend is a traitor to my country.

"As for lying to my friend, I consider what I'm doing role-playing. That falls into a category that the Word of God teaches is not a sin when it is done in defense of my country."

"You mean, it's a sin, but it's forgiven."

"No, Sir! It is not a sin. The Word teaches that there is a special category of morality applicable to legal activity against enemies of my country and against criminals. Didn't King David send his friend, Hushai, to befriend his own son, Absalom, and deceive him with bad advice so David would have time to prepare for war against his son?"

"Danny, I think your theology is a little off."

"Sir, does that matter?" The point is, I believe it! Now, I ask you. If I believe that, can I do this?"

"I see your point, Danny, but I still have to recommend, for your sake, that your part in the operation be terminated."

As he left, he handed me his business card. After he was gone, I left the hotel to eat lunch and think over this new challenge. I was scheduled to meet Mr. Romski in my room later that afternoon. I was back before he arrived. I had no idea what to expect. Romski began immediately with a question.

"Danny, what do you think Clyde is guilty of?"

"I'm aware that he is capable of jacking us around, but I believe he is guilty of espionage."

"And how does that make you feel, Danny?"

"I'd rather not get into that, Mr. Romski, because I have to insulate myself against such personal indignation. I don't want to take a chance that I might display a negative attitude with Clyde when I discover indisputably that he is a traitor to my country."

Romski seemed to understand that. He even seemed pleased, but I was concerned about the FBIs recommendation. I quickly added, "When that becomes evident, I will have no difficulty fulfilling my duty as an agent, even though Clyde is my friend."

Romski's expression of confusion at my statement suggested he had no knowledge of any recommendation from the behavior specialist. His next question confirmed that. "Danny, do you want me to address any particular issues before you depart for Germany?"

I explained about the two Battalion agents I had bumped into at the Frankfurt Airport and my handling of the situation. I also stated why I would prefer the CI Field Office in Mainz not be used for debriefings or writing sworn statements. He said he would address those issues. We parted company and I took a taxi to the airport.

During my return flight, I decided I still had a part in this operation. I just wasn't sure what changes I would have to make. I put that concern aside and took the time to reflect on my friendship with Clyde.

I've been Clyde's friend all these years not because I've agreed with or even needed to know everything he did or believed, but because I've respected his skills in a profession I consider honorable. Now that I know his professionalism has not always been based on the oath he took or the soldier's creed, but on hiding his espionage activity, I'm extremely disappointed, but not shocked. His decision to betray my country has limited our friendship to an impersonal one, but I will always respect his mastery of the military skills and leadership he has demonstrated and taught me.

I know he has also been my friend, because he has often expressed admiration for my professionalism, appreciated my unconditional friendship, and in spite of himself, respected my integrity. When he learns that I haven't changed any more than he has, I believe he will respect the path I've chosen.

In the mean time, he will keep trying to corrupt me, because that's his nature, and I will do my best to gain the evidence that will put him in prison, because that's my sworn duty. We will still be friends, but neither of us can escape his destiny.

Grant met me at the Frankfurt Airport with my BMW, which, to my chagrin, he had been using while I was gone. He asked how the trip went. I told him I thought it went fairly well. We didn't discuss the details. We parted company, and I drove to BK.

Because I had crossed the international dateline twice, I was returning the day after I left. As I neared my BK hotel, I realized I needed to assume my usual paranoid, operational attitude. At that moment, a thought overpowered me.

Clyde will be waiting for me at my hotel. I will have to leave my luggage in the trunk of my car and unload it very early in the morning.

I parked the BMW in front of the hotel and walked into the lobby. The owner's son was behind the desk and called me over.

"Your friend just left. He said he will return in about an hour. He's been here a couple of times this weekend. He's very anxious to see you."

"Thank you very much. I'll come down to the restaurant in a few minutes. Please send him there if you see him."

Clyde returned that evening and several evenings after that. He embarked on a concentrated campaign to subvert my normally idealistic and tolerant view of the world and what he considered my narrow sense of morality, a misplaced faith in principles which don't matter. To justify his views he referred to some articles he had been reading.

"Haven't you read lately about all the corrupt politicians, government leaders, and businessmen around the world? These are the very people who make the laws we are expected to obey. I have a rule I call my golden rule: the one who has the gold makes the rules.

"None of it makes any difference. We've both worked for incompetent officers and we've had to clean up their messes. Don't you ever just get tired of it? I never work with anyone unless I like them and want to see them do something good for themselves. Aren't you fed up? Aren't you ready to do something that counts for you?

"I'm getting that way, Clyde."

"Danny." He paused and thought hard before continuing. "I tried many times to steer my commanders in the right direction. Most of them disregarded anything I tried to tell them and kept right on doing it wrong. They had the power. Many times I just sat back and smiled to myself and thought, *We'll see who has the power. I'll just sell all your secrets.*

"The Hungarians are the same way. They've tried using their power as a country on me. The Czechs have tried wielding their power over me too. I let them think they've succeeded, but the money I've taken from them is my ruler to measure my power over them.

"My two friends who are surgeons, the one who is an expert with weapons, and another who's putting together that kit with lethal drugs in case I need them, have taught me a lot of things about foreign intelligence services.

"I have an Atlas in my car. I've marked the locations of all the military units in Germany and others in Southern Europe. I also have the location of foreign intelligence centers where workers are trained."

Clyde retrieved his Atlas from his car and showed me the location of a hotel in Austria, used by the Hungarians to train workers. He preferred the term "workers," over recruited agents. He also showed me the location of a Russian ship, moored in Austria, used for the same purpose. He was careful not to let me see any pages in his Atlas except the ones he wanted to show me.

At my debriefings, I tried to convey Clyde's indirect recruiting method, explaining that he would not recruit me the way they were expecting, but with questions like, "Aren't you ready to do something that counts for you?" I knew he was expecting me to answer, *Yes, what do you have in mind?*

My superiors seemed to ignore my conclusions, insisting, "Clyde will ask you to join him in espionage if you pressure him enough. Just be careful not to volunteer for any involvement with Clyde. Let him make the offer."

Apparently, Grant was sensing some danger in that approach and asked me, "What would you do if Clyde decides you are working against him and threatens you with bodily harm?"

I answered truthfully, "I'll do what I have to."

SECURITY

Grant's superiors were determined to direct my conversations with Clyde and eventually implemented what I considered the second most dangerous and unnecessary investigative tool in any operation involving a controlled source. The second most dangerous is surveillance. Wiring a source is the worst. With that unspoken reservation, I agreed to being harnessed with a recording device.

I stood passively for hours while various attempts were made to settle on the best arrangement of wires, recorder, and microphone to be strapped to me. The contraption was strung from my ankle to my chest, requiring me to lower my trousers to change the batteries and recording tapes.

I diplomatically tried to point out that the adhesive tape used to secure the recorder to my ankle would not hold if I had to walk, sit, climb in and out of the car, and pull my pants up and down. The experts assured me everything would work just fine and treated me to a lecture on the vast experience that led to the choices they had made.

After the technicians left, Grant reiterated the subjects our superiors wanted me to discuss with Clyde to get him to incriminate himself on tape. I was glad they hadn't accepted his stated commitment to selling all his commanders' secrets, or even his reference to his association with the Hungarians and the Czechs, as enough incrimination to arrest and interrogate him. I was sure they would get nothing that way.

They also wanted me to be sure to ask him what he knew about the "Status of Forces Agreement" between the US and Germany and again challenge his belief that his family could not be investigated if something happened to him. I said I would do that, then

I shared some thoughts with Grant about getting some clues from Clyde that might reveal the identity of some of his associates.

"I've been thinking of a subject that might entice Clyde to discuss characteristics of some of his friends and associates, at least enough to determine if some of them are in fact U.S. soldiers. He has mentioned before that he has friends with talents he considers assets. I can ask if he has trained a replacement to take over his operations when he is gone."

"No, you can't ask him that. It sounds too much like volunteering your services."

"Believe me, Grant, I will ensure that the context in which I ask the question will not sound like volunteering to Clyde, because I plan to combine it with a request for characteristics and qualifications he has looked for in all the people who have worked with him."

I was surprised when Grant responded angrily, "If you're going to insist on doing things your way, Danny, and not following orders, the operation can terminate right here!" I was dumbfounded when he spun around, opened the hotel room door, and charged down the hall.

I stepped into the hall and called after him. "Please wait a second, Grant." He returned to the room, and I immediately attempted to calm him.

"Grant, if you think this operation should terminate, then it should, but please hear me out. Okay, I'm an asshole, but what you see as a lack of cooperation, I view as enthusiasm. I have absolutely no desire to countermand any orders. All I ask you to do is recognize that I'm the one who faces the target every day. I'm the one he is still a little suspicious of and the one who has to convince him otherwise. I'm also the one who has gotten him to give us the information we have so far.

"I consider it my obligation to tell you what I see going on out there, what I think I can do effectively, and what I think will work for me with Clyde. I only ask that you listen and be willing to discuss it. When you don't agree, once you've heard me out, you can tell me to shut up. I have no problem with that.

"I'm still aware the Justice Department does not want me to say anything that can be construed as entrapment. I would never do that. I assure you, I would never say anything that isn't clearly a part of the natural context or that could possibly be understood by Clyde as a request from me to become involved in his activities."

"As long as you can guarantee that, Danny, I have no problem. I agree you should give us your impressions, and by all means I will listen, but a lot of factors have to be considered. The Justice department appears to be running certain things. They're the ones who have to prosecute."

"I understand that."

Grant instructed me to meet him again early the next morning before meeting with Clyde, to be fitted with my electronic straight-jacket. That morning they gave me extra micro cassette tapes and batteries to stuff in my coat pockets. After having me sign the necessary legal documents a judge required for electronic surveillance of U.S. citizens, they sent me on my way.

I had breakfast with Clyde at the Hotel Viktoria. When we finished, he asked me to take a ride with him in my BMW. He directed me through BK, north to the Bingen Autobahn, then east along the Rhein River. Along the way, I reminded him of a previous conversation.

"Clyde, you threw me a curve the other day. I think you enjoy throwing me curves."

"No I don't!" He had a smirk on his face.

"You said that you had told me some things, and when I indicated what I thought you meant, I was wrong, but you just let me keep that wrong impression. Why would you do that to me?" He smiled but didn't answer, so I continued.

"There are a few areas in which I want to be sure I don't have the wrong impression." His cool attitude told me he wasn't ready to answer the questions I wanted to ask, so I started with some questions he might be more likely to answer. I thought up the questions as I spoke.

"What do the words 'contract out on you' mean? Do they mean you are going to be murdered and put six feet under?"

"That's exactly what they mean."

"Then, on the same subject, what do you mean when you say, 'It's inevitable?'"

"I went to the guy I knew would get the contract and told him to volunteer. I made a deal to make it easy for him, for half the money. He came back and said he got the contract, and he paid me the money."

"Clyde, why would the guy need assurance that the job would be easy if he's like the surgeon you told me about with special training, who's in it for the excitement?"

"Everyone likes easy money. He will call me one day and tell me where to go, and that's when it will happen. I use the term, 'inevitable,' because I have a friend who was at the meeting that was held, who heard them say, 'He will be taken care of.'

"I know I might postpone it, possibly forever, because they will wonder if I have put some information in some safe place where it will be released if anything happens to me. But you never know when one of those guys will get a wild notion, and I go out to my car some day with my family and it blows up.

"They've done a profile on me and know where to hurt me. I didn't want to go to school to pick up Jeurgen someday and he wouldn't be there."

"I can understand that, Clyde, although that doesn't make it easier to accept. Would you please clarify one more thing? Since I have had to reconcile myself to the fact that you sell classified U.S. information to foreign countries, am I right about that?"

He didn't answer. He didn't even look at me, and it was clear he was going to wait for me to make the next move. I looked over at him as I inquired, "Are you having trouble putting that into words after you made me reconcile myself to it?"

"Well, I have to be very careful about what I put into words. Let me tell you a story.

"I was sitting in front of an officer once. He was providing something for me. Then, all of a sudden he asked me if I had a tape recorder. I said, 'Yes,' and took it out and laid it in front of him. He asked me if I was going to record what he was going to give me. I said I was going to offer in case his memory needed any help."

Clyde and I both laughed, but I knew this was no funny story. He continued. "I said it wasn't on right then. He asked if I would really do that. I said, 'You're doing it.' He looked very surprised, but I could see it on him."

At that moment, Clyde leaned over in the passenger seat and looked hard under the sport coat I was wearing, unbuttoned, as I drove. I sensed he wanted to startle me enough to make me look down to see if anything was showing. Instead, I gave him a confused expression and pretended not to realize what his gesture implied.

Just then, we approached what I remembered was the last gas station before we would reach Mainz. It had become obvious Mainz was our destination. I pulled in for fuel. We both stood behind the BMW while I put gas in the tank. I finally responded to his story.

"Clyde, I can't believe you would walk into someone's office with a tape recorder."

With a mocking laugh, he looked at me sideways and stared awkwardly under my coat for a couple of seconds, then looked at the pavement and paced as he spoke. "Once I was accused by one of the people I do business with of some activity he didn't approve of. They have a special test to find out things. They put this thing around your head and give it a quick twist when they want to know something and don't like your answer.

"So I pulled a bluff. I told him I wanted to take the test, but I reminded him of my reputation with his bosses. He decided not to give me the test, and he was right about me! You see what I did?"

"Of course I do, Clyde."

He didn't take my word for that and said, "He ran the risk of looking foolish if he insisted on the test and was wrong."

To make sure I understood the implication of his story, he turned toward me and pulled my coat open further with his right hand so he could look closer. Every muscle in my body strained against the temptation to pull away from him, but I simply wrinkled my forehead at his gesture, while I quickly formulated a plan.

If you start patting me down, I'm going to pick that time to remove the

*gas nozzle and return it to the pump, and accidently let some gas spill
on your hand.*

Clyde suddenly backed off. If he had intended to pat me down,
he changed his mind. As I put away the gas nozzle, I couldn't help
wondering if Clyde's stories were going to be too subtle for the
guys back at Headquarters listening later to the tape, since they
couldn't observe his actions. When we were back in the car and on
our way to Mainz, I changed the subject.

"Okay, I can understand your need for caution. Just give me an
example of my impressions that are incorrect."

"For one thing, you thought I wouldn't let you come to the
house because you might say something stupid or my family
might say something stupid."

"Alright, Clyde! It's not that I believe your family knows more
than you say they do. You told me you would allow me to challenge the logic of your reasoning about the solution you have
planned for yourself. I was only going to suggest that any investigation might not stop just because you're gone."

He did not respond to that statement. The subject was closed.
He started repeating the story of the meeting that was held
concerning him. He didn't hesitate this time about naming the
Hungarians as the ones who had held the meeting.

In describing the meeting, he referred to their investigations
into activity they didn't approve of, not only his, but also others
who were involved with him but were telling the Hungarians
stories he had coached them on. He called these stories "truth the
Hungarians could accept." I wondered if the guys listening to the
tapes would ever realize that all I would ever get by just letting
Clyde talk would be truth he thought I would accept.

115

DAMIAN and MONGOOSE

It was Clyde's contention that the Hungarians had to be careful what they decided to do about him, not only because he knew so much, but out of fear of losing a very important source.

He had learned that the basic philosophy, which dictates most of their actions, is, "Where the source leads, we must follow." Always referring to himself as a source, he conceded, "In spite of my importance to them, I can't take a chance on that guy who might get a wild notion to go through with their plan to eliminate me."

When we reached Mainz, Clyde showed me where to park and led me to a pool hall a couple of blocks from the Bahnhof, where he challenged me to a game. I had kept track of the time elapsed since I started the recorder, so I went directly to the men's room while Clyde looked for some cigarettes.

In one of the stalls, I quickly changed cassettes. I noticed the recorder had become a little loose on my ankle, and it worried me some, but nothing was broken, and I didn't want to keep Clyde waiting. I wrote the time and date on the recorded cassette and placed it in my coat pocket.

As I approached the pool table, I reached into my pants pocket and activated the switch to restart the recorder. Clyde insisted I take off my coat and hang it on the wall. It seemed important to Clyde, and since my heavy, loose-fitting sweater concealed the microphone well, I removed my coat. I kept an eye on it because my CI credentials were in it.

My leg was hurting considerably from a pinched nerve I had suffered several days before, of which I had informed Clyde. Bending was awkward and painful, but it gave me an excuse to be careful not to disturb the recorder and wiring too much. As we started the game, I resumed the discussion about the contract on his life.

"Clyde, when you figured out it was inevitable you'd be departing the scene, did you train a replacement?"

"You can't really do that."

"Because of the investigation, or you couldn't find anyone with your qualifications?"

"No. The system doesn't allow it. Common sense, Danny. That's the biggest qualification."

"Besides that and abstract thinking, what qualifications have you looked for in the people you work with?"

"Those are the two primaries, but—" He interrupted himself to concentrate on the game. After several shots between us, he continued, "Virtually impossible to find anybody to do my job. Qualifications? Abstract thinking; a combination of someone respected, professional, hard working; makes friends easily; super con-artist."

"And what happens to the associates you already have?"

"If they want to do anything when I'm gone and enjoy themselves, all they need is a little imagination."

I was getting no information or clear personal characteristics, so I changed the subject to one Grant had directed. "Clyde," I said with concern in my voice, "I have conducted some investigation that involved liaison with the Germans. I discovered they didn't always stick to the letter of the Status of Forces Agreement and often insisted on prosecuting American soldiers. It worries me a little that you don't think they will investigate your family."

"Gitta won't be bothered by the Americans, and the Germans

won't care where her money comes from as long as she pays the German taxes on it. I've talked this over with an attorney.

"Gitta will receive proceeds from two insurance policies totaling one million one hundred thousand dollars, as well as an inheritance of two million dollars. A lawyer will show up on her doorstep. Forty thousand is in a trust to be paid to Jeurgen in monthly installments. Jeurgen will also receive any training he desires."

"What kind of training?"

"Whatever training he's interested in. You see, I've taken care of everything. Whatever he wants, someone will be waiting to provide training in whatever areas he shows an interest in. I've spent hours teaching Jeurgen philosophy.

"I've been teaching him rhymes since he was very small. They contain more information than I've told you. When he is old enough, he will understand them. You could question him all day, and he wouldn't know what you're talking about, but when he needs the information, he has it."

After three games of nine-ball, Clyde suggested we go to a restaurant to eat and drink some more beer. As he started toward the bar, looking for the waitress to get him some cigarettes, I put on my coat. Turning from the coatrack, I felt something hit my right foot. I knew immediately what it was.

I looked around to see that Clyde had stopped about fifteen feet away and turned to wait for me. I caught a glimpse of the tape recorder lying on the floor next to my foot, still attached to the microphone wire that ran up my leg.

I had no doubt that Clyde had seen it, even though the light was dim. I expected him to do an about-face and head for the door, but

118

instinctively I rotated my right shoe over the recorder to hide it and stood there with my weight on my heel.

At the same time, I raised my left arm and motioned toward the men's room, saying I needed to take care of some business. I complained that my leg was hurting and told him, "Get your cigarettes; I'll be with you in a minute."

When he started off to look for the waitress, my heart was in my throat. Although I realized he hadn't seen the recorder, I was afraid to bend down to pull it from the cord because he might turn back. I limped as I pushed the recorder along the floor the twenty feet to the men's room, shielding it from Clyde's view with my right foot, should he turn around. There was no one else in that part of the poolroom, and Clyde was still walking away from me.

In the stall, I discovered that all the adhesive tape holding the recorder just above my ankle had broken. In anger, I swore aloud.

Realizing I was wearing a pair of thick, stretch-knit socks, I loaded a new recording tape, wrote the time and date on the used one, tied a loop in the cord to shorten it, and stuffed the recorder into my sock. Clyde was waiting for me on the sidewalk when I again flipped on the switch in my pocket.

There was a festival in Mainz that day, and many of the streets were lined with booths selling all sorts of merchandise, especially food, beer, and wine. Hundreds of people crowded the streets and the booths and watched musicians and costumed entertainers who paraded randomly up and down the streets. As Clyde led me to the Chinese restaurant where he wanted to eat, he told me about a scheme he had never gotten around to. The story was purposely cryptic as usual, but he finally revealed some characteristics of associates who were clearly not American soldiers.

119

"Danny, let me ask what you think would have happened. I stopped it—"

"You what?"

"Something I was thinking of doing. I did the background work on this, and I figured it would work. I was sitting and somebody was reading the paper and talking to me. There was this sad story about a big-ass doctor's sweetheart in East Germany. He couldn't get her out.

"The comment was made, 'Yeah, it's very sad. The guy works hard and has all that money, and it doesn't help him; he can't get his sweetheart out.' Well, later when I was looking, you know, doing abstract thinking, running qualifications. I run qualifications, such as language, locks, you know, any special talent. And uh, cross borders without being checked—"

"Yeah?"

"That's one of the qualifications. So in a click, I thought, *Well, shit, if you can say, 'I'm bringing out a few items, and I don't want them checked.'* They don't check at all! So I talked to the guy. 'Would you bring somebody out?' And, you know the obvious: 'How much would I get?' 'Could you do that?' 'Oh yeah.' 'Oh yeah?' 'I can do that!'

"So I looked at it, some of the mechanical stuff. How to make sure the person being transported doesn't see the transporter, how to contact the people who want somebody out. It came down to there was nothing to it. The money and contacts you could work through a lawyer. Then the guy says to the guard at the gate, 'I can get an escort; don't open the trunk.' 'Oh, yes Sir, yes Sir!' That'll work."

Clyde seemed to have satisfied himself that I wasn't wired when he proceeded to enlighten me concerning training made available to him. "I received specialized training from the East in only one area. They offered me several others, but I refused them because I didn't want to accidently reveal such knowledge in front of the wrong people. Watch this:

"For the acronym GDP (General Deployment Plan), the Hungarians use EDP. I didn't want to pick up any bad habits and say EDP in front of the G-2 (General Staff for Intelligence).

"Once, after I was already retired, I was having a conversation with a major who was still working for G-3 (General Staff for Training). The major said, 'You will never believe what they've done to the GDP.' I reminded him that I had retired and no longer had a clearance for classified information. He said, 'I know' and kept discussing it.

"Surveillance was the one area of training I allowed myself, both on foot and by vehicle. The training was conducted by people who didn't know what they were doing. My real interest was in those skills which would help me determine if I was under surveillance. I demanded that training, and I was given a special instructor. The first thing out of his mouth was, 'common sense.'"

As Clyde described the techniques in surveillance detection he'd been taught, he kept asking me if I understood them. I finally admitted to him that surveillance and surveillance detection were two of the subjects I had taught in special operations. He didn't ask me if the techniques were the same. Either he suspected they had to be because they were common sense, or he already knew they were the same.

He explained that he had exploited their rule, "Where the source leads, we have to follow," in demanding and receiving this special instruction. He also explained that he had allowed himself to be tested by one of the services.

He suddenly reverted to his well established habit of avoiding naming the service that had required him to provide a psychological profile. His reason for even revealing this test was to further demonstrate his power over this particular service.

"After eight hours completing the test, I saw the guy returning that evening. I met him and demanded to see the results of the test. The guy was torn between his fear of his bosses if he showed it to me and fear if he didn't. He decided not to risk losing such an important source, so he showed it to me. I had anticipated the results. Someone who had taken the test told me how to convey the profile you want them to have of you.

"One intelligence service interviewed me and asked if they could call my wife and give her the code word to activate an escape plan if I got into trouble. I told them, she wouldn't know what you were talking about.

"I tried to teach the Hungarians and the Czechs that they didn't have to ask anyone to work for them if they would use my recruitment philosophy. I told them, 'I never recruit. I prepare a guy until I know exactly what he will do, then I find something for him and just say, 'Go. Do it!'

"One of the services pays me three thousand a month just as a consultant. I listen to what they want done and say, 'Here's how you do that.'"

"Is that dollars or Marks, Clyde?"

"Marks."

I realized Clyde often failed to say which currency he was referring to, but he usually meant Deutsche Marks. I became convinced that I might have assumed that he had been referring to dollars when he offered me three thousand a month back in 1977. I made a mental note to make that correction the next time I talked to Grant.

Clyde continued reminiscing. "I once approached the Hungarians with a suggestion that they open a video store outside one of the American Posts. I told them they would have all the American soldiers filling out applications. They could collect personal and financial data on all of them. Their reply was, 'We'll give you the money to open a place and stock it, and we will guarantee you a profit. Then you stand by and we'll tell you what we need.' I finally turned down the offer because I didn't like the idea of staying in one place. I don't know if they used the proposal themselves.

"One of the intelligence services told me they had brought in a computer specialist to organize their collection effort. They declined my offer to help the computer specialist. They were afraid to lose their compartmentalization.

"An intelligence handler from the East offered me forty thousand dollars plus expenses to go to the States and find out where the president of the United States goes in the event of a nuclear war. I already knew the five locations where the President goes, but I waited until I returned from the States to tell the guy, who promptly paid me the money."

After considerable pressure, Clyde told me the five locations he had given the intelligence handler. Then, he said, "The guy already knew them too but wanted confirmation. I believe it was just a test to see if I could deliver. I actually spent his money traveling around the States, to Mexico, to New Jersey, all over, looking for computer components and chips.

"I had been in contact with a high-ranking member of the Hungarian Intelligence Service, who offered me the opportunity to bid on the procurement of the computer components and chips on the master list. He offered the short list of the components they were seeking, for me to prove I could get them. I demanded the entire list and got it. I just took advantage of their philosophy, 'Where the source leads—'" Clyde assumed I would fill in the remainder of the philosophy.

He eventually decided procuring computer components himself was too much work. He said, "I tried to get my contact at the U.S. Embassy in Bonn to buy the thirty components on the short list in exchange for the master list. He offered me ten thousand Marks for the entire list, then raised the amount, but I refused."

Clyde's eyes narrowed at the realization that he had inadvertently revealed he'd been dealing with the U.S. Embassy. Then he relaxed and proceeded to describe another deal he'd attempted to make with them.

"I offered them the name of the top Hungarian agent. They said they would take the name and then tell me what it was worth. I refused their offer. The Americans have the largest budget and pay the least. They can't make a decision. They have to get on a plane and fly back to the States before they can make a decision."

I cringed at that remark but couldn't detect any subtle meaning in his voice, so I tried to tie up a loose end. "Did you actually do any business with them, Clyde?"

"They came through with a hundred thousand Marks several times for other things. They knew I'd never given them anything that wasn't good. I'd have my man tell them it came from David. I am David! Don't use that name in the wrong circles or you'll have some people down on your neck!

"I'd never mention the name, Clyde. Have you used other names?"

"When I traveled, I used several names. I had passports for all the names, but I got rid of them."

"Were they provided for you by East Block intelligence services?"

"Yes."

His hesitation made me doubtful. By then, we were sitting in a very nosy Gasthaus. Clyde pulled a piece of paper from his wallet and copied three telephone numbers from it onto the corner he had torn off a beer *Deckel*, which he handed to me with an explanation.

"I want you to have these. The first one is a number in Budapest for the Hungarian Intelligence Service, used by agents and couriers who call in when they want to meet with someone. The second is the same type of number for the Czechs in Prague. The third is the number of a highly placed Hungarian Agent I haven't been able to check out yet. He's a sleeper, living in Germany, still waiting for an assignment."

"Why are you giving this to me, Clyde?"

"You may want to use it to make some money, or you may just want to make some bennies. You'll think of something. The first two numbers are current, but unless the caller has the daily codes, the phones will shut down."

That was clearly his opening for me to ask for the daily codes, signifying that I was interested in working in espionage. I knew I would have to wait for my debriefing before I gave him any response at all, and maybe someone would have to fly to the States before a decision was made. Clyde added one more element of persuasion without actually asking me to do anything.

"The Hungarian Intelligence Service is second only to the Russians. The Czechs are next. Everyone knows the East Germans are the largest intelligence service in Europe, but they have the largest turnover. They lose more agents than anyone else. As with most of the revelations he made discursively along the streets of Mainz and at several noisy Gasthauses, he wasn't revealing many personal details, but he soon surprised me.

"I received a call, Danny. From Chicago." He mentioned who the caller was, but the noisy Gasthaus drowned-out everything but the word "father." It sounded like "the girl's father" or "my stepfather." He moved quickly to a description of the call.

"He called me to tell me someone was asking if I sold secrets. The guy says, 'If I'd known you were into that, I might have been able to help you.' He dabbles a little in drugs anyway."

"Clyde, I interjected, I've been meaning to tell you something about that. I'm not saying there's no investigation. You would know best about that, but I've conducted a number of five-year bring-up investigations in the past that should never have been conducted.

"INSCOM gets behind on investigations by the thousands. I've spent weeks on a background investigation for some guy's security clearance, only to discover he retired or left the Army years earlier.

"I remember you told me they never did your last five-year bring-up. If the investigation goes away, maybe that could be what it was. As for the surveillance you detected, could that be those guys investigating you for activities they don't approve of?"

126

"I thought of that. I don't know."

Grant had warned me not to put words in Clyde's mouth, but I'd suddenly thought of a way to turn some of Clyde's own words against him. "You said you told the Hungarians you don't recruit. What have you been doing with me, Clyde, with all this information you're giving me: preparation?"

"How can you say that? I'm just giving you an opportunity to take advantage of this information, to make money if that's what you want to do, or for the glory."

"Is that an offer, Clyde?"

"Danny, I'll never make you an offer. You're a friend."

I couldn't help thinking, *If that's not clear enough to the Justice Department, I don't know any way to explain it to them. What I have to do is answer in the affirmative one of his questions about whether I'm ready to do something for myself, and I'm recruited.*

My superiors refused to believe that Clyde was still at least cautiously suspicious and wasn't going to ask me to sell secrets. He again demonstrated that suspicion after a lengthy discussion about Zolton Szabo.

"One day I was sitting with friends. One of them made the comment, 'Szabo pulled a fast one by getting himself into trouble.' They considered Z's trouble a blessing because his loss of clearance allowed him to retire from the U.S. military, something the Hungarians wouldn't have let him do otherwise.

"Z's bennies for being a Colonel in Hungarian Intelligence include a house in Budapest in addition to his house in Austria and villa in Spain. He travels a lot.

"He is very clever and intelligent. He knows the history of numerous buildings and other landmarks we've passed on our journeys through Germany and farther. He speaks French, Hungarian, English, Italian, German, and a little Russian.

'He's as busy as I am, but I'm the best. Between Szabo and me, there's no more knowledgeable person about the activities of intelligence services in Europe."

"Did Szabo recruit you?"

"No! My first business transaction with Z was when he wanted me to translate something for him."

His distortion of this story was already obvious. I challenged him with a slight smile. "Clyde, I saw Szabo translate for Captain Webb. He didn't need any help translating."

He looked at me sideways, then said, "I went to Z with a proposal. He just said, 'You can't know those things.' I said, 'I know you're a Colonel with Hungarian intelligence!' Z got real mad and asked me how I knew that, and I just said, 'The important thing is I do know, so will you translate for me?"

Even with his correction, the story sounded like a mixture of the invented product and the video of soldiers and controllers, but his point was that he was already working for the Hungarians and had learned about Szabo from mutual friends. I was only convinced that Clyde wanted me to believe he had not been recruited by Szabo.

I did believe the position of Colonel with Hungarian Intelligence was more plausible for Szabo than Russian Military Intelligence (GRU). He continued by repeating his other scheme involving Szabo.

"I made another proposal to Szabo to make a video of soldiers and controllers going into the same hotels so I could sell it to the Americans, but he went to the Hungarians with the plan."

"And, you say he's not dangerous, Clyde?"

"He might be like you, Danny."

"Like me? Wait. What are you trying to tell me?"

"I don't know." His sarcasm was obvious.

"What do you think was Szabo's motive for telling them about your scheme?"

"Same as yours."

"What's my motive to do what?"

"A patriot!"

"Oh. What kind of patriot is Szabo?"

"Hungarian!"

While I was trying to think of a response, Clyde closed his fist, raised his thumb, and pointed his index finger like a gun, pretending to take shots at a group of black performers parading by. When I turned to see them, he smiled and said, "I've always known you were prejudiced, Danny."

He punctuated his remark with uncharacteristic pokes of my chest with his finger. At the same time, he smiled as he turned his head from side to side looking intently under my coat. I understood his implication that his accusation of my prejudice might be recorded, and I recognized his attempt to get a reaction.

I stiffened and held my breath, because each poke of his finger landed squarely on the microphone taped to the middle of my chest under my sweater. One millimeter to either side and his finger would have slid off the microphone. When it didn't, I hoped he thought he was hitting my chest bone. He assumed an expression of at least temporary satisfaction as we walked to the car.

When I dropped him off at his car in Bad Kreuznach, I explained that I needed to take a long walk because my leg was hurting. I needed an excuse to leave my hotel right away in case he stayed around to check on me.

I would need to cross the river and walk into the woods a couple of hours later to meet with Grant to return all the recording equipment. I hated having that meeting so soon after my visit with Clyde and so close to my hotel, even though I knew Grant was worried about the evidentiary chain-of-custody of the recorded tapes.

My instructions were to call Grant when Clyde departed. I didn't want to use the phone at the hotel desk because the manager might have to dial the number, but I remembered there was a pay phone in a pub just down the street, between my hotel and the Kurhaus. Once I had called Grant, I had an hour and a half before our meeting, so I joined about a dozen Germans strolling along the path next to the Nahe River.

In my sport coat and tie, I blended nicely with the walkers on the path and the couples cruising down the river on paddle boats. Germans always dress up to stroll in the evening. The pain in my leg slowed my pace considerably, but I needed the time to think through the information Clyde had given me.

Suddenly, I realized the information was starting to run together in my mind. I couldn't sort it out. I couldn't even remember how the conversation began that morning. Then I realized they would have everything on tape, and I relaxed, thinking the recorder might be a blessing in disguise, in spite of the near disastrous mishap. I didn't stay relaxed long.

Whoa! What the hell are you thinking, Williams? Half the reason for these damn tapes is probably to test me. From now on, they will already know the answer when they ask if those were his exact words.'

SECURITY

My integrity is on the line. It always was. I won't be allowed a single mistake. They've never believed I could accurately remember all I've been telling them; now they'll expect me to remember every word.

Surely they can't deny the volume of information I got today, after only six weeks, but will this backfire? Will they think they have enough to arrest and interrogate him? They'll lose him if they do, and they'll never learn who his associates are. Damn, I have to stop arguing with myself. I have to get ready to regurgitate ten hours of information in another hour.

I tried picturing myself at breakfast at the hotel Viktoria that Saturday morning. I saw myself greeting Clyde when he came in. I recalled the conversation we had at breakfast, on the road to the gas station, to Mainz, at the pool table. Slowly, methodically, it all came back to me, but as portions of the conversation popped into my head, a sense of frustration and anger swelled up in me. I contemplated the pressure I would endure from questions about my technique and my failure to get the specific responses they wanted from Clyde.

Why do I have to be continually on trial? Will Clyde's demonstrated suspicion of me be wasted on them? Will they appreciate any of the information and understand how much more there is to be learned, or will they consider it all just so much delusion of grandeur or Clyde's jacking us around?

I had crossed the river and started up the winding trail toward the top of the wooded hill. I was passing walkers on the trail. I shuddered as if somehow my thoughts were so loud they might be overheard.

I walked as fast as the pain in my leg would allow, almost desperate to separate myself from the crowd. I found a short,

131

dead-end spur off the main trail, where I could stop and gather my thoughts. I tried to put aside my anger and frustration and get organized, but I began instead to analyze my own motives.

Am I all wrong about Clyde and just too arrogant to recognize it? I was wrong before! Is Clyde inventing all these stories? Is he what they think he is, just a soldier who sold classified documents and nothing more? If I stop trying to read his expressions and sit back and let him do all the talking is there no danger of blowing my rapport with him? Why does that scare the hell out of me? Why can't they accept the consisten- cies in his stories that I know Grant has seen? Damn, Williams, there you go again.

I glanced back at the main trail and saw a young boy standing, watching me pace. I wondered if I'd been talking aloud. I relaxed, took a shortcut through the trees to a spot near the lower end of the main trail, then sat down on a log and finished organizing my thoughts.

It was fairly dark, and I had only ten minutes left, so I started down the hill to the meeting place. As I approached Grant's car, I remembered how much beer and wine Clyde and I had consumed. I wondered if our superiors would consider Clyde's revelations the ravings of an alcoholic.

As soon as I had greeted Grant, I suggested he give me a field sobriety test. He agreed, and I passed the test. I hoped that would assure him that Clyde had also been lucid when he made the statements I was about to report. In my case, I knew adrenaline was keeping me sober.

Before I could get started, Grant informed me that he only wanted to collect the equipment and tapes and would arrange a debriefing at a later date. I couldn't help wondering about the possible significance of that arrangement. *No doubt you want a transcript of the tapes in front of you when you debrief me.*

I handed over the equipment with a brief statement that the recorder had broken loose but I had prevented a compromise, which I would explain later. I knew I was wasting my breath, but I mentioned that it would be good to relax a little, not having to remember statements verbatim. He corrected me immediately.

"Oh! You will still have to be debriefed the same in spite of the tapes, in case of some mechanical failure."

I insisted on giving him a few bits of information before he left, so he took me for a thirty-minute drive, then let me out where he had picked me up. During that drive, I told him to be especially attentive to the first tape, which illustrated Clyde's continued suspicion of me and his serious caution against making incriminating statements. I also told him about Clyde's dealings with the American Embassy and his code name, David.

The surprise and slight smile on Grants face told me there had already been some cooperation with FCA by the people Clyde had dealt with at the Embassy, and they didn't know Clyde was David. I also told him of the call from Chicago about their investigation.

On Grant's instruction, I stayed away from my hotel Sunday and continued my war plan coordination the following week in order to avoid another meeting with Clyde until my next debrief. My debriefing, late Tuesday, provided several disappointments.

Something had happened to the recorder at the outset, and nothing was recorded until the second tape, when Clyde and I were at the pool hall in Mainz. That meant they would have to accept my word that Clyde was suspicious of being recorded.

I was only half surprised that, after three days transcribing the tapes, they required me to execute another hand-written, sworn statement of my ten-hour conversation with Clyde. I completed the statement in a hotel room at two o'clock Wednesday morning. My greatest disappointment came when Grant surprised me with a question.

"Danny, why did you ask Clyde what qualifications he would consider for someone to replace him after I told you not to ask him that?"

I was confused and embarrassed. I told Grant I had come away from our discussion with the distinct understanding that he had concluded as long as I could guarantee I would not ask that question in a context that might suggest I was volunteering to work for Clyde, it was allowed.

"I never made that statement," he said, bitterly. "I'm just waiting for the Justice Department to decide if you have completely blown the mission. In the mean time, we will proceed as usual."

"I'm sorry, Grant. I promise I will pay better attention and avoid such confusion in the future. I believe, and I certainly hope that the Justice Department will conclude from the tapes, that Clyde did not think I was volunteering for anything."

4

<u>SPY SCHOOL</u>

On further instructions, I had been too busy with my cover mission to meet with Clyde the week following my second, handwritten statement. Clyde had said he would be busy for a couple of weeks as well. I hoped that meant he was traveling. I dreaded the possibility he might look for me at my hotel, then worry about where I was, after he had told me so much on Saturday.

I had told Clyde I was scheduled to take the train from Mainz to Bremerhaven where my private auto had arrived from the States, drive my auto back to Frankfurt to pick up Shirley at the airport, then drive her to our apartment in Steinenbronn just southwest of Stuttgart. I had also scheduled a week's leave to move Shirley into the apartment before returning to Bad Kreuznach.

Grant arranged to meet me once more the evening before my

departure for Bremerhaven. We met in a huge park in Wiesbaden where we had met before. As we walked along the park trails, I explained my schedule and we made arrangements for emergency contact while I was on leave.

It grew dark rather quickly, and we seemed to be the only people left in the park. We had walked onto a large veranda of a park building and were leaning forward against a railing looking out into the night, when Grant took a deep breath and began to speak without looking at me.

"Danny, I want to prepare you. After considerable deliberation, it's been decided that we are going to shut down the operation."

I could hardly catch my breath. The darkness closed in around me, and for several seconds, I felt I was standing there alone. Slowly, reality crept back into my mind as if I had just stepped out of the twilight zone. I was certain immediately that the impending interrogation of Clyde, which Grant's announcement implied, was doomed to failure, but I knew that any argument from me was likely to fall on deaf ears. As we walked off the veranda toward the lake, I was overwhelmed with disappointment, but I tried to reply calmly.

"Well, you guys have all the data on which to make that decision. I just hate to see you arrest Clyde expecting to break him down in an interrogation. Obviously I've been wrong about him before, but I think you'll lose him." Apparently I wasn't as calm as I thought.

"Danny, I know you don't like the idea! Hell, I don't like it either, but you said yourself, Clyde is not going to recruit you! Didn't you say that?"

"Yes, I said that, Grant."

"Then there's nothing else we can do! We can't justify continuing indefinitely! What would you do?"

That's not a question. That's a challenge. I've tried unsuccessfully to convince you Clyde will recruit me, but not the way you want him to. No one seems to get that. But you asked, so I have to come up with something.

"That would depend on what you would consider important enough to continue this operation." I needed time to think, not only of something they would buy, but also that Clyde would appreciate. I formulated an idea as I spoke. "Would you be interested in learning exactly how various foreign intelligence collection services are operating at this time, what information they are requesting, what they are getting?"

I knew all they wanted was Clyde's head on the wall, but I doubted they could refuse this kind of information. The only question was how the hell I would get it. Fragments of plans were floating around in the right side of my brain like in a toy crystal ball. I was thinking of ideas that might lead to my recruitment in a way that would satisfy the Justice Department. Grant's next question forced me to make a choice.

"How would you get him to give you that information?"

I decided to give Grant a taste of my thinking process, believing he would appreciate it. "Okay, Grant, pretend you're Clyde.

"Clyde, I've finally thought of something you could do for me before you depart the scene permanently. I'd like to learn everything you can teach me about how the various intelligence services work so I can decide, after you've departed, just how I can use the information."

"That might work." He was hesitant, but he seemed pleasantly surprised. At the same time, he started glancing around, worried I was talking too loud. The still night air and the lake next to the trail would carry my voice even farther than usual. I apologized in a whisper.

"I'm sorry. I'll be quieter. Let's change his name to John, but seriously, you know how he thinks by now. Put yourself in his place and answer me the way you really think he would.

"John, like you said yourself, you are one of the two most knowledgeable people in Europe concerning foreign intelligence collection. I'd like to learn everything you are willing to teach me before all that knowledge is gone forever."

"I believe I would be willing to do that, Danny"

"Great, John! And I agree with you, Grant. That's exactly what he would say. I don't know if there is any hope, but if you run that up the flagpole—"

"We're the one's on the front line here. I can make a command decision. Unless you are notified otherwise, proceed with that approach."

Now you're talking my language, Grant.

"Danny, no one has said exactly when the operation will terminate, only that they are seriously considering it. If this approach changes that, I will inform you. Certainly it won't be terminated before you return from getting your wife settled in."

"I'm really glad to hear that! One question, though: did that mistake I made about asking Clyde about his replacement have anything to do with the decision to close down the operation?"

"No! As a matter of fact, the Justice Department didn't seem to have any real problem with that."

"Thanks. I guess I got lucky."

"But, Danny, that doesn't mean that's the end of it. Not everyone agrees."

"I understand."

I believed Clyde would only accept my request for this special education if he expected it to lead to my expressing an interest in espionage, but it would give me time to figure how to do that and avoid any hint of entrapment. However, the uncertainty of the operation suddenly made me apprehensive about taking leave. Relief from that concern came unexpectedly.

Next evening, while I was having dinner at my hotel before departing for Mainz to catch the Bremerhaven train, Clyde surprised me with a visit. After an exchange of greetings and a short conversation with our waiter, the hotel owner's son, Edward, I got right down to business.

"I'm glad you came by, Clyde. I finally figured out what I want from you."

"First, Danny, maybe I'd better tell you what happened to me."

"What, Clyde? Did you get that call?" His eyes flashed as if I wasn't supposed to know about some call, so I quickly added, "From that guy, telling you where to be for your accident."

"No, but go ahead and tell me what you want from me." He seemed worried, so I proceeded cautiously.

"It wasn't until last Saturday in Mainz I realized how much you had to offer. What I want from you is an education." I waited until he relaxed, but before I could explain further, he answered me.

"I can do that. I can give you an education, but let me tell you something first. Guess who showed up at my doorstep last weekend?"

"Not Zolton Szabo?"

"Right! Z says to me, 'I've got a problem, Clyde! I need help!

DAMIAN and MONGOOSE

Nobody will talk to me. I can't do anything. I can't live like this! I don't know what's wrong!' Z is not a saver, Danny. He's a spender. Z says, 'I don't know what's wrong. I'm hurting!'

"I told him to sit down, then I said, 'I don't know what I can do, Z. I've been lying low myself. I've been getting some bad vibes.' Then Z says, 'Well, I've gotta tell you something.' Z doesn't know that I know everything he said at that meeting. Z says, 'I told them about that proposal you made.'

"He told me what he said, Danny. He told the truth. I couldn't believe it. I said, 'You didn't?' Z says, 'I did.' I said, 'I'll bet you didn't tell them that other thing you did.' 'No, I didn't.' 'I bet you didn't tell them about that little deal on the side.' 'No'

"I asked him, 'Why would you do something like that?' He tells me, 'I had no choice!' Z is cagy, Danny, real cagy. He says, 'For all I know, you were testing me. When I went in to give my report, I can see me getting up to leave and these guys tapping me on the shoulder and asking, *Isn't there something else you want to tell us?* I wouldn't be coming back, Clyde.'

"I asked Z, 'What can I do? I'm not in a position to help you.' Z says, 'I want you to go tell them it was a lie; you were just testing me. That way I look good for telling them, and they will believe you, Clyde!' I told Z, 'We're going to have to talk a lot more before I go see them. You call me this weekend, and we'll get together.' Z will call and tell me when and where to meet him."

"You're not going to meet with those guys until you're certain they'll buy your story, are you, Clyde? On the other hand, they might pretend to believe you, then they will have you where they want you."

"I'm not sure I'm gonna go. Unless Z tells me everything he

140

said at that meeting, and I know exactly what he said, I'll know something is wrong, and I'm not going. On the other hand, Danny, I can't help but think, call this bragging, they want to believe this didn't happen, because they know I'm the best. But you never know who's pushing.

"I called that guy and asked him about the contract, and he said, 'It's on hold.'" He shrugged his shoulders like he didn't know what to make of his situation. Then he continued. "On the other hand, Danny, if they do believe me, I've got to go away for a while for a new citizenship."

Damn, Clyde! That's the kind of statement that will scare my superiors into thinking they have to take you before you slip through their fingers.

"Where do you have to go, Clyde?"

"Oh, Sweden or Switzerland."

"Wait a minute, Clyde. Does that mean you're going to leave your family?"

"No. I've got to leave my wife here to keep a permanent residence, but she will live with me."

"Wouldn't it be easier to get new citizenship if you weren't under investigation?"

"I'll buy a new citizenship."

"What do you plan to do?"

"Oh, I'm going into business."

"What kind of business?"

"Videos, if somebody buys my proposal. If they believe me, I'm going to make a proposal."

"How's that going to do you any good in Sweden or Switzerland?"

"No, Europe, a chain of them in the name of my German-born wife with a permanent residence. I went to the Hungarians and suggested they open a video store outside an American installation to identify and learn information about the soldiers who would join the video club to rent movies."

"Are they the ones who said they would guarantee you a profit?"

"Absolutely."

"Clyde, if you're leaving, you won't have time for my education."

"Oh, I'll educate you."

"I'm my own boss here, Clyde. I can easily swamp these commanders with so much work they'll beg me to hold off for a while. When do you want to do it?"

"I'll make it convenient for you."

"I thought you said you're leaving right away."

"Two or three weeks, after I'm satisfied with what Z has to say. The kind of proposal I'm making won't be decided at their level."

It was clear to me the chain of video stores was not the proposal itself, but collecting personal information about soldiers was related to a proposal he planned to make to the Hungarians, one he wasn't ready to explain to me. I wanted to press him, but I thought it more important, in the short time I had, to pin down his timetable.

"Clyde, if Szabo tells you what you want to hear, where will you meet with the Hungarians?"

"Austria."

"About this education. You told me I can do what I want with the things you told me before, so I don't have to decide now, right?"

"As long as you don't stick me with it."

"I'm sure you're well protected. The one thing I have decided is what I might do about those things you said are stashed in England. Shirley and I may go to England next week during my leave. If we do, I might check those things out."

I hated bringing up those vials of strychnine, believing that story by Clyde had been more of a trap to see if any agencies showed an interest, but Grant had directed me to address it. I was surprised at Clyde's response.

"Good! Make sure you don't use this information where it will get you in trouble." He suddenly stood up to leave and said, "I have to go home to give Jeurgen's piano teacher a ride home. I'll be back in about forty-five minutes."

"Sorry, Clyde. That's too late. I have to get to Mainz to catch my train to Bremerhaven, and I have to drop the company's BMW at the Mainz detachment first."

He said, "That's too bad." Then he departed, and I finished my dinner. For the next twenty minutes, I reflected on the change in Clyde's demeanor.

His meeting with Zolton Szabo had clearly altered his status with the Hungarians. He was now contemplating resuming his business of supplying material and would view me as a possible asset. He would certainly provide the information I had promised Grant, but only as a recruiting tool or at least a tool for preparing me to want to do something for him as well as for myself. I was still thinking about his renewed enthusiasm as I paid my dinner bill.

When I rose to leave, Clyde walked in with a smile, saying "Hanelore was visiting her mother, so I talked her into taking the music teacher home. I'm going with you to Mainz."

"Clyde, I know it doesn't bother you, but I can't afford to let you be seen with me by the CI guys at the Mainz detachment where I'm leaving my BMW. I hope you can appreciate that. I'll have to find a place within walking distance for you to park your car while I deliver mine. I can join you there, and you can drive me to the Bahnhof."

As we approached the foyer of my hotel, another idea came to me, and Clyde agreed to it. I walked to the hotel desk, picked up the phone on which the owner had started letting me dial the numbers, and dialed Grant's number in Wiesbaden. Grant answered the phone. I knew he would recognize my voice and Clyde would hear every word.

"Hello, this is Master Sergeant Williams. I'm supposed to bring a battalion BMW to your detachment tonight for you to use while I'm on leave for a week. Are you aware of that?"

"Yes. That's correct."

"Well, a friend of mine has offered to give me a ride to Mainz. Would it be possible to leave the keys here with the manager of Hotel Viktoria and have a couple of your agents pick up the car sometime this weekend? It would save you having to wait for me this evening."

"I think that would work just fine. Is your friend standing there with you now?"

"Absolutely. I'll arrange this with the manager. You can pick up the key from him anytime. The car will be on the street in front of the hotel."

I left the keys with Edward. As we walked to his car, Clyde asked a totally unexpected question. "Do you know a CI agent named Banners?"

"I worked with an agent named Banners in the 165th MI Battalion some years back."

"Banners was in my German class at DLI (Defense Language Institute). Do you know about Banners' problems?"

"No. I haven't heard from Banners since I left Giessen in eighty-three."

"He loaned his car to a German who didn't have a license. The guy got drunk and had an accident. Banners is no longer in your business, Danny. I had a lot of conversations with him while we were in German language class and after class when we went bowling together.

"He was really arrogant. He thought he spoke better German than I did, and he thought he was a better bowler. I usually let him win. I used his arrogance against him to extract a lot of information."

I couldn't tell if Clyde was already in his teaching mode, but he dropped that subject. I wondered if he just wanted me to know that he had made other acquaintances in CI. Now that I knew, I feared he might also know more about my daily business than I had hoped.

Clyde drove an unusually circuitous route through BK. When I asked why, he said he didn't want Hanelore to see us together when she drove the instructor home.

I asked him, "Are you concerned about Szabo seeing me?"

"Oh, no! He's not here. I'll see him in Munich or somewhere like that."

"I realize my education would be something of a legacy, Clyde, with you and Szabo being the most knowledgeable sources in Europe. Have you changed your mind about taking him out?"

"I didn't say that. If this thing goes through when I visit these people, I'll have to let some time go by, but he will be taken care of. And I'll tell you this: I will know everything he knows, because he will be questioned. Would you like to be there?"

"Speaking of being there. I was going to ask you if I could be in the vicinity if things didn't work out and that accident is arranged for you. Someone should know exactly what happens."

"That can be arranged, as long as you don't get in the way."

"I'm no fool, Clyde" I was buying time to decide how to answer his question about Szabo. I knew he wanted me to prove I was unencumbered by scruples, but I would have to remain noncommittal until CI ruled on my answer. I also realized he was already confident he was going to be around to take care of Szabo himself. I leaned my head back and smiled.

"Clyde, I would probably find it hard to pass up an opportunity to be present when Z is questioned."

He seemed pleased and immediately launched my first lesson. "Danny, let me give you some highlights of your education. First, let me tell you this: politics is the key to everything. It took me a long time to learn this.

"There are these guys who make things, devices with secret compartments, fire extinguishers which have nothing inside, and you put in whatever you want. Fruit cans that have a compartment for real fruit. And they work! The bottom part, after you put something in the can, snaps once you close it. You can't open it up again without cutting it. That not only protects the worker but keeps the courier from opening it. That also gives somebody a job.

"They've got a whole section of people that make these things. I told them, 'That's stupid. Why have guys out there to get caught

146

with those things?' They said, 'If you don't use them, you put somebody out of work.'

"Take radios. They buy them in bulk. They buy all the same brand. Every worker has one"

"What do you mean by 'every worker?' Spies?"

"I don't like that word. Workers."

"Okay. Why do workers need radios?"

"Each worker gets his own frequency, which he monitors twice weekly. They get their own transmission for no more than three minutes."

"What does it tell them, Clyde?"

"Anything they need to know, including where to go for a meeting. Workers are supposed to monitor them twice a week, but I asked some, and they said they never monitor more than twice a month. Can you believe that?

"Take cameras. These guys buy cameras in bulk too. They just say, 'Here's a camera.' I asked them, 'Why don't you give them the money to go out and buy a camera of their own? That way they'll be able to explain where it came from.' I asked them about this on several occasions. They always give me the same answer: 'There's a man whose job it is to buy these cameras and he saves money by buying in bulk. If you don't use them, the guy's out of a job and his kids don't go to school.'

"I tried to offer them ideas. All they would say is, 'How many people will this take?' If I said something like, 'Two or three guys could do it,' they weren't interested. It's all political. Everything's measured by how many people each person has working for him.

"They ask each other, 'How many people do you have working for you?' It's a status symbol. The more people they have involved in something, the better they like the idea or operation because it's good for the organization."

We parked near the Mainz Bahnhof and strolled along the street. He became silent, so I asked, "Will you be able to give me comparisons between the different intelligence services, some details about their controllers, how and where they meet their people?"

"I'll show you that, Danny. When they pay in Deutsche Marks, they pay in one thousand Mark bills. When they pay in American, they roll off one hundred dollar bills."

"Who, the Hungarians or the Czechs?"

"Both! That's one of the discriminators, you know. Ask anyone in your unit the color of a one thousand Mark bill. Whoever knows it's brown is probably working. I'll also show you on a map one guy's favorite restaurant and the restaurants he uses to meet workers."

"How do you know that, Clyde?"

"I sat down and talked with the guy. Whenever they go to a meeting, they always go two days early. Do you know why?"

"No. Why?"

"To shop! Another thing they do is always drive with a CD sticker on the back. That stands for Corps of Diplomats. If it were up to me, Danny, I could stand on the overpass above the Autobahn going into Salzburg. As soon as I saw a CD car come through, I wouldn't know where a meeting was, but I would sure know when: two days later.

"Before they return through their border, they will have already arranged for their car not to be searched because there will be operational stuff in the back. They also will be smuggling, either for themselves or for the black market. I figured out they could probably do the same thing leaving their country.

"Actually, they have some pretty sophisticated stuff. Take the one-time pad for codes. They put their codes on paper that will dissolve in your mouth or in the commode. Watch this: when the CIA gives out their code pad, they actually type it out on bond paper. When an agent gets a message, he has to pull this out and decipher his message, then destroy this bond paper somehow."

As Clyde looked at the ground, trying to decide what he wanted to tell me next, I reminded him how little time I had before the train departed. I tried to make a quick list of the specific information Grant had insisted I obtain from him. "I'd like to eventually learn details about the training you've received, what you liked about it, why you thought your surveillance training was taught by someone who didn't know what he was doing, what they want to know, and what they already know."

He looked up with a troubled expression and said, "Regarding the right and wrong type of training, I'll tell you all about that. I can tell you this: none of that matters. They think their system can't be penetrated. All you have to do is penetrate the system, then you can use the system against them.

"For example, I was sending guys with their family to meet with people that didn't exist, and they didn't care! They said, 'Well, we'll try again some other time.'"

I knew I would have to get him to clarify that story when I had more time, but he started a new story. "This guy brought in some hot information, two rolls of film, really hot. This other guy brought in a really big stack of information that turned out to be nothing but garbage. They fell all over this guy with the garbage and asked the guy with the two rolls of film, 'Is that all there is?' It doesn't matter what you bring, Danny; bring it in volume. You remember the story about the shoe salesman who went to Africa to sell shoes?"

"You mean the guy who said, 'There's no market there; no one wears shoes,' and the other guy who said, 'There's a great market there; no one has any shoes.'"

"Yeah!"

We had finished a cup of coffee and were laughing as we walked to the track where my train was about to depart. I realized Clyde was telling me he had exploited the Hungarian Intelligence System and he wanted to teach me how, but I was almost sure my superiors would not be interested or believe it. Since time was short, I quickly addressed a compelling issue.

Concerned that I might have cast suspicion on the wrong person in a previous report to Grant, I reminded Clyde of his statement about someone calling him from Chicago to warn him of an investigation. Then I said, "I didn't quite hear whether you told me that was the girl's father or your stepfather.

"Since you introduced me to your stepfather when he and your mother visited you in Germany, I wondered if he could have mentioned me as a friend of yours." When he answered so emphatically, "No, it's never come near them," I was relieved that I had reported correctly, it was the girl's father. I also knew his mother and step-father lived in Ohio.

Clyde and I had drunk only coffee all evening. He had sworn off beer and was eating only salads since his visit from Szabo. He wanted to lose enough weight to fit into his tailored suit and look his best if he met with the Hungarians in Austria. He left as I boarded the train.

I had left the recording apparatus with Grant, so I spent most of my trip to Bremerhaven organizing the details of my unplanned conversation with Clyde. I hoped for an early meeting with Grant in Stuttgart to give him Clyde's tentative itinerary and what I hoped was plenty of justification for continuing the operation.

Grant debriefed me in a hotel in Stuttgart. He was pleased with my meeting with Clyde and reasonably confident that the operation would continue with the new approach.

Unfortunately, I also received a call from a doctor through the Red Cross, informing me that my younger sister was dying of cancer and my presence in Houston would soon be required. I called my brother in Houston, who assured me that he had everything under control and I wouldn't be needed. I was still deciding what I would do.

I had taken Shirley to Bad Kreuznach over the weekend because I knew Clyde would be out of town. We enjoyed dinner and a carnival in Wiesbaden with Edward and his girlfriend.

Shirley had never asked me details about my job in counterintelligence, and temporary duty had not been uncommon for us over the last several years. None of that made it easier for me to leave her alone with her two cats in Steinenbronn, but Shirley was a tried and true military wife. I left her with a promise that I would complete my special assignment as quickly as possible. The evening I returned to Bad Kreuznach, Clyde joined me for dinner at my hotel.

Almost every question I asked him revealed more of his knowledge of foreign intelligence procedures, but he only stayed on that subject long enough to demonstrate how antiquated their procedures were. Though Clyde wasn't completely sure of his status, he was not only preparing to resume his espionage activity, he also intended to escalate his manipulation of the Hungarians.

151

I tried to determine his current timetable. "Clyde, did you talk to Szabo and to the Hungarians?"

"Yeah."

"Did Z tell you everything you wanted him to tell you?"

"He was lying through his teeth, but I knew the lies he was telling."

"Tell me what happened?" He didn't answer me. He seemed not to want to talk about Szabo, so I asked, "Did things work out for you with the Hungarians?"

"If I knew that, I'd tell you, Danny." He shrugged his shoulders.

"Are they going to let you know? Don't call us; we'll call you?"

"No. No. After I explained, the guy said, 'Everything's okay. Forget it. We put a curtain in front of everything. It's in the past. Come visit us.'" He shrugged again.

"Wow. And that bothers you, Clyde?"

"It doesn't. I don't know. I really don't. I'm dumber now than before I went to Austria. There was a lot of fear of me. They're wondering, because I have a lot of information, *Is it written down? How busy was he? Did he take pictures?* Everyone is nervous."

"Whom did you meet?"

"If I said 'committee level,' would that mean anything to you?"

"Not really."

"If we had a committee, it would be like the Secretary of Defense, Director of the CIA. That's a committee. This guy is a committee member."

"Did you know him before?"

"No."

"Did you tell him the truth?"

"No."

152

"Can you give me an example of what you told him?"

"No." He seemed to have something else on his mind.

We were interrupted at that point. Edward, our waiter, brought us more coffee and informed us he had wrecked his new Mercedes sports car and was currently having it repaired. After a short conversation, he left, and Clyde continued to answer my last question but used his answer to switch to his teaching mode.

"It's not only fear. I have something they want. Hungarian Intelligence primarily recruits workers among expatriates, someone who left Hungary, joined some military service, then returned to Hungary for a visit. Their couriers are usually Hungarians living in neutral countries, who were recruited when they returned to Hungary for a visit. When they recruit workers among soldiers who are not expatriates, they usually take one or two years to recruit them.

"I told them that last approach was idiocy. By the time a recruiter identifies and assesses a potential worker and recruits him, it is time for the worker to rotate back to the States.

"In most cases, these recruiters are dumber than dog shit. The only direction they give a worker about the procurement of classified information is, 'If you have the opportunity, do it. If you don't, don't.'

"Some of them are intelligent, but they lack the necessary knowledge of the way soldiers think or act. I tried to convince them they could recruit soldiers without ever having to do anything illegal and do it in three months instead of two years. I explained the whole system to them."

The fact that this system was the proposal he had for the Hungarians became obvious.

"I told them they should hire people in neutral countries; train them in the distinctive thought patterns, language, and life styles of soldiers; then send them to make friends with soldiers in designated areas of Europe.

"By exploiting circumstances and weaknesses that make good soldiers vulnerable to recruitment, the trained neutral would identify and befriend soldiers with the proper access to classified material. The neutral would never ask anyone to do anything. He would prepare the soldier until he is ready to do something for some extra money, then take him to a neutral country and introduce him to a controller, who would attempt to recruit him.

"If the soldier says, 'No,' the controller would be safe under diplomatic immunity, and the neutral would be safe because he has not actually done anything illegal. Beside which, the neutral would never know what the soldier decided. He would already have moved to another designated area to identify and befriend another soldier.

"My plan would provide incentives for the neutral to produce someone every three months. In addition to a ten thousand Deutsche Mark monthly salary, he would receive funds to buy computers, electronic equipment, or any item he deemed necessary to cultivate the friendship of a prospective recruit. He could fly to Spain or anywhere soldiers vacationed. He would drive a nice car, live in nice hotels, and enjoy unlimited entertainment funds. He would work directly for a controller to preserve the compartmentalization the Hungarians require. That's their greatest fear. They never want anyone to have more information than absolutely necessary to do his job.

"Of course, I know these concepts are beyond the Hungarians' comprehension, and they will need my assistance to implement my plan. A major part of the plan is management of a recruited soldier's career.

"A Hungarian soldier has no control whatever over the assignments he receives. I assured them that a U.S. soldier, with my assistance, could develop the exact profile his assignment branch would require to guarantee an assignment to the job which would give him access to classified documents of interest to the Hungarians.

"I offered to help their computer guy set up a database to manage that. I said I would supply the prerequisites for all military schools, the criteria for promotions and assignments, and all the tricks employed by smart soldiers to get preferred assignments throughout the military services. They were afraid the computer guy would have too much information about recruited agents, so I set up a demonstration for them.

"I persuaded them to describe only the rank, type of job, basic skills, and previous training of one of their agents in the U.S. Army, without revealing his name, unit, or location. They picked the type of assignment they would like for him to receive next. After they followed my instructions, he received that assignment."

"What instructions did you give them?"

"The same things anyone does who wants a particular assignment. Number one, look in the phone roster of the place where you want to be assigned to see if you know anyone there with influence. Work your dick in the dirt, soldier like a motherfucker, get a letter of release and a letter of acceptance, then take them both to your assignments officer and watch what happens."

I understood Clyde's directions, even in his crass, military vernacular, but I felt a little guilty knowing where he first learned that technique. When he was assigned to Fort Ord, California, he asked me how he could get a quota for German language school in Monterey.

I told him, "Ask the G-3 Sergeant Major of 8ID in Bad Kreuznach, where you want to be reassigned, to check on a vacant assignment slot in G-5 (Civil Affairs) requiring German language. If that slot is still open, ask the SGM to send you a letter of acceptance. Then, get a letter of release from your current commander and call the schools branch and tell them you have those letters for a slot specifying German language. Tell them you are practically in Monterey and you want a quota for German language school.

"Next, send your assignments branch the letters and your language school quota. The SGM will assign you against the G-5 slot with duty in your old job in G-3 Operations. That's how the SGM assigned me when I first started working at 8ID, G-3 in 1975."

It worked out exactly that way for Clyde, and unfortunately, it would work that way for agents recruited by the Hungarians, with his help. This switch in my education to the plan Clyde wanted to sell the Hungarians became a double-edged sword.

To my superiors, his plan was preposterous, and they expected the Hungarians would reject it while stroking Clyde's ego until he produced more documents. The plan also hinted that he might want to turn me over to someone else for recruitment, which they forbid me to allow.

To Clyde, however, his plan was the solution to his problems with the Hungarians. He made that clear by saying, "If they accept my plan, I will know they have actually put a curtain in front of everything."

At our next meeting, Clyde suggested we visit a park in Bad Muenster, about five kilometers south of BK. As I drove, he continued to explain his plan. "I'm in the process of designing the plan so that the Hungarians will require my assistance in training the neutrals for preparation of soldiers.

"I'll teach the neutral to shed his European habits while he's around Americans. He'll learn to cross his legs at the ankles instead of the knee, hold his coffee cup with his hand instead of his fingers, and hold his cigarette between his middle and index finger instead of his thumb and finger. I'll teach him the slang expressions and the accepted gestures. He'll understand the needs, desires, problems, and vulnerabilities of soldiers during that critical phase when they first arrive at their military assignment in Europe.

"I'll make sure they know all the rules, so they won't ever do anything illegal. They won't take cigarettes from a soldier, eat in an establishment on a military post, or accept an invitation to enter the barracks or any building where they're not authorized. And they will especially never ask a soldier to do anything. They will only prepare soldiers for recruitment."

The way Clyde explained it, preparation would involve identifying or even subtly creating a soldier's disenchantment with the military's failure to recognize his true worth, a condition Clyde had found so prevalent in the military. This was exploitation of what Clyde believed was a good soldier's inherent need to find a way to make his talent count for himself.

Since the neutral would never ask the soldier to do anything, Clyde insisted, the neutral would have done nothing illegal. I knew preparation was criminal subversion, but I never pointed that out to Clyde. He also had plans to train the controller.

"The controller will teach the workers the proper procedures for collection, storage, and delivery of stolen, classified information, as well as payment procedures and even procedures for quitting or taking a vacation anytime the worker chooses. He will never order the worker to do anything. Service will always be voluntary, to insure continued loyalty.

"After initial training by the controller, all contact with the worker will be maintained by two couriers who will know him by a code name. Only the controller will know the actual identity of the worker. Since the neutral will have moved to a new location, he will never know whether or not the soldier he prepared was actually recruited, but I will.

"If I train the neutrals, I will co-opt them. I will learn, without the Hungarians' knowledge, the identities of all recruits, and I will eventually create my own organization."

"After all your troubles, Clyde, you think that's wise?"

"The benefits far outweigh the risk. If the Hungarians don't come through, I'll set up the plan myself. I'll do the hiring and the training. When you're talking training, Danny, there are few people who can do it, train somebody like that. I only know two: me and you.

"To train and put someone in the field, we'd need one red-pass guy, the computer guy, and two couriers." He continued to call a controller a red-pass guy because he carried a pass guaranteeing diplomatic immunity from prosecution.

When we reached Bad Muenster, he took me for a short walk through the park along the west side of the Nahe River. He said he wanted me to see what a nice place it is. But as we walked along the river, he pointed to the high cliffs on the east side of the river and said, "I've scouted out some places on those cliffs overlooking the park that give a person with a pair of binoculars and a high-powered rifle complete coverage of the park area." He narrowed his eyes and waited without a smile for my response.

I allowed myself a slight sneer, as I shook my head slowly in disbelief and disgust. I resigned myself to the obvious implication that he could easily take me out if he decided I was working against him. There was little I could do about it, and he knew I understood that. We entered the Gasthaus located in the park next to the river and ordered coffee. Clyde said he had been there many times.

"Eighth ID, G-3 and G-2 have had several combined parties here. The G-3 Sergeant Major invited me to his parties even after I retired from the Army.

"I made friends with the Sergeant Major a while back, when I provided him with a number of critical tools and other equipment that had come up missing just prior to an inspection of his vehicles." His smile implied he might have helped the tools come up missing.

"I also showed him how to use some sophisticated, electronic office equipment that was being wasted in the headquarters' basement. I've kept in touch with most of the people in my old unit as well as other units around southern Europe."

After we ordered more coffee, Clyde resumed his critique of the Hungarians. "Under the current system, classified material is taken to the East and evaluated. A fair price is determined and paid directly to the source. Only a real good source might be allowed to dicker for more.

"With my system, every agent would be taken to Switzerland

to open an account in which a monthly salary, like two thousand Deutsche Marks, would be deposited automatically. Bonuses would be deposited for special merchandise delivered.

"The worker could confirm his account balance by phone but would not touch any money until he retired from the military. Small sums of money would be given directly to him periodically for vacations and special needs. This would eliminate suspicion.

"Szabo gets a salary, and he contracts various jobs, like looking someone over for them and making friends with certain people. He also enjoys bennies commensurate with his rank, such as retirement benefits and commissions for certain material he helped deliver.

"But I'm certain Z will soon be persona non grata with the Hungarians. I made sure of that by dropping a few hints during my discussion in Austria with the committee man, calculated to intensify the Hungarians' distrust of Z. His monthly salary as well as mine is reserved for very special people under the current system. I plan to apply those arrangements to all workers.

"Next to not touching their payments until retirement, the most important security aspect of my plan is reduced danger time. That's the time when a worker actually has a stolen document in his hand.

"Under the current system, a controller tells a worker what documents are of most interest from a list of documents to which the worker has access, and says, 'Look for opportunities.' The time between acquiring the document and actual delivery can be extensive, and the worker has to expose himself to that risk over and over again"

Clyde's hesitation, while he pondered how to explain his remedy for this risk, allowed me to address one of the subjects

Grant had emphasized. "Clyde, what are some of your techniques for acquiring and delivering documents?"

He sidestepped the question. "Basically, I do anything I want, Danny. I'll give you an example: I found a courier."

"Found?"

"Found."

"You want to say how?"

"No, but I found him. I talked him into working for me with an extra salary. He thought that was great. And because I knew that courier, I knew some people and another courier. Now, by siphoning off things, you can flip-flop them, create people that don't even exist. And everybody is saying, 'Boy, that's great! That's great' within the system."

This reference to things that don't exist was no clearer than his mention of it before, and he still wasn't ready to clarify it. He only wanted to make the point that he had exploited the Hungarian system and considered that the most important thing for me to learn.

I knew that wouldn't make my superiors happy because they thought he was basically blowing smoke. I hoped they would eventually realize that selling his plan to the Hungarians was one way to insure a better relation with them and establish a need for my services in supplying documents, but I tried again to get something personal out of him.

"You must have been a mighty productive worker to reach the point where you could exploit the system."

"I'll say this, Danny. No, that is not a requirement." With an expression of realization that he had inadvertently implied I would never have to be a worker, he quickly modified his statement.

"No. No, that's not required, although anybody who doesn't work has to be a smart motherfucker or nobody will ever trust him. Once a guy works, they say, 'Okay. Now we know. Good, now we can do business.' Until that point, everybody is saying, 'We don't know about you, and you don't know about us.'

"A worker is told to arrive at a certain hour for his meeting. If no one meets him, he is to depart the area and return every two hours until he is met. If he is meeting a controller, he will be met when the controller's surveillance team is satisfied the worker has not been trailed. If he is never met, he is to go home, sit for six months, and do nothing.

"Your first exercise after six months will be, 'Well, you go here and walk around, and we'll check to see what's wrong.' If they detect trailing at that point, their mind runs wild. They usually drop you completely, within reason, depending on how productive you've been.

"Believe me, Danny; I'm not like most people that are floating around. The guy who came to see me, I don't know of anybody else he would come out to see under any circumstances."

"But he is a friend?"

"No, not this guy."

"Then why did he come out to see you?"

"He was told to. The Hungarians sent him to ask for an explanation from me about suspicions they had developed from their own investigation. What he really wanted was any plausible excuse which would allow them to put a curtain over the past, and I knew just the kind of truth they would buy.

"I expect it will take a while for the people in a position to make a decision to translate and study my proposal, then they will

162

summon me to Budapest to hear their decision. I've been there before, and I know they will expect me to make the trip as a show of good faith. I'm content to wait for their decision, then go back there."

We crossed the river on a raft we pulled by a rope. We ordered dinner at a restaurant halfway up the cliff. I had fresh trout and coffee. Clyde had his usual salad and coffee.

When we descended the cliff, I started toward the raft. Clyde grabbed my arm and led me along the east side of the river on a very dark trail overhung by trees. We were headed toward those places he had scouted out as he began describing equipment the Hungarians used.

"They use thirty-five millimeter cameras and a camera with up to a hundred frame roll of film, depending on what you need it for. They give shortwave radios to all workers.

"You can stand outside the home of anyone you suspect, and around 2200 hours you'll hear that radio come on. They insisted on giving me all that equipment, but I promptly tossed it into the river."

He lit another cigarette as we walked. I didn't realize several seconds had passed with neither of us saying anything until he chuckled and said, "You remind me of the committee man in Austria."

"How's that?"

"He did that: just went silent and waited to see what would develop."

That surprised me, not because I hadn't suspected for some time that he had learned from his foreign intelligence contacts how to recognize most elicitation techniques, like the one he was ascribing to me, but because I hadn't used it on purpose. My superiors had insisted I use it often and just let Clyde talk, but I'd always feared he would think exactly what he was vocalizing now. Then another thought came to me.

I remembered I had intended to change the tape in the recorder once we reached the Gasthaus on the other side of the river. I knew the tape had probably run out by now, and Clyde's remark about the transparency of certain elicitation techniques would not be recorded. I was disappointed my superiors would have to trust me to relay this conversation, but I started thinking up an excuse for appearing to be eliciting information.

"No, I was just thinking of something I wanted to ask, but I didn't want to imply that you had to answer."

"Hm." His obvious doubt was disconcerting, so I started my answer before it was solidified in my mind.

"Clyde, I know you keep saying I shouldn't ask you about what you've done personally, but I'm interested in your thought process, how you've made these concepts work, even mistakes that taught you something. I don't know exactly why I do that. I really don't want you to tell me anything you don't think you should."

"I know why you ask me those things, Danny," he interrupted with a smile.

I welcomed his interruption and his change in attitude. "Really, Clyde?"

"Curiosity! You just want to know everything!"

"Yes, I guess I do." He seemed satisfied for the moment that I had not tried to elicit anything from him, and he appeared to dismiss the question I hadn't even asked.

I hoped I might accidently have succeeded in laying some

groundwork for future personal questions, the one's my superiors demanded.

We both had been using the military courtesy of addressing each other by name occasionally, each for different reasons. His primary reasons were to alert me to the importance of a statement he was about to make while he carefully selected words that wouldn't incriminate him, or to convey persuasion without transmitting an offer. I'd used that courtesy with him for years for other reasons.

Clyde never argued. When he made a statement, you could take it or leave it. When he addressed a subordinate or a friend, if you disagreed, he would usually respond with "bull shit," then turn and walk away. With a superior, he would just say, "Yes, Sir," with no further comment. The worse thing he might do is agree with you and leave you unconvinced. I had been one of the very few, in those early years, who could get by with challenging him, but not very often and only with respect.

Lately, I found the technique useful, along with a reflective expression, to suggest concerns that I needed resolved before I could make a decision while I remained almost persuaded.

We crossed the river and returned to my hotel. Along the way, we discussed past military experiences together in and around the Taunus Mountains we had just visited.

For the next few weeks, Clyde overwhelmed me with enough foreign intelligence modus operandi to satisfy my promise to my superiors while astonishing me with details of his personal plan for revamping the Hungarians collection system. He included details he never intended the Hungarians to know. He even requested my assistance in finalizing his plan.

5

OPLAN.001

My training became fast and furious. Clyde's next meeting with
the Hungarians kept getting postponed because the Hungarian he
needed to meet with was on another assignment. The Hungarians
even failed to show up for one meeting they had arranged with
Clyde. He managed a meeting of his own near Fulda with a friend,
from whom he learned that the Hungarians' attitude toward
him was cautiously friendly. His friend described some of their
comments.

"One high-ranking official lost his job over you. They consider
you a rotten bastard but a smart one who needs to be watched like
a hawk. Be extra careful, because they will probably have a surveillance team in your neighborhood. They'll want to know whether
any Hungarian controllers or couriers are friendly with you."

OPLAN.001

Clyde intended to be careful, but he also intended to continue meeting with this friend. He wanted to be certain their improved attitude hadn't changed before he accepted their invitation to Budapest. He accepted the Hungarians' explanation: "It might take considerable time to translate the plan, staff and approve it, and appropriate the money."

In anticipation of his return to Hungary, where he expected to receive approval for his OPLAN, Clyde had already lost sixteen pounds. He continued his diet and his abstinence from beer to ensure that his tailored suits would fit him perfectly.

When I asked him the title of the man who would give final approval of his plan, with a whine in his voice, he answered with one of his favorite responses: "Iiiii dooon't knooow!" That meant I shouldn't expect him to know, but also that it wasn't important to him. I was reasonably certain, every time he used that expression, that he was being truthful, not withholding information. He seemed to be holding back less information and even clarifying previous stories.

He had not only made friends with controllers and couriers, then elicited information he wasn't supposed to have, but had exploited established meeting procedures in order to gain knowledge and even photos of the people they sent to meet him.

He often arrived a day early for planned meetings, rented a room near the meeting site to set up a telescope and observe their procedures after purposely missing the first rendezvous. He catalogued characteristic dress, walk, and personal actions of a number of officials and their support teams.

He also entered into schemes with couriers and controllers, allowed them to make trips, even take their families on vacations, allegedly to keep appointments with Clyde, which he had arranged for delivery of classified material.

Clyde would fail to make those meetings, make an excuse to the Hungarians, and reschedule. They would pay their people for the aborted and the rescheduled meetings. He said his friends were grateful and their Hungarian superiors didn't care.

Clyde talked one courier into persuading a source to quit the Hungarians in order to go to work for an independent for more money. He then told the Hungarians he had recruited someone on his own. He said, "It was tough convincing the Hungarians to accept documents from me that I had received from another source. I demanded, 'He's mine. You don't get him. You just take what you get and pay me for it.'"

In addition to payments for the documents from this recruited agent, Clyde demanded a commission for himself. They wanted the agent's name, but since he had stolen the agent from them, he gave them the name of another soldier in the same unit, who had already rotated back to the States.

He learned later that the Hungarians had made some calls to the unit trying to verify the identity of the source. Apparently they weren't successful, but he didn't say how he learned that. Having succeeded with this scheme, he eventually invented his person who didn't exist, which he described in detail.

"Watch this: I contacted the Hungarians myself, pretending to be someone who wanted to sell them classified documents, and arranged to deliver them at certain locations. I instructed the courier I knew would be selected to pick up documents in those particular locations to give his superiors a bogus description of the source from whom he received the documents, which were actually delivered by me.

"I later changed the numbers on the same documents and delivered them again myself. Because of my status with the Hungarians, this not only gave them the means to verify the authenticity of the documents from the invented source, it also guaranteed me double payments. Once this source was established, I notified the Hungarians that I had in fact recruited this source, and I demanded a commission."

Clyde also further clarified his schemes with the U.S. Embassy. "I persuaded a Hungarian friend, whose dialect would prove him to be from Budapest, to write a letter in Hungarian to the U.S. Embassy on stationery containing the letterhead of an intelligence office in Budapest.

"The writer described himself as a records clerk at this office in Budapest, who reviewed all the documents that were delivered to the Hungarian Intelligence Service. He offered to provide excerpts from these documents for one hundred thousand Marks. He told the Americans that excerpts were all he could safely copy.

"The excerpts we delivered were from documents classified NATO, COSMIC, ATOMAL, and TOP SECRET. I directed the Americans to place an advertisement in the paper: 'Dog lost, ID# -------.' The ID number would represent the amount they were willing to pay.

"The writer, who called himself, David, eventually offered the Americans the name and photo of one of Hungary's top controllers. He even offered the controller's Budapest address and the purpose and schedule of his assignments throughout the world."

He described the Americans response with contempt, at the same time revealing who he thought they were.

"The CIA found this information uninteresting. They were also uninterested in obtaining the KGB's want-list of computer components, uninterested in debriefing Hungary's top Intelligence computer specialist, and uninterested in receiving a list of border crossing locations frequented by Hungarian couriers.

"They even refused to pay for a description of a working agent, which David provided them, because they couldn't identify him without a name. All they wanted were more excerpts. My associates were very frustrated at the Americans' refusal to deal in good faith.

"Actually, had the Americans bought the list of border crossings, I intended to sell the Hungarians the same list as locations the Americans were monitoring. I also had plans for one of the American agents and a Hungarian agent to meet unwittingly, then photograph them together for the purpose of blackmailing them."

"I had an ultimate goal for this operation. I figured I could establish David as such an important source to the Americans that I could leverage him as protection for my own associates, should any of them come under the scrutiny of U.S. Counterintelligence. I figured I could say, "Leave them alone; they work for David.""

Clyde was almost as frustrated as his associates, trying to figure out why the Americans had been stalling David on many of his offers and had become so preoccupied with excerpts. He even asked me what I thought their reason was.

I couldn't tell him what I really thought. I said it was probably just a matter of red tape. Actually, I thought their motive should have been obvious to Clyde based on a story he had told me a short time earlier:

"While assigned as document custodian for 8ID, I once received a message from a CI, NATO, COMSEC (Communication Security) officer, tasking all commands to send a copy of each of their wartime general deployment plans (GDPs) to him. I was jealous of his being in a position to score such a coup.

"I never responded to the tasking for my command, but I tried to think of some plausible reason I might send out such a message myself. I already had several techniques for gaining access to all GDPs from 8ID and higher."

When Clyde relayed this story to me, I wondered why he wouldn't have suspected the COMSEC Officer of trying to match up his excerpts with GDPs. I was also reminded of a tasking I had received while I was NCOIC of the 165th MI Detachment in Giessen in 1983.

At that time I was directed to identify every person who had accessed the GDP of the 11th Armored Cavalry Regiment (11th ACR), located in Fulda and Bad Hersfeld. I could tell at the time that the tasking was coming from the CIA.

With Clyde's clarification of the meaning of excerpts, it seemed logical to me now, that agents at the U.S. embassy thought they had matched some of David's excerpts to 11th ACRs GDP and were trying to identify any soldier who could have delivered the GDP to the Hungarians. I could see now that the COMSEC officer had not attached any significance to Clyde's failure to respond to his tasking.

Since Clyde was busy all day and most weekends working on his proposal, I stayed busy during the week days coordinating

171

with 527th and local units and spent as many weekends as possible with Shirley in Steinenbronn.

The time we spent together was absolutely necessary for Shirley and me. Being apart for over two months had been hard on both of us. She wasn't one bit happy that I had returned to my TDY assignment so soon after she arrived in Germany, nor that I had left her rattling around in a twelve-room, five-level townhouse with little more than a few dishes, three pieces of furniture, a TV, and two cats.

Her cats, a blue Persian named Bobo and a Himalayan named Aristocrat, were about the only entertainment she had. Although the cats had seldom meowed in the six years we'd had them, they quickly learned to run down to the basement just to listen to their meows echo through the empty house.

When I could visit with her, we took a lot of walks through the beautiful, wooded valley and surrounding farmland. Shirley really enjoyed walking. We enjoyed each other and the many restaurants along our walks, restaurants that had been converted from old mills. Since joining the Army, we had made a hobby of running or hiking to the best restaurants. Shirley often said the only occasions we really had time to talk were when we were sitting in restaurants and taking long hikes.

Our household goods finally arrived in Steinenbronn, and I helped Shirley unpack. She also found herself a teaching job around the end of July, on the Army Post in Heilbronn, about fifty miles from our condo. School wouldn't start for another month and a half, and we still didn't know how much longer she would be alone.

She never asked me about my work. She knew what everyone

knew: I caught spies. I had always worked incredibly long hours: before I joined the military, during my five years in the infantry, and for nine years in CI. She never got used to it, and she never hesitated to register her complaints that the Army was unreasonable and I was working too hard.

Lately, I acknowledged her indignation by sharing my own complaints about bureaucracy, politics, and general lack of common sense. I would voice my frustration with the unnecessary work and complications caused by the hesitation and lack of imagination of the people who called the shots. Even though she'd heard it all before and knew it to be true, she wasn't distracted from her perception of the reason I was spending all those hours away from home.

Sometimes she let me know she wasn't buying my complaints with remarks like, "You don't fool me. I know you love it. I can see how anxious and excited you are the minute you start getting ready to leave."

I would smile at the realization that she knew me so well and still respected my commitment to my mission despite her disappointment at being left alone. I had the same respect for her total commitment to the teaching profession.

However, she never hesitated to voice her displeasure the next time I finally returned for a short stay with no explanation of how much longer I would be on TDY. Sometimes she was mad for the first few hours, sometimes she couldn't help crying, and sometimes she couldn't resist using her notorious sarcasm. When I entered the house, she would often say to Bobo and Aristocrat, "In case you don't know him, boys, this is your daddy!"

I was always back in BK by Sunday evening and spent most

evenings with Clyde during the week. While continuing my education and describing his plan for revamping Hungarian intelligence collection, which he titled his Operational Plan 001 (OPLAN), he became engrossed in completing and delivering it. He even started bringing me a computer print-out of the draft OPLAN. I would read it aloud to make sure it was recorded, then Clyde would ask for my comments.

He had written his proposal in a format similar to a tactical field order. Under the definitions paragraph, he defined the field man, his new term for the neutral, as the citizen of a neutral country who would be hired and trained to prepare soldiers for recruitment into espionage. He also defined the controller, the courier, the worker, and the trainer.

He devoted separate paragraphs to responsibilities, logistical support, training, and security. Clyde was in the process of outlining the OPLAN but hadn't yet filled in all the details. He did discuss many of the details with me, including those aspects of the OPLAN he didn't intend to reveal to the Hungarians. He mentioned there were others, which he wouldn't even reveal to me.

In addition to having the trainer develop scenarios to duplicate various aspects of military life, Clyde planned to have each field man live for a short time with a soldier in off-post quarters to enhance his understanding of the soldiers' way of thinking.

A trained field man would identify a newly assigned soldier with a key position in control of classified military documents. He would apply Clyde's formula for making friends with the soldier by offering much needed and appreciated logistical and monetary assistance during the soldier's period of transition into his European assignment. Once a friendship was established, the field man would steadily exploit those frustrations and disappointments shared by all good soldiers.

Clyde believed soldiers developed these frustrations as a result of the U.S. Army's consistent failure to recognize certain soldiers' basic desire to excel, failure to utilize these soldiers' talents, and failure to properly reward deserving soldiers. Clyde expected the greatest disenchantment and his greatest success among potentially the best soldiers, those with two years of college, eager to work, well disciplined, and not involved in drugs or any other criminal activity.

He was also prepared to assure the speedy success of his OPLAN by enlisting his own, previously recruited military associates as ringers, to pretend to be recruited by the field man. This would not only guarantee the Hungarians' continued support of the OPLAN, but also aid him in eventually usurping control of agents and the material they delivered.

The only obstacle Clyde anticipated in the recruitment of any soldier was the soldier's fear of being caught. His solution to that problem was to minimize all the danger areas. He planned for the field man to address those danger areas and Clyde's solutions in hypothetical discussions in his preparation of soldiers. At my insistence, he gave examples.

"Watch this, Danny. The field man is sitting with a soldier and says, 'You read about that soldier arrested for selling secrets?' 'Oh, yeah!' 'Well, I've thought about that. The only way somebody like that could get caught is if he starts throwing his money around. There's no other way CI would ever be interested in that guy. Think about it.'

"Once the documents are gone, they're gone for good. His money could have been paid to a Swiss Bank and he wouldn't touch the money until he was ready to get out or retire, when he could just sit back and enjoy his money. In the mean time, he could check on his money with a simple phone call.'

"The field man will identify and address every concern hypothetically until the soldier reaches the point when he is desperate to do something for some extra money or to make his talents count for himself. But the soldier will have at least a vague understanding that espionage is being proposed.

"Another danger area the field man will address is the critical time when the soldier will have stolen documents in his possession. This will be the most important part of the OPLAN and the hardest for me to sell the Hungarians.

"I plan for each worker to copy every classified document he has in his vault in one or two carefully selected days, have the Hungarians deposit up to a million Marks in the workers Swiss account, then have him stop collecting for a couple of years or until he has a new, critical assignment. He'll be able to do that with a digital video camera, and he'll know how to exploit U.S. Army security procedures and control his personnel so he has two uninterrupted days.

"I'll have the Hungarians research and test the proper video cameras, lenses, and computer interface for copying all these documents on a video cassette and then retrieving them. I'll also have them build a device for concealing the camera. The device can be wrapped and mailed from anywhere in Germany to the worker at his unit.

"You know, the accepted U.S. Army security practice is for a designated person to pick up all mail at the U.S. Army Post Office and deliver it to the desk of each person who works in a classified vault. The box containing the camera will stay unopened on the desk of the worker until he is ready to use it. He can say it's a present for someone. Should the camera be accidently discovered, the worker is free of guilt since someone else delivered the unauthorized, electronic device to his desk in the vault.

"On the day selected, usually a weekend, the worker will set up the documents on his desk, open the box enough to reveal the lens and a few switches, and turn the pages while filming the document.

"Since the vault always remains locked, the worker will have ample warning should someone activate the code to enter the vault. He can turn off the camera and close the box so it looks like it's never been opened. He can resume copying when the intruder leaves.

"If necessary, I will place an assistant outside the building with pictures of everyone with access to the vault. The assistant can notify the worker telephonically if one of those people enters the building.

"When the tape or disk is full, the worker will arrange telephonically to meet a courier for delivery. The worker will carry a large magnet with him to erase the tape or disk if he is stopped while the video is in his possession. He can claim it contained pictures of his wife, which he didn't want anyone to see. Beyond that, he will say nothing without a lawyer. There is no evidence except what comes out of a worker's mouth."

Clyde would not say whether he had ever used a video camera for copying documents, but he eventually admitted that he was waiting for the digital technology to be perfected and tested. He did describe having sat for up to four hours reading documents into a recorder in a vault from which he could not safely remove any documents.

He later typed the documents from the recordings and used the appropriate security stamps, which he had acquired for himself. He preferred copying classified documents to a computer disc. He gained access to those documents through his mastery and exploitation of Army security procedures.

Clyde had earned a reputation for his knowledge of regulations governing the marking, storage, and control of classified documents and in the writing of war plans and tactical field orders. He had not only copied every document in his vault, one way or another, he also had corrected every document and sent or personally delivered each corrected document back to its originator as a courtesy. He often manipulated requests to correct other units' documents in order to help those commands prevent any derogatory findings in future security inspections.

According to Clyde, commanders of a number of military units throughout Europe had issued orders to their personnel: "No documents leave this command until Clyde Conrad has a chance to correct them." His access to these documents in the first place was usually directed by his own commanders throughout his career.

He developed a strong relationship with each of his commanders by anticipating and meeting their requirements. He made a habit of keeping them informed of the status of all their personnel, equipment, and projects as well as all requirements from higher headquarters.

With this established trust and dependence, he often persuaded his commanders of the need for copies of war plans of any and all NATO units who would be adjacent to or even remotely connected to his unit in time of war.

Clyde's commanders had provided him with signed requests for the plans of all units mentioned in his own war plans. Eventually Clyde gained access in this way to plans of the units mentioned in other unit's war plans, to include those of the Germans, the French, the Belgians, the Canadians, and all the U.S. services.

On one occasion, Clyde informed his division commander during a field exercise that his unit didn't have the war plan of a major command that was going to send a patrol into his area during the exercise. His commander supplied Clyde with his personal pilot and helicopter and a written order to fly to that command's field headquarters to retrieve a copy of their war plan. Clyde described the event with enthusiasm.

"I left the pilot in the hot seat, trying to explain to the military police what the hell he was doing landing on their general's helicopter pad. In the mean time, their document custodian was so intimidated because I had arrived in a general's helicopter, he started offering me copies of other documents, which I gladly accepted without even signing for them. I usually insisted on signing the proper documentation, but not this time."

As with other documents, once he had copied them, he sent them back loaded with paperclips marking multiple security and technical errors he had voluntarily corrected. His expertise also prompted an order to purge various security files throughout his own command of outdated classified documents.

"During the last few months of my army service, the division commander ordered me to purge the files of the entire division before I retired. I retired from the Army with two large plastic bags of classified documents that were documented as destroyed."

I immediately concluded that Clyde had to have had an espionage associate in the division headquarters to sign the destruction form as a witness. Outdated documents would have been almost as valuable to Clyde as current ones.

I knew when we were in the infantry together that even on a manual typewriter, with half of his ring finger missing, he typed eighty words per minute. As an expert in the development and writing of war plans, he could update the old plans and use his own stamps to classify and number the new documents. He told me he had even discovered the Hungarians didn't know how to read many of the plans they had received.

"I once listened to a Hungarian Intelligence Officer complain that some stupid soldier had delivered a war plan that didn't even include the grid coordinate for the various locations in the field of the headquarters and other elements. I had to explain to the Hungarian officer that every plan has a separate section devoted to grid coordinates. Even then, I had to explain how to match the coordinates with the respective elements."

This kind of assistance to foreign intelligence agencies had eventually earned Clyde an invitation to Hungary for a week or so to teach the Hungarians how to better exploit the documents they received, how to inflict the maximum damage on NATO troops, and how to anticipate certain commanders' decisions on the battlefield.

He taught a whole room full of Hungarians, sharing the platform only with his British-trained female interpreter. It was during this training session that he determined he had met the

Hungarian Defense Minister. He described the scene in the room where he conducted his briefing.

"One officer was introduced to me as Head of Hungarian Intelligence. A few minutes later, a man in civilian clothes entered the room and everyone stopped talking and stood at attention. I was introduced to him. I figured he had to at least be their defense minister."

I agreed with his assessment. I asked him why the defense minister was there, and he gave me his opinion: "I figured anyone connected with the high quality of intelligence information I had delivered to them would want to be able to say, 'Yes, I've met him.'"

Eventually Clyde offered foreign intelligence organizations a number of ways to ensure the defeat of NATO forces, although he wouldn't confirm which ones they accepted. He offered them tape recordings of classified command briefings, profiles of key commanders to help them predict their actions under various battlefield conditions, and the identities of all priority targets which NATO forces would likely destroy with tactical nuclear weapons, in the event they were about to be overrun by the enemy. He even offered to deliver to them a truck load of tactical nuclear weapons during a field exercise to which he had been granted special access.

One of his most ambitious plans was to plant remotely activated electronic homing devices in the walls of all the command vehicles, to include the new ones scheduled to be issued at the outbreak of war, because he had access to the POMCAS Sites where they were stored around Europe.

He did indicate that some of his offers, such as planting the electronic devices and stealing the tactical nuclear weapons were considered too risky by the Hungarians, who didn't want to take the chance of losing such an important source.

Determining what specific documents Clyde had delivered to foreign intelligence was next to impossible. He did say that wartime GDPs were priority for the Hungarians, and all documents involving nuclear information were the Czechoslovakians' priority. He said he saw a six-foot-long computer printout of eight digit coordinates for all GDP locations as it was in route to the East. He also stated, "All security plans and exercise GDPs classified COSMIC, TOP SECRET, ATOMAL, and LIMITED ACCESS, and all NATO wartime GDPs from Hannover south have gone."

Clyde eventually brought me a copy of his OPLAN on a computer disk and allowed me to take it home with me to Steinenbronn for a weekend to study. After studying it, I gave the disk to Grant, then told Clyde I had followed his advice and burned it. I brought my computer back to BK with me, and Clyde began leaving updated disks with me to study in my hotel room.

He had already given the Hungarians the concept on which to make a decision. Now he was filling in the gaps. He asked me to study each update, correct the grammar, make it clearer, then offer my opinions. Before making any corrections, I would make sure Grant got a copy, as I did with everything Clyde gave me.

I learned that Clyde's methods for storing his OPLAN on a disk, and his codes for accessing the file, were the keys to accessing most of the files produced on his computers. Rather than formatting a blank disk to store his files, he would replace unnecessary files on a commercial program disk or in the programs on his computer, such as Apple Writer, with files he wished to hide. He kept several copies of Apple Writer word processing and other programs on which to store his OPLAN and other documents. I had only to type in the sequence code Clyde provided me to access the OPLAN file.

Copying the Apple Writer program, with the embedded OPLAN, onto another disk for Grant proved a little tricky. I anticipated the difficulty and secured several copy programs from an expert in my battalion headquarter supply section, which would override Apple's copying safeguards.

The rules for maintaining a proper chain-of-custody of evidence required me to take my computer and the disk from Clyde to Grant's apartment in Wiesbaden. There we could discuss the plan during my debriefing and Grant could have the disk copied.

I unloaded my computer from the trunk of my BMW and crossed the street to Grant's apartment in the middle of the day. I envisioned Clyde driving down this priority street in Wiesbaden as I lugged my computer across it. I wondered what I would tell Clyde if he questioned me later. A story came to mind as I climbed the stairs of Grant's apartment building. I would tell Clyde or anyone else who asked me, *My computer crashed and I located a guy working at Wiesbaden Air Base who said he could fix it while I waited.*

First sight of the interior of Grant's apartment stopped me in my tracks. I glanced around the living room/dining room/kitchen combination as Grant made a space for my computer on the dining table. He shoved aside huge mounds of American and German coins, partially eaten pizzas and sandwiches, dirty clothes, sex magazines, and several things I didn't recognize.

He made a quick pass around the room collecting laundry, including a pair of underwear hanging on the TV antenna. He gathered fast food packages and a few of the magazines and dumped them out of sight in the bedroom. He did the same in the bathroom, then cleared a chair for me in front of the computer on the breakfast table.

I recognized the motif as that of a base for a surveillance team working all hours of the day and night, emptying their pockets between each change of clothes, which they left where they landed. There must have been several hundred dollars and Marks in piles of change all over the room and at least two dozen magazines open to photos of nude women in all the popular poses and a few new ones. Even with some of the laundry removed, there was scarcely a place for Grant to sit, so he stood.

I felt a little sorry for Grant, realizing the kind of hours he and his friends had to be keeping on this operation, so without comment and suppressing a smile, I sat down to the computer, opened the OPLAN file, and explained to Grant how to make a copy for CI. I was afraid Clyde might have made some mark on the disk he gave me, and I wanted to make my corrections for him on the original.

Grant informed me he would have to take the original to his headquarters for their Apple Computer expert to copy it while I waited in his apartment. I gave him one of the commercial copying programs and wrote down the instructions for its use and the code for accessing the OPLAN file.

Grant returned in about an hour and explained that their expert could not execute the copy program or access Clyde's embedded files. I ran the expert through the sequences telephonically, then Grant retrieved the original copy of Apple Writer with the OPLAN from his headquarters. When he returned, he debriefed me concerning my last meeting with Clyde. He also made new arrangements for delivering copies of future disks.

OPLAN.001

During this and several debriefings in the month of June 1987, I perceived that USAI was only interested in Clyde's OPLAN because they hoped to retrieve incriminating evidence on one of several disks I provided. At one point, Grant indicated they had found classified material embedded in one or more of the disks, but he never specified anything.

I knew that Clyde was preparing a cover letter for his final submission to the Hungarians, explaining some of his actions of which they didn't approve, but he didn't let me read it. I fully understood why Clyde would not want me to read the truth the Hungarians would accept. He was still trying very hard to determine the truth I would accept, and he wouldn't want me to make comparisons. I never knew if they contained anything classified or incriminating or if USAI had found it on the disks.

Completing and obtaining approval for the OPLAN became Clyde's driving obsession. While USAI saw no redeeming qualities in it, my appreciation of it eventually produced the results which had eluded USAI and would fully justify the continuation of the operation.

6

RECRUITMENT

Everything Clyde said, every story, every illustration, was part of a determined effort to get me to volunteer for espionage, which he hoped he could later claim was entrapment. With the same determination, and at my superiors' insistence, I tried to force him to recruit me. One approach I tried was to get him to admit that what he called preparation was actually recruitment.

Always on guard as if he might be recorded, he answered with comments like, "I'm only providing general information on which you can base your own decision." He even tried reverse psychology, saying, "You are the one person I could never work with. You're the type, Danny, that if I took you as a junior partner, a year down the road I'd be working for you." He was just as careful with the subject of actually delivering documents.

RECRUITMENT

He had made the point on several occasions, that there was no alternative to delivering documents. He emphasized the Hungarians' natural fear of traps and their belief that no one can deliver genuine, classified documents unless that person is genuine. Claiming to want to allay any fears I might have of the Hungarians, he also described what documents they preferred, how they verified authenticity, and some of their current security practices.

"The Hungarians are interested in war plans, including exercise plans. They will ask for three things, one of which they already have. All documents are cleaned up before they are handed over to the Russians. Names or identifying data associated with the source are removed. A worker can quit anytime or just take a vacation."

He almost got personal when he said, "The hardest thing in the world, Danny, is to find someone I can trust." He clarified his own definition of trust with, "Mutual trust is only possible when each party has dirt on the other."

I began to recognize that his difficulty making it clear he wasn't recruiting me, while still trying to get me to volunteer, was becoming very frustrating to him. The random thoughts he was sharing often seemed contradictory, but my volunteering to deliver documents was implied.

"Being a worker is profitable, while controlling workers is more profitable. Being a worker may provide credentials, Danny, because any connection with me or any of my friends is a strike against you. One can be a worker and still exploit the system. You might decide to work for a year, then branch off into schemes on both sides.

"The best thing might be to remain in a legal status until you can leave the army and focus on exploiting the system, but as a really productive worker, you could demand an escape plan.

"I am among the limited few who have been provided an escape plan. I've had an escape route forever, for years, Danny. I have travel documents, routes, safe houses, and an offer to bring the whole family to the East to work for them.

"A few years ago, the Hungarians got a commendation from the Russians for 'Foremost Source.' I represented ninety-five percent of the Hungarians' production. Around December 1986, when I just said, 'Stop,' everything came to a screeching halt. Couriers were sitting there."

Clyde's frustration peaked a few days later. I thought he was out of town, but he surprised me with a visit on the patio of my hotel restaurant. I ordered us both coffee, then excused myself to retrieve the latest printout of his OPLAN from my room so we could discuss my corrections. I strapped on the recording apparatus before returning. Following our discussion of the OPLAN, Clyde leaned back in his chair and cocked his head to the right.

"Danny, my primary concern when I talk to you is, 'Now, if he told me this, what would I think?' Sometimes I think that and I say, 'I don't know. I really just don't know?'

"Why don't you ask me, Clyde?"

"Uhh—"

"You can't?"

"No!"

"Oh. Then don't ask"

"Uh, because I figure in the end if you benefit, that's good, and if you don't, that's okay. But I still wonder."

RECRUITMENT

"Then ask me."

"What do you think?"

"About what, Clyde?"

"See, Danny, the crux of my problem in coming out and saying, 'Now this is the way that works.' The things I tell you, when I first thought of them, they were incredible when they worked, and I saw they worked. You say, 'That's unbelievable. I'm not really sure I believe this.'"

I saw a showdown coming, but I knew I had to tread lightly because of constant warnings by my superiors not to put words in his mouth, so I tried to use his own words against him. "Clyde, back in 8ID when you offered me a chance to make some money, was this what you were trying to recruit me into?"

"No. If you had expressed an interest, I would have found something for you to do. Then—" With a smile, he purposely left that sentence incomplete, but he seemed to realize I had understood it as an admission and quickly added, "Danny, you've never voiced an interest in that area."

"What area?"

"This area."

"Weren't we talking about recruitment? What was your intention ten years ago?"

"Like I said, Danny, you could say, 'Yeah!' But you didn't. What I'm saying now, I'm telling you the way things are. You look at it as it applies to you. Don't do that."

"Clyde, how can you say I apply it to me personally and at the same time say I've expressed no interest in any of these activities?"

"You've never voiced any interest in that area, Danny." He quickly dropped that subject.

DAMIAN and MONGOOSE

I was convinced this had been a legitimate attempt to recruit me and I could legally express an interest, especially in his original proposal, which I believed he had just admitted was a recruitment for espionage. However, the nuances, subtle as they were, would have to be discussed with Grant, who would have to discuss it with the Justice Department.

After my next debriefing, I stayed away from my hotel until Grant could get back to me with a decision. When we met again, he told me the first tape had not recorded, but based on my verbal report, the decision was made that I could accept Clyde's original offer made ten years earlier. He then directed me, "Get Clyde to identify the specific documents he wants."

I was aware that their normal procedure would be to arrest Clyde the moment he accepted documents from me. I was concerned that an early arrest might cost us a valuable opportunity to identify Clyde's associates.

Just in case they might be willing to adjust that procedure, I was determined to ensure my status with Clyde, after recruitment, would justify his continued flow of information in addition to receiving documents from me.

I knew the actual release of any of the war plans he wanted would prove difficult, if not impossible. I also knew the Justice Department needed the information that had not been recorded at our previous meeting. With these challenges in mind, at my next meeting with Clyde in the Hotel Viktoria restaurant, I quickly took over the discussion. I made this my showdown and didn't allow him to interrupt.

"Clyde, you say I haven't voiced an interest in your activities. Seems to me that's all I have done. I admit I didn't know what you were offering me ten years ago. Now that you've explained that you were offering me a chance to make some money selling secrets to foreign countries and explained several schemes I can take advantage of, assuming that offer is still open, I'm very interested. If you haven't been able to tell how interested, maybe it's because I was trying to figure out just what you have left me to be interested in.

"First you tell me you have an incredible operation I can be part of, then you say you're probably going to be taken out of the picture. Next you tell me I should leave the Army, move to a neutral country, and work with you as a trainer for your OPLAN, then you say they probably won't accept the plan because they'll realize they don't know how to do it. Finally you tell me I can be a worker for a year, then branch off into schemes on both sides, but you warn me that any connection with you or your friends is a strike against me."

Clyde's expression of realization and calm reflection lacked his usual, threatened demeanor when he responded. "I see what you mean, Danny, about removing options. It's still true; I'm dumber now than ever. Until they accept the OPLAN, I don't know.

"I've tried to give you dozens of alternatives: wait 'til the end of your military career, then step out and become legal or step out and say, 'I've got something to offer.' What I pictured was actually somebody to help exploit the system."

"Alright, Clyde. So you're telling me you're offering me all those options?"

"That pretty well says it. If you say, 'I want to stay in, and I want to work,' great!"

"For whom would I be working?"

"The Czechoslovakians. The Hungarians."

"And work with?"

"Me. And when the Hungarians get the full packet, they're gonna want it so bad they can taste it, and they front the money, I'll say, 'He's gonna be the trainer.'"

Clyde assumed I was recruited and immediately began discussing my role as a trainer of field men in the implementation of the OPLAN. He also suggested, and I agreed, that it would be beneficial for him to give the Hungarians my name and personal information. He said he would tell them he had recruited me ten years earlier, he had sent me to learn all I could about CI investigative procedures, and he is now activating me.

His immediate plan, as I had expected, was for me to implement that concept of the OPLAN that called for delivery of as many verifiable war plans as possible, not only to establish my credentials, but also to help him reestablish his and sell the OPLAN.

I bought some time by reminding him I would soon be completing my TDY assignment and returning to my duties as Operations NCO in Stuttgart, at which time I could start to identify just what documents were stored at B Company Headquarters and what I could access outside my own unit. In the meantime, I asked him to suggest documents in the intelligence arena that would establish my credentials with the Hungarians. He was clearly disappointed.

"The Hungarians want war plans, Danny, and they have to be verifiable. Anything else they're going to suspect I invented." He said that as if I already knew they suspected him of inventing some documents, but he gave me no chance to ask. "I know anyone who carries your credentials can gain access to those plans."

192

RECRUITMENT

"Oh I don't deny that, Clyde. All I want is to first get a clear picture of my unit's security procedures before taking any risks."

"The Hungarians are not going to be interested in any counter-intelligence documents. That's not their preferred area."

"Not even to establish my credibility until I can take control of my surroundings in Stuttgart?"

"I don't know, Danny. There might be one area: the schedule of electronic sweeps of classified briefing rooms throughout Europe to locate any listening devices. That would tell the Hungarians when to place and remove any recording devices."

Clyde knew those electronic sweeps were conducted by a CI unit, and the schedule would be classified SECRET. We had both seen those schedules when we were in the infantry together. I said, "I'll be on the lookout for one, if they haven't yet implemented a new policy of making the sweeps unannounced."

I knew of no such policy, but I hoped Clyde would consider that a possibility, because I doubted USAI would consider that choice of documents any better for them than war plans. Clyde asked me to set aside some time the following Sunday for a meeting with him in my hotel room for some concentrated training.

At my debriefing, Grant agreed that I had been sufficiently recruited and that Clyde had satisfied their requirement that he request specific, classified documents. In response to my concern that Clyde did not really want to offer intelligence documents to the Hungarians, Grant said, "He's just blowing smoke. He'll gladly accept any classified documents."

In preparation for my concentrated training session with Clyde, Grant arranged access to my hotel room while I was out. We met again that week, and he told me a larger recording device had been placed in a box filled with bottles of drinking water, which I kept on top of my closet. He told me how to activate the recorder just before Clyde arrived, but instructed me to wear my micro cassette recorder as backup.

When Clyde arrived on Sunday, he explained that he had spent the last few days at his computer completing his OPLAN for the Hungarians so we could have this training session. I procured a pot of coffee from the restaurant, then pulled out a small notebook and pen.

Clyde started a rapid-fire discourse on being the best soldier and supervisor in my unit. As he paced the floor, he delivered a lecture I sensed had been given to others before me. I couldn't help wondering how many. At first, I resented the fact that Clyde saw the need to lecture me on professional soldiering, but I soon learned his underlying purpose.

"To succeed in this business, a soldier has to wear the sharpest uniforms, be in the best physical condition, and observe the strictest military courtesy in order to earn respect from his subordinates as well as his superiors. You have to demand those same standards of subordinates, administer impartial discipline, and recognize subordinates' achievements. That's the only way to ensure their fear of you and have complete control of your people and your surroundings.

"By enforcing the military concept of chain-of-command, no one can give a task to any of your soldiers directly. All tasking from my superiors came directly to me. It was the only way to be sure where my soldiers were at all times. This is vital if you want uninterrupted time to conduct your business without risk.

"I kept a spiral notebook open on my desk at all times. I used it to organize, schedule, and assign all tasking. I listed everyone in my unit who was my responsibility. It would show where they were any time during the workday, whether on leave, at an appointment, on assignment, in the motor pool, at their desk, or otherwise occupied. Each supervisor would write any changes in the notebook on a daily basis. If anyone failed to be where the notebook said he was, his immediate supervisor would be disciplined by me.

"The notebook is vital for you to know where everyone is at all times in order to schedule your time alone with documents, but it's also where you keep track of everything going on in your unit, so you can keep your superiors informed. They eventually become dependent on you.

"Another section of the notebook lists the unit's security requirements and document controls, with rules so stringent everyone will avoid the responsibility, and the commander will naturally insist that you assume complete control of all classified documents related even remotely to your area of responsibility, and eventually all documents in the unit.

"Never do anything yourself. I always relied on fear of me, and I ordered a soldier to copy documents or send a letter requesting documents. I would usually back that up with written orders from my commander. Never be observed engaging in those activities yourself."

Clyde still continued to avoid the use of terms like spy or espionage. He referred to himself as an independent information broker. Delivery of documents was clearly the focus of this training, and my speedy delivery of the documents the Hungarians wanted would represent the first implementation of the OPLAN. He added that I would certainly become a trainer when the OPLAN was adopted. With that reminder, he abruptly ended the session with the revelation that he had already arranged to deliver his completed OPLAN packet to a Hungarian courier later that afternoon in Mainz.

I asked him, "When will we meet again to continue this lesson?"

"You're driving me to Mainz."

I had informed him earlier that I had to move out of my hotel that afternoon to make room for a special guest who booked the same room every year, and I would have to put all my things in my BMW until my new room became available late that evening. Because he had forgotten and had a schedule to meet, he insisted on helping me carry my things to the car.

To ensure that he didn't stay behind and accidently discover the recorder in the box on the closet, I placed several folded clothing items on top of the box and handed it to him to carry down to the car. I quickly grabbed a load of hanging clothes and followed him to the car, where I took the box from him and placed it in the back seat with the clothes still on top. I locked the car and took him back for a few more loads to make sure he was never alone in the car.

Once we started for Mainz, I summarized Clyde's earlier recruitment of me in case the recorder in the box was better than the one I was wearing. I usually got Clyde to repeat conversations when there was trouble with my recorder or I thought the tape had run out before I could change it.

I only changed the tape when I could manage to go to the toilet alone, except once, a few weeks earlier, when Clyde followed me into an unoccupied toilet and continued a rather important

196

subject. I excused myself and went into a stall because I knew time had run out on the tape, but Clyde stood outside the stall and continued his story.

Because the recorder was in a cloth bag closed at the top with Velcro, I realized he would hear it open, so I managed a rather loud bodily noise to cover the sound of the Velcro, then changed the tape. As we were leaving that Gasthaus, I got Clyde to repeat some of the points I hadn't recorded.

When Clyde and I reached Mainz, Clyde left me at a Gasthaus two blocks from the Bahnhof. On his return, an hour later, he said very little about his meeting with the Hungarian courier, except that the courier told him to expect a long delay while the Hungarians translated and studied the one hundred revised pages he had given them. He said he was willing to give them that time, citing his familiarity with the way the system had worked over the years.

On the drive back to BK, Clyde continued my training with a lesson in document control and marking regulations. I saw this as an opportunity to address what I viewed as a complete change in his attitude. I wanted him to know I was interested in more than selling documents, so he would include me in all his activities.

"Clyde, I respect your expertise in this area, and I understand it's importance to developing complete control of documents in my unit. I've spent years inspecting document custodians for commanders all over Germany. While that's no longer a CI responsibility in Europe, many commanders have requested my help with that and in writing their entire security program in compliance with Army Regulation 380-5 and others regulations.

"What concerns me right now is that I detect a change in your attitude toward me. I know you thought of me as the guy who didn't have a price, but now that I've agreed to your offer to sell secrets, you don't seem to have the same respect for me. I don't have any problem working for you, in fact I insist on it, but I want to be that guy who can help you continue to exploit the system, and you're the only one who completely understands how to do that."

"Absolutely not. I assure you I have nothing but respect for you, Danny, and I intend to eventually tell you everything and keep you informed of the progress of the OPLAN. Your delivery of documents will demonstrate the effectiveness of the OPLAN and enhance its chances of adoption. The money we will make, even with the OPLAN, will always depend on production.

"Speaking of money, Danny, the Hungarians will even let you deposit the money you make in their banks, where you can earn sixteen percent. Or you can store it in Swiss banks, where I keep most of mine. I have a few accounts in Zurich and another in Lucerne because the Swiss will never release information concerning my accounts.

"I've demanded a large monetary commitment from the Hungarians to implement the OPLAN and to prove to me they have really put a curtain over the past. I've already approached the owner of a video store in BK, who is willing to sell his store to me. I included that price with my packet and emphasized its importance in creating a database to be used by the field men, to identify prospective workers."

He still wasn't entirely convinced the Hungarians would accept his OPLAN, but during the next few days, he became enthusiastic about financing it himself. He proposed a partnership between us in a neutral country. He doubted the Hungarians' ability to fully understand the OPLAN, even with our help. He also worried about their lack of motivation.

"The political climate is changing in many Warsaw Pact countries, Danny. A war in Europe is no longer contemplated. Mark my word. There will soon be only one Germany. I'm serious. We probably ought to become independent brokers.

"I could help you manipulate the Army into giving you an early retirement. Some friends of mine offered me the same thing after Gitta's crying on an Army doctor's shoulder failed to help me get a release from my assignment to drill sergeant school, before my commander stabilized my tour in BK.

"These Hungarian friends gave me a list of symptoms with which to fake back problems. They even went so far as to offer to break something for me so I wouldn't have to fake it. I could get the same thing for you." We both laughed, and Clyde began detailing our partnership.

"We can set up in a neutral country, hire and train field men, and recruit our own ring of workers from various military services. We could easily broker documents to various countries."

"I'm willing, Clyde. I've been to the hospital in BK about my lower back and leg, and I had some X-rays taken in Stuttgart of the pinched nerve or whatever it is. I haven't heard back from the doctor, but I'll let you know if it's debilitating enough to get out of the Army."

I wasn't looking forward to relaying Clyde's plans for an independent brokerage to Grant, who had let slip some of the comments made by our supervisors expressing their total contempt for Clyde's OPLAN. For that reason, I did not express my opinion that U.S. Army Intelligence could be overlooking an opportunity to gain control of an entire espionage ring, to include the soldiers who would join it and the information to be delivered, eventually identifying every person ever connected with Clyde's activities, even foreign agents and controllers, and influencing decisions made at the highest level of several foreign intelligence agencies.

During my next debriefing, I couldn't resist mentioning the possibility, although I tempered my personal enthusiasm, believing they would never consider such a complicated operation. Grant's response staggered my imagination. "You know that scenario is not beyond the realm of possibility, don't you, Danny?"

"Well I certainly would be willing to do whatever it would take to make that work, Grant.

It could be an excellent way to control a sizeable portion of foreign intelligence collection, at least until we identify all his associates. I can pick up those X-rays from Stuttgart and make them available to you so they could be considered."

"Do that, Danny." Grant informed me that my TDY would end shortly, and they would move the operation to Stuttgart.

I began preparing Clyde for the transition. That preparation included some subtle suggestions that I intended to change some bad habits I had picked up from him. I jokingly accused him of being a bad influence with his raunchy infantry vocabulary. I vowed to break that habit before I returned to my job.

In reality, I had started using some of his vocabulary on purpose, to help him believe I had lost a lot of my old inhibitions. Even in my infantry days, I seldom resorted to that vocabulary. In those days, Clyde had jokingly accused me of self-righteousness, which he said he hated. I just wanted one less obstacle to gaining his trust. When I told Clyde I needed to make this change in order to protect my reputation as a gentleman, he said, with conviction, "And you should, Danny."

Just before my TDY ended, I received another call from my sister's doctor that suggested I might have to spend two or three weeks in Houston after all. I told Clyde I would probably have to go because the doctor's message said my presence was absolutely imperative. I called the doctor for an explanation. He was emphatic.

"Your sister is dying. There is nothing we can do for her but make her as comfortable as possible. We try to give her anything she wants. She wants you!"

Shirley had become extremely impatient for me to complete my TDY. As soon as I returned to our condo in Steinenbronn, I told her about the doctor's second message. She insisted I leave for Houston right away. She had seen my sister's animosity toward me the few times we'd visited her over the years, and she understood my fear that my presence would only cause her more pain, but she said, "You have to go, Danny. She's your sister!"

I met with Grant to discuss my predicament. I left the final decision with them, but I emphasized the doctor's concerns. I even made an offhand remark that I could still leave everything in my brother's hands unless someone might need an out-of-the-way place to meet me and do some planning. Grant's response came a few days later.

"As a matter of fact, Danny, we do want to have a meeting with you in Houston. I'll be returning to the States myself. I'll give you a number to call when you get to Houston and know your schedule."

I assumed USAI would take this opportunity to spell out an

operation contingent on Clyde's decision to resume his espionage activities with me in a neutral country. I was prepared to at least pretend to leave the Army, even become a citizen of some neutral country, and spend as many years as necessary to strike a blow against foreign intelligence collection. I believed the possibilities were unlimited, but before committing to such a plan, I had one arrangement I had to make.

"Shirley, before I go to Houston, I have one very serious question to ask you about our future. Would you be willing to leave the Army and move to another European country where I would start a new profession for a few years?"

"Okay, Danny, what have you done?"

"Humm, very funny, babe. You know what my job is, honey. I catch spies. I promise you will be told more than you've ever been told about my job, if such a drastic measure becomes necessary. It would be strictly voluntary, and I wouldn't do it unless you agreed."

"You know what my answer is, Danny: I go where you go."

"Yeah, I know. I'm not sure it will come to that, but I'll give you plenty of notice. I should know more when I return from Houston."

I was sure USAI would allow me to devote my time primarily to my sister, but I was definitely ready to work in some meetings to discuss the requirements for my participation in an even more extensive operation. I had made arrangements for my brother, David, to meet me on 9 July 1987 at the Houston Airport and drive me to my sister's home, where I would stay as long as she needed me.

7

<u>HOUSTON</u>

My sister's husband, a Harris County policeman, took me to the hospital, where I met with the doctor. The doctor thanked me for coming, then he explained again my sister's rapidly deteriorating condition and his desire to keep her as comfortable as possible and to grant her every wish within his power. Her husband and I entered her room, and he gave her a kiss while I greeted her nurse and an aide. Then I greeted my sister.

"Hello, Pauline."

"Well, it's about damn time. Everybody, this is my brother, Danny. He's the only one who can call me Pauline, so don't get any ideas. Everybody please leave us. I need to talk to my brother."

I was shocked by her extremely gaunt appearance. Her every move was punctuated by pain, and I wondered how much she would suffer from this talk with me, which was obviously very important to her. I hugged and kissed her, then moved a chair next to her bed.

At forty, Pauline was the youngest of my two sisters. She was tall and pretty, like her mother. She had long blond hair, big blue eyes that took in everything, and a very sharp tongue. She had always dominated her men, but she could be sweet. Though she tried, she had never been able to intimidate me.

Everyone else knew her by her first name, Linda. She never really minded that I called her by her middle name, Pauline, and I knew it. I didn't even know when she had started calling herself Linda. I had only seen her a half dozen times in the past thirty-five years or so, after we'd spent a year together in my first and her only foster home.

I knew from my brother that she had been unhappy a good bit of her life, but she always seemed to face life with defiance. Today seemed to be no exception. She had something on her mind, and she was determined to address it as she pushed herself up as high as she could on her pillows, enduring the agony, and raised her chin.

"Danny, how long are you going to be here?"

"I'm here as long as you need me, Pauline. If you get tired, I can come back. I'm staying at your house."

"Are you here on business?"

"I'm here to see you, Pauline."

"But are you here on business?"

"Just a little. As soon as CI heard I was coming to Houston, they gave me the name of someone to look up for them, but I only have to do that if I have time."

"Good. Thelma came to see me a few days ago. There was one thing she wouldn't tell me. I want you to tell me." She had narrowed her eyes, and she had her usual, demanding tone when she started, but she softened it to a request.

I smiled and said, "I'll tell you anything you want to know, Pauline."

"Who is your father?"

"Pauline," I answered as tenderly as possible. "I meant it when I said I will tell you anything, but I don't know who my father is."

"Haven't you asked Thelma?"

"Yes, I've asked, but I don't remember the names she's given me. I doubt if she remembers. She's told three or four different stories over the years. She told our first caseworker, Mrs. Vickers, one thing, then she told me something else. She told our last caseworker, Mrs. Johnson, another story. I've known all along she wants to protect him and probably hasn't really told anyone who he is. I respect that. I think Mrs. Vickers knew she was protecting him and never pressed her about it.

"Why would she want to protect him? Don't you want to know who your real father is?"

"I guess he was married and respected in his community. No, I don't need to know who he is. Even if I asked her again, for your sake, I doubt we could believe what she told us.

"I'm sorry, Pauline. It just doesn't matter to me. I never considered you and June and David any less my brother and sisters because Bill Williams was your father. Thelma is still our mother."

"Alright, but I have another question. Why have you all hated me all these years for letting the Smiths adopt me?"

My heart was suddenly in my throat. Learning for the first

time that Pauline had suffered such needless emotional pain and unhappiness was a shock, and I took a minute to respond.

"Pauline, I promise you, I have never hated you. I've always loved you, and David and June have always loved you. They certainly know what I know, that you didn't let the Smiths adopt you. In the first place, you were just a child. You had no choice in the matter. It was a court decision. In the second place, if anyone has to take responsibility for your being adopted, I do.

"Mrs. Johnson came to me one day and asked for my help. She told me that the court had decided you were growing up knowing only one mother and you should be adopted by the Smiths. Mother had refused. Mrs. Johnson told me if Mother didn't volunteer to let the Smiths adopt you, the court would take you from her. She asked me to persuade Mother.

"That wasn't easy for me, and I didn't want it either, but I didn't want to see Mother or you hurt even more. I finally persuaded her it would be easier on you in the long run, and when you turned eighteen, you would want to get to know her.

"Once Mother gave her consent, Mrs. Johnson told me no one in the family would ever be allowed to visit you again. Of course, David never accepted that. I know he used to wait for you after school and visit you all the time. He got in trouble over it too."

"Okay, Danny, then tell me why you got a divorce and why you never see your three children."

"Pauline, I have to explain something to you. If you need for me to tell you things that happened in my past and in our past, I'll do that for you. It won't be easy for me, because I don't concern myself much with the past. I like to look at the past the same way David does since he got out of prison the last time. June asked him why he seemed to have completely changed his attitude about life. He told her, 'I used to be a fool. I'm not a fool anymore.'

"I hope I've learned a few things from my mistakes. I just don't like to dwell on them. Not that I don't remember."

"But, why don't you see your kids?"

"I have seen my two sons when the oldest turned eighteen. That was the agreement with their mother when I allowed their stepfather to adopt them. She believed their new family would have a better chance that way. I couldn't see my daughter because she was only fourteen, and her mother didn't want to upset her. I asked my two sons if there was anything they wanted to know, anything that bothered them over the years, and they both said there was nothing. I gave them my address and phone number and told them I would love to hear from them. They never called or wrote. They have their own lives to live, and I respect that."

"Danny, please give me a hug. I'm getting tired. Early evening is the only time I can have visitors because of my therapy. I want to talk to you some more tomorrow. Now that I understand a few things, I keep asking myself, 'Where have you been all my life.'"

As I left the hospital, I asked myself the same thing about her. In less than an hour, we had become brother and sister again, with little or no time left to enjoy it. I was losing another friend.

I had come here for Pauline, and I had put Clyde Conrad in the back of my mind. I hadn't even thought of Clyde's friendship as a loss until now. I had allowed the role I was playing to replace the genuine friendship I once enjoyed with Clyde.

Realizing my role might be perpetuated for some time, if USAI had half the imagination I did, I knew this might be my last opportunity to visit friends of mine in Houston, my brother and my younger sister, June, and Pauline's husband. As the visits with Pauline became shorter and fewer, I knew within a few days I would have plenty of time for USAI, so I called Grant.

I was a little surprised when the first meeting was scheduled in a restaurant. I assumed it would be followed by planning sessions in a hotel room. Grant introduced me to a gentleman who didn't volunteer the name of his agency, if he even told me his real name. As we exchanged comments about the weather, Grant and his companion began reminding each other how little time they had before they would have to start for the airport to catch their flight out of town.

We sat at a table next to the wall in a crowded restaurant, and I answered questions about my sister's health. Between their chit-chat and constant reminders about having to rush their lunch, I was having difficulty figuring out what the hell was the purpose of this meeting. I surmised that Grant's companion was the ranking man when he leaned forward to compliment me.

"Danny, I want you to know, you have changed the way we conduct counterespionage investigations. I can't thank you enough for the great work you've done."

I wanted to ask how investigations had changed, but his tone suggested a "but" was coming soon. Or maybe I was just worried that I had completely miscalculated the direction of this operation and was concerned that Grant and I would remain the only two who had seen potential beyond hanging one more spy's head on the wall. With my frustration and disappointment mounting, the question which followed sounded like another trap.

"Danny, I have one question. I already have some theories of my own, but I'd really like to hear your opinion. Why is Clyde Conrad confessing everything to you?"

Slowly the heat began to rise to my neck. Not only did I hate having this conversation in a restaurant, I was apprehensive about answering the question. Grant's companion was busy eating, so he waited while I thought.

If that isn't obvious by now, you don't know what's going on between me and Clyde. If you still think he's confessing, you'll never understand. If I insinuate I'm conning him, the Justice Department will translate that as manipulation or putting words in his mouth, and USAI will call it trying to run their operation. No matter how I answer, someone won't like it.

"He's not confessing because he doesn't believe he's done anything wrong."

Grant quickly interrupted me with, "Danny, I think he knows that." His eyes revealed a fear that his companion had been insulted. I looked back at the man and continued.

"Good. Then you understand that his arrogance has convinced him that everyone has a price and he can con anyone. I'm only trying to make that as difficult as possible so he will tell me whatever it will take to convince me and keep me convinced."

"That's basically what I figured." That ended the meeting, and I returned to my sister's house.

Pauline had asked the doctor to stop her therapy and let her go home to spend her last days with her husband. Before she returned, I mowed her yard and weeded her rose garden. A few days later, I returned to Stuttgart.

A few weeks later, I received a call from her husband telling me, "Danny, Pauline is gone." I was very sad for him, but I took great comfort in the realization that she and I had enjoyed our short time together as the brother and sister we had never been to each other.

DAMIAN and MONGOOSE

That memory, the time I could now spend with Shirley, and the fact that I was fully employed as Operations NCO, B Company, 527th MI in Stuttgart made it easier for me to resign myself to whatever plan USAI had for me and the operation. I knew they would inform me of very few details and expect little or no input from me. I wasn't sure they even had a plan, but Clyde certainly had one.

8

FRIENDSHIP VERSUS HONOR

Clyde Conrad didn't wait long getting in touch with me in Stuttgart. He called my office, identified himself to the sergeant who answered the phone, and asked to speak to me. His sudden lack of secrecy didn't surprise me. I imagined him listening intently for any indication of surprise or hesitation at the mention of his name. He would have listened as well for conversations in the background that might reveal that anyone other than I knew who he was.

He invited me for dinner that evening, saying that he was in Stuttgart to visit another friend. I agreed to six-thirty to be sure I wouldn't have to make any excuses for leaving early, because I was usually the last one to leave.

211

DAMIAN and MONGOOSE

I had quickly brought myself up-to-date on the message traffic of a number of ongoing espionage investigations, while expanding my coordination with local units for development of Company Bs War Plans. I attended war planning meetings at 527ᵗʰ Headquarters in K-town, and met with G-3s and S-3s of several combat units throughout southern Germany. I gave myself a rather unstructured schedule similar to the one I'd had in Bad Kreuznach.

At a hotel restaurant in downtown Stuttgart, Clyde resumed my training as if I hadn't been away, and nothing had changed. Disregarding my earlier insistence that I was well schooled in classified document control, he gave me a refresher course in the writing, marking, and safeguarding of war plans and related classified documents, then he detailed one practice in U.S. Army document control procedures, which he expected me to exploit immediately, for the benefit of the OPLAN.

This exploitation was one of those aspects of the OPLAN that Clyde hadn't described to me and didn't intend to describe to the Hungarians. It was designed for his personal manipulation of the OPLAN.

U.S. Army Regulation 380-5 required that the names, addresses, and nighttime phone numbers of personnel who had the combinations to classified storage facilities be displayed on a Department of Defense Form 727 on the front of all vault doors and safes. This gave the Charge of Quarters for each building someone to notify if they discovered a door or safe unlocked after duty hours.

He expected me to use my access to the buildings containing these vaults to copy the names of document custodians off the form 727s for our future recruitment targeting. Stalling Clyde on the implementation of this concept was going to be a bit tricky.

FRIENDSHIP VERSUS HONOR

I began by informing him that the regulation had been changed in the past six months to require the Form 727 to be posted inside the vaults and safes, where a Charge of Quarters would still have access, but only if the door or drawer was left open.

I assured him I would look for those units who were slow to implement the regulation change. He reminded me that a little ingenuity would gain me access during duty hours to Form 727s, even if they were on the inside.

My training that evening in Stuttgart continued with a strong suggestion that I join and frequent the noncommissioned officers clubs in the various communities and get myself nominated to the local Masonic organization as soon as possible. One purpose was to develop a network of acquaintances throughout the military who could be called when critical assignments were sought for agents we would recruit. The more important purpose was to identify newly assigned document custodians who would need a friend to help them adjust to a foreign country, the beginning of their preparation for recruitment. Newly assigned document custodians would have plenty of time left on their tours to deliver all their documents.

Following this increment of concentrated training, Clyde handed me two thousand Marks and instructed me to buy a new set of military dress blues and a tailored suit. He asked me to bring him the receipts so he could eventually make the Hungarians reimburse him. I asked him what was wrong with the sport coat and slacks I was wearing, and he smiled and said, "They're off the rack."

At my next debriefing, I exchanged the money with Grant so he would have original bills given by Clyde, then I followed

Clyde's instructions as far as the money would allow. He could see from the receipts I gave him that there wasn't enough money for tailored suits. He was proud of his own suits, as well as the diamond studded Rolex he wore on special occasions.

Clyde also requested I supply the unclassified line and block charts of my unit and units I supported, which contained the command structure and identified personnel, duty positions, and office phone numbers.

I followed Grant's instructions and gave Clyde the line and block charts he requested. I also implemented the use of a spiral notebook to demonstrate to Clyde my complete understanding of his concepts and to lessen the appearance of stalling. I didn't have to stall for long.

Grant surprised me with a classified document that USAI had decided to make available to Clyde. It was a lesson plan from my old office in the special operations section of the Intelligence Center & School at Fort Huachuca. It had been written by my officer friend who had housed me on the night I arrived in Frankfurt.

I had previously edited the document, designed practical exercises for it, and taught it to hundreds of CI students, including my Company B operations officer, Mr. Beard. Since the subject of the document was surveillance detection, it was easy to understand why USAI considered it no loss to give it to Clyde, but it caused me problems immediately.

I thought I had persuaded Clyde that a document not related to war plans might suffice to establish my bona fides with the Hungarians, but when I described the classified, intelligence document from Fort Huachuca, that no one in Company B knew I had, he argued that the Hungarians would not want the document, especially on a subject with which they were already so familiar. The Hungarians had already warned Clyde to be very careful about his association with a counterintelligence agent.

I tried to convince him he would know the document was genuine and so would the Hungarians. I wasn't sure Clyde would even accept the document, but Grant directed me to have it with me at a meeting Clyde had arranged in Heidelberg and to make sure Clyde asked me for the document. I had it in a large, brown envelope sitting beside me in the booth of a crowded, noisy Gasthaus when I brought up the subject.

"Clyde," I said almost apologetically, "The reason I selected the document I told you about was that I had arranged to have it mailed to me for training purposes when I left Fort Huachuca. No one told me it had arrived, but I found it unopened and addressed to me in one of the safes. I know you will recognize it as a current document."

"Where is the document now?"

"I have it right here, Clyde."

He seemed shocked and very uneasy. He sat there silently.

"Are you interested in it, Clyde?"

"He took a deep breath, then tightened his jaw and said, 'Let me see it.'"

His next few moves were smooth and calculated and couldn't have taken more than ten seconds. He reached for the envelope, lowered it to his lap, and pulled the ten-page document about three quarters of the way out of the envelope. He quickly skimmed over the first three pages, shoved the document back into the envelope, and laid it on the seat beside his left leg.

He was already sliding out of the booth to his right with the comment that he had to go to the latrine. He hurried down the aisle faster than I'd ever seen him walk. I watched in admiration. As he quickly distanced himself from that document, I reflected on what he had just accomplished.

He had taken just long enough to establish that the document was SECRET and genuine and placed the document where it couldn't be easily seen by anyone else in the room. Then he removed himself so rapidly it would be hard for anyone in the room to see that he didn't still have the document.

If anyone was planning to arrest him, they would only succeed in revealing that intention to Clyde. He could claim he was on his way to the telephone to report me to CI. I cringed and glanced around the room hoping not to see any movement in his direction.

As I watched Clyde turn the corner toward the toilet, a mysterious sensation overpowered me. I felt a tightness in my shoulders and chest and a sense of apprehension washed over my consciousness. I had never experienced such a phenomenon. Straining to comprehend it, I remembered the warning I'd received from the FBI behavior specialist, and I wondered about it.

Could he have been right? Is my emotion going to rule my mind so I can't bear continuing this operation against my friend? Do I not have the moral courage I was so sure I had? Even if I fight this, will it happen again when Clyde returns?

Not being able to control this emotion, or even understand it, made me angry. I decided not to fight it. I needed to know what kind of person I really was, what this power over my grasp of reality meant. I wanted it to express itself in thoughts, no matter what they turned out to be. I sat quietly, but only for a few seconds.

FRIENDSHIP VERSUS HONOR

From somewhere deep in my subconscious mind, this emotion identified itself. It was guilt, pure, unadulterated guilt, but not for what I was expecting.

I had just given a classified document to an agent of a foreign country, and the guilt was overwhelming. It didn't seem to matter that I had the authority to release the document. I marveled at the paradoxical nature of that emotion, but I realized what had caused it.

I had read about the dangers of playing an undercover role too well or too long. I knew a person ran the risk of becoming enslaved by the role. That depended entirely on the strength of character of the individual.

I had just experienced the opposite. I involuntarily responded emotionally to the true norms and standards of my conscience, standards obviously so entrenched that even the ease with which I was playing the role of a traitor could not fully suppress them. I hated the thought of giving a document to a foreign agent, and I was glad to know that about myself. I relaxed and returned to my role.

I thought about the document on the other side of the booth. I reached under the booth to retrieve it so it wouldn't appear to Clyde that I was trying to leave it in his possession. When he returned, I chided him for leaving it unsecured.

He paid the bill and followed me toward the toilet, then went looking for more cigarettes. When I caught up to him, I realized I had accidently left the document in the toilet and hurried back to retrieve it. I took a few jibes from Clyde when I joined him again, then he surprised me.

"Danny, let me see it."

"Sure. To tell you the truth, I decided you weren't interested in the document at all, or you still don't trust me."

"Danny, you know how I know I can trust you? Because if I couldn't, they would be arresting me right now. Am I right? Can they give away a classified document?"

"Not that I'm aware of, Clyde."

"No, they can't. I'll study this, make a copy for myself, then deliver it. Then we'll have to wait for the Hungarians to verify it, determine its value, and deliver the money."

After several weeks, I delivered two more intelligence documents, classified SECRET and CONFIDENTIAL, even though the Hungarians hadn't paid me for the first document.

I knew USAI was having trouble getting commanders to release the documents Clyde really wanted, although I kept trying to convince Clyde he would eventually get them.

I used the Hungarians' delay as an excuse for dragging my heels about mass delivery of war plans. He assured me that waiting for the Hungarians to pay was routine. My excuse didn't impress him. What's more, my superiors were unimpressed with my part of the operation.

At my next debriefing, I was surprised to see that Mr. Romski had joined us in the hotel room. No one asked me to sit down, and Romski's displeasure was obvious. He took a step toward me, lowered his eyebrows, and raised his chin.

"Danny, why didn't you tell us about Allen Crammer?"

I was dumbfounded. Although I was bad about names, I always told them when Clyde mentioned someone, even if I didn't remember the name. I would sometimes forget to tell them something, then be reminded of it by another subject. I considered all that when I responded.

"I don't know any Allen Crammer."

"I'm not saying you know him, Danny, but why didn't you tell us that Clyde mentioned him?"

"I admit that I sometimes forget to tell you something right away, Mr. Romski, but Clyde has never mentioned such a name to me."

Romski was livid. He said, "Wait just a minute," as he spun around to the hotel desk and opened his briefcase. He pulled out a cassette recorder and a set of headphones. He started listening to a tape in the recorder to find the portion of tape he wanted. Doubt and dread began to flood my mind.

If the name is on the tape, I must be wrong, but how is that possible? Even when I forget a name, I recognize it when someone says it. I always remember what interests me. How could I forget Clyde mentioning a person? How can I explain such a thing?

Romski turned to me and handed me the headphones while he held the tape player. He punched the button, and I listened intently. The voice was Clyde's. It was clear and easily understood.

The statement he was making was so innocuous I couldn't picture where we were when he made it. Not only had there been no mention of Allen Crammer or anything that remotely sounded like it, the subject wasn't about a person.

Romski turned off the player. When I looked up, he glared at me and growled, "Did you hear what he said?"

"Yes, I heard what he said. I can't tell you why he was saying it, without hearing more of the context, but I heard what he said."

"What did he say?" Romski's tone was mean.

"If you will let me listen one more time, Mr. Romski, I'll tell you every word."

He found the beginning of that portion again and I listened. When I finished, I repeated it verbatim. Out of the corner of my eye, I saw Grant flash a glance in Romski's direction, as if he didn't want to miss his reaction.

Romski raised his eyebrows in total disbelief, grabbed the headphones from me, and sat down at the desk. He listened to the tape several times, then put the recorder back in his briefcase before dismissing the subject with disdain.

"That might have been what he said, but that's not the only problem, Danny. You constantly interrupt him. Why would you interrupt him when he's explaining something so important as the way controllers and couriers conduct their meetings? Don't you know there are people who want to know what he can tell us?"

I knew he was referring to a subject unrelated to the one I'd just heard on the tape. I was glad I recognized this particular conversation.

"I interrupted Clyde that time because we had just come off the bridge and he was turning left down a path that was pitch black. He had his head down and didn't realize how dark that trail was. All I did was turn him around to walk in the light. He resumed that subject right where he left off, Mr. Romski.

"Yes, he did resume that subject, but you seem to forget, Danny, that you're a counterintelligence agent. You're out there to collect evidence. You even let an opportunity go by that could have cleared up a very important point for us, when all you had to do was challenge him."

FRIENDSHIP VERSUS HONOR

He was very angry and not looking at me as he began to pace. He had clearly jumped to yet another subject. I tried to calm him.

"Mr. Romski, I know I interrupt him sometimes. There are times when his expressions or gestures warn me not to press him on something, but I remember those subjects so I can challenge him at a more appropriate time. Tell me some particular subject you have in mind, and maybe I can tell you why I decided not to challenge him right then."

"You tell me, Danny. You're supposed to have such a great memory."

Even though I was irritated at his sarcasm and unreasonable challenge, I was fairly certain I already knew what Romski was referring to. I had been studying his expressions. I sensed his exasperation and disappointment, the kind one feels when he sees a golden opportunity slip by and believes it could be lost forever. I saw it as soon as he said, "You even let an opportunity go by."

I had experienced that frustration many times with Clyde, but never any stronger than during the conversation brought to mind by Romski's expressions. It had been just as strong a disappointment for me as it must have been for Romski when he listened to it on tape.

"Oh, I know what you're talking about: that conversation while Clyde and I were standing behind his car."

"I don't know where you were standing. I wasn't there!"

"Yes, I know, Mr. Romski. Clyde was talking about that document he sold to the embassy. Then in the next breath he started talking about Szabo."

"Yes, that's exactly what I'm talking about."

221

Romski couldn't hide his astonishment. Neither could Grant, but Romski continued in his same contemptible tone.

"I know what I would have said, Danny, something like, 'Why, you sly dog. Why didn't you tell me it was Szabo who helped you with that?'"

"Yes, Sir. I could have said something like that. I had to bite my tongue to keep from doing that, because just as soon as he mentioned Szabo's name, he raised his head and cringed like he was sorry he had identified a name, and he quickly changed the subject. I also knew if I was wrong about Szabo being the one, he would let me keep that assumption.

I decided I could bring that up later in an entirely different context. I've thought of one or two ways to bring it up since then. If it's something you need to clear up right away, I'll bring it up at the next opportunity."

"Okay, Danny. You do that. You and Grant take care of your business, then I need to cover some other things with you."

Romski sat quietly while I signed and dated the judge's orders for electronic surveillance. That was the procedure before every taped conversation with Clyde. I sat on the edge of the bed and Romski leaned back in his chair and gathered his thoughts. Then he turned to me with a stern expression and began to lecture me, to remind me in no uncertain terms who was in charge of the operation. USAI was not interested in hearing me talk on the tapes.

"We want you to stop interrupting Clyde. We want you to allow him to do all the talking. We want to hear everything Clyde has to say. We want you to conduct yourself like a counterespionage agent attempting to collect evidence. We want you to follow instructions as to any questions you should ask or your part in the operation will be terminated. And if you intend to purposely cause the operation to fail because we aren't doing it your way, you can be terminated right now."

As I listened, I couldn't decide if they considered most of the information I had provided so far worthless, or they were simply in a hurry to arrest Clyde, or they just knew they could do a much better job than I was doing, or all the above. I wondered if letting him do all the talking included the abstract thinking they had no use for.

However, I realized I would have to start doing things exactly the way Romski had spelled them out. It was one hell of a challenge, but I resigned myself to it. I was already searching for some way to justify to Clyde such a drastic change in my personality.

However, I couldn't suppress the uneasiness that overwhelmed me. I feared that Clyde would take the opportunity to provide only the truth he thought I would accept or that he would not even reveal his suspicion of the change in me but slip out of the country.

Although Romski had made it clear they weren't interested in my opinion or my impressions, I still considered it my duty to state the dangers I perceived. Once I'd fulfilled my obligation to warn them, I would follow their instructions and hope for the best. I only knew of one way to even get them to listen. I had to test my theory that Romski was a peacemaker.

"Mr. Romski, I think you're right. I think you should terminate my participation in this operation right now. If you believe I would purposely do anything to sabotage this operation, or I would purposely withhold some of the information I get, there's absolutely no reason to continue using me. It's clear that I've been ineffective, and none of the information I've provided is of any value. I did volunteer for the job, and I'm sorry I wasn't able to accomplish anything for you. I have another job, so I'll return to it, but I would at least like to give you my perception of this one before I leave."

I had already started walking toward the door when Romski and Grant, still reeling from shock, both said they would like to hear my thoughts. I turned around and started pacing as I spoke.

"Mr. Romski, I've been unable to convey to you exactly what I see when I'm with Clyde, that you can't possibly detect from the recordings. Perhaps those glares and startled looks he gives me when I ask certain questions, or even show an interest in a particular subject, are not suspicion on his part.

Maybe I'm too cautious, especially when he asks me, "Why do you want to know?" I may even be overly concerned about his reminders that he's been testing me or that he won't hesitate to put a bullet between my eyes. I'm not really concerned about that, but maybe I shouldn't even consider the danger of compromising this operation and causing him to slip off to a neutral country.

"Perhaps I was wrong about starting off as the same talkative Danny Williams I thought he would expect and wrong about interrupting him when he starts to roll his eyes in the middle of a story he's starting to fabricate. Maybe I'm wrong about challenging him to convince me he's telling the truth, the way I always did in the past. Maybe the truth he thinks I will accept is all you need to hear.

"Perhaps I should ignore his insistence that he's been around a lot of foreign intelligence people who employ the same obvious interrogator techniques you employ, Mr. Romski, like when you sit back and say nothing, creating that awkward silence you think will force the other person to volunteer more information without being asked. But I keep asking myself, 'Why take that chance?'"

"You say I've forgotten I'm a counterespionage agent. I should use your interrogator techniques to challenge him to give me information he has already said he doesn't want to give me, instead of waiting until I think of a plausible, less threatening reason for wanting to know it, at a time when he might be more receptive.

"No, I've only tried to forget, tried to get him to forget, that I'm a counterespionage agent and he's been warned by the Hungarians to be careful of his relationship with such an agent. I'm trying not to forget that he's just waiting for me to start acting like a counterespionage agent to confirm what his instincts keep telling him about me.

"I don't have a problem with your insistence that I talk less, Mr. Romski. Hell, sometimes I hate to hear myself talk when I'm just trying to convey to Clyde the idea that I have some subject I'm concerned with but trying not to make it sound like someone is directing me to ask about it. I don't even have a real problem with the fact that you guys treat me like Joe Shit the Rag Man or that you don't trust me.

"What I don't understand, Mr. Romski, is why you make these debriefings as hard for me as you possibly can. Why would you make sure your source knows how little you trust him, how little you regard the information he's supplying? Why wouldn't you want him to be as relaxed as possible when he faces the suspect? Why wouldn't you want him to use the approach with which he's most comfortable, one with which the suspect is most comfortable?

"I'm not telling you how to run your operation, Mr. Romski. I'm just confused about why it should be easier for me to deal with Clyde, who's promised to kill me if I slip up, than it is to deal with the people who are supposed to be on my side. I just don't get it, Mr. Romski."

I wasn't sure if Romski knew I never intended or even wanted to quit the operation, but his response seemed to take that for granted. He was sitting with his head down when he spoke very slowly and deliberately, as if he were making a very difficult pronouncement. As he made it, Grant seemed as surprised as I.

"Danny, I'm going to do something I've never done before. I'm going to eat my words. I want you to continue just as you have been. I will see to it that the debriefings in the future don't cause more pressure for you than you already have. I understand some of the things you've explained. I do have one question for you though. How much of what he's telling us do you think is true? How much damage has he really done?"

"Personally, Mr. Romski, I think he's killed us."

"So do I, Danny."

From his tone, I thought he might be saying that he shared mine and Grant's view that most of what Clyde was telling us was true but someone was overruling him. If that was the case, he would probably have hell to pay for deciding to eat his words.

Grant was genuinely concerned when he said, "We can arrange to have Shirley returned to the States if you're afraid of what Clyde might do if something goes wrong and he discovers you're working against him." I assured him that would not be necessary. I didn't bother telling him the truth: Shirley wouldn't go.

I hated the thought that I might have won a reluctant concession from them only because they thought I was afraid of what Clyde might do. Knowing Clyde's threats were genuine, and letting him know I believed him, showed Clyde I had no reason to fear him because I wasn't sent. That was part of my role; it had to be played that way. Those threats also reminded me to never drop my guard.

As I left that meeting at a hotel in downtown Stuttgart, I walked toward the elevator, thinking how easily I could run into someone from my unit or even Clyde. If asked why I was there, I could say I had met with a member of a U.S. Army reserve unit, here to coordinate war plans, who needed my help in arranging a conference with his seventh corps counterpart in Stuttgart.

I decided that would not arouse suspicion or even interest, because no one was ever concerned with my daily war-planning. My story was ready by the time I reached the main floor.

I always did that when I left a debriefing with Grant or a meeting with Clyde. I had stored a dozen plausible stories in my head. I always tried to anticipate situations that might cause my three lives to collide.

No one in B Company knew I was working with this operation, to include my commander, Major Daniels. I managed that by keeping a schedule that began with exercise at 5:00, a shower and breakfast at 5:30, and work from 7:00 to 7:00. I worked much later if I had to travel to one of my detachments.

When I had appointments with Grant or Clyde during the day, I would tell Major Daniels or First Sergeant Fry I had a meeting on the other side of Stuttgart to discuss war plans. I never took a day off or arrived late, even when I hadn't returned from a clandestine evening meeting or debriefing until 3:00 in the morning.

I lived a busy life the way I always had in the Army but still made time for that second life with Grant and the guys from the

States, known only to my battalion commander in Kaiserslautern, my brigade commander in Munich, and a couple of people close to them. My third life was the role I had now assumed for Clyde as a traitor to my country.

Shirley made keeping those three lives separate a little easier for me. She knew enough about my job not to ask questions. I reinforced the secret aspects of my job by reminding her that many of the investigations my unit conducted were compartmentalized. Since there was no way for her to know who had knowledge of what I was working on, she would tell anyone from my unit who might call for me, when she didn't know where I was, that I was out with some friends. She'd offer to give me a message when I returned.

She also knew, although she didn't like it, that there was no way for her to get in touch with me during after-duty hours. I did tell her she could call my battalion commander in an emergency.

Shirley was not aware that I was still in touch with Clyde. I didn't tell her for the same reason I refused USAIs offer to tell her about the operation: I didn't want her to worry about how to act if Clyde called me at home and she answered the phone. I suspected he might do that after the call he made to my office. He confirmed my fears one evening. Fortunately, I answered the phone.

He wanted to see me the next evening in Stuttgart, but I informed him I was leaving the next morning for two days TDY in Kaiserslautern. That suited him just fine, and he arranged to meet with me for dinner in a restaurant near the K-town Bahnhof.

Since Shirley had overheard the conversation, I told her the truth: I was meeting Clyde to repay him the one hundred Deutsche

Marks he had paid for the bill from the lab in Idar Oberstein for analyzing my sample of lapidolite.

Following a day spent on the Sergeant Major's promotion board at battalion headquarters, I spent several hours with Clyde in downtown K-town. Reminding him of the continued delay by the Hungarians in paying me for my classified documents, I challenged him to produce some clearer evidence that he wasn't jacking me around.

"Clyde, when I walked up to your table at the Bahnhof this evening, you were reading a book. As soon as you saw me, you tore the book in half and threw away the pages you'd already read, then you stuck the rest in your back pocket."

"I always do that. I do a lot of waiting and a lot of reading."

"Yeah, I thought you might, but I've never seen that done before. Have you read any of Ernest Hemingway's works?"

"Never heard of him."

"He was pretty famous around Monterey, California. I thought you might have heard of him while you were in language school."

"No. The best book I ever read was *The Day of the Jackal*."

"Yeah, it was a good movie too. I think you would have liked Hemingway's book *Of Mice and Men*. It's the story of two friends traveling from ranch to ranch, hiring on as cowhands. Lenny is a giant, very strong, and very retarded. He gets into serious troubles that cause him and his friend to have to move around a lot.

"His friend takes care of him and calms him when he's upset or depressed. He constantly reminds Lenny of the ranch they're going to buy someday. Sometimes I feel like Lenny, Clyde."

"I see what you're saying, Danny. Here, let me show you

229

something." He pulled out the Casio electronic dairy he always carried and started punching buttons.

He had suggested I buy one so I could type whole documents into the secret compartment, which he could later type and mark with the appropriate dates and classifications for delivery to the Hungarians. I watched him type his code for access to his secret compartment, D-A-M-I-A-N." I recognized it as his son's middle name.

He scrolled to the name of an associate of his, Imre Kercsik, whom he described as a Swedish surgeon, serving as a Hungarian Courier. He said he would talk to Imre about meeting with me and answering some of my questions.

He walked me out to a pay phone and called Imre in Sweden. He asked Imre for the frequency he listened to on the radio to get his instructions from the Hungarians and the day and time his instructions were broadcast. When he hung up, he said he would talk to him again to see if he would agree to meet me. In the mean time, he wanted me to have that frequency and schedule.

After another hour of hopping bars with Clyde in K-town, I had to keep a rendezvous at the bar in my hotel with some of the agents in my battalion. Clyde insisted on joining me. I could see this was another test, so I invited him to follow me to the hotel where we sat at the bar for an hour or so.

Although I talked across the oval-shaped bar with some of my fellow agents, I never had to introduce Clyde, and no one showed any unusual interest in him. He seemed content with that. He volunteered to take me back to Stuttgart the next day, so I let another agent drive my company vehicle back.

In Stuttgart, we stopped at a park behind the Bahnhof, where

FRIENDSHIP VERSUS HONOR

Clyde provided me some hands-on training in the procedures the Hungarian couriers usually use when they meet with agents to pick up documents from them or pay them. He indicated that couriers would only have a description of the agent and a code name and would never have a conversation with an agent.

"If a courier talks to you, Danny, report him. He is not a genuine courier. He's probably CI. The courier should only direct the agent to follow him to a restaurant where he will make the exchange required, then they should both leave."

Clyde demonstrated the procedure to me. He walked, and I followed. Later, he discussed an occasion when a courier left a meeting, then stayed around to follow Clyde for some distance.

"I suspected I would be followed, so I ducked around a corner to confirm my suspicions. I complained to the Hungarians about the courier risking my security, and I demanded a different courier. The Hungarians refused, and I quit. I did nothing for about a year, until they contacted me requesting a meeting.

"They asked me what courier I wanted. They named a few code names of couriers who had serviced me in the past and asked me to choose one. Thinking they might have suspected one of the couriers of becoming too friendly with me, I purposely berated the courier I really wanted. Predictably, the Hungarians chose the courier I said I didn't want, and I reluctantly agreed to resume production.

"You see, the new courier had been forced on me in the first place because one of my regular couriers, the one I said I didn't want, had gotten into trouble with the Hungarians and was no longer being used by them.

"He had become a friend and business associate of mine. His

code name is Rodnas, which is his nick name, Sandor, spelled backwards. I call him Alex. His real name is Alexander Kercsik. He is Imre's older brother. He's a Swedish surgeon too. Alex doesn't even know this, but my one year hiatus was calculated to get Alex back into action."

In subsequent meetings, Clyde showed me how the daily code was determined, the code used with the phone numbers agents call to arrange meetings to deliver merchandise. He also gave me a sample sheet of dissolving paper containing the Hungarians' one-time-codes for decoding secret messages. He even invited me along with him when he met with a courier in Vienna, Austria. I sat in a restaurant while Clyde met elsewhere with his courier, whom he wouldn't name.

Even though the Hungarians still hadn't paid me for my documents, Grant eventually directed me to make available to Clyde the entire set of lesson plans I had used in the classified portion of my Special Operation course at Fort Huachuca. They hoped to substitute volume for substance, which Clyde had stated the Hungarians had occasionally preferred. After Clyde had studied all the documents, his imagination went a little wild.

He started planning for me to take leave for two weeks in order to set up the CI Special Operations course in a hotel in Stuttgart, to teach agents whom Clyde would persuade the Hungarians to send.

He envisioned that as the only way the Hungarians would understand the lessons, no matter how many times they read them. In addition, Clyde and I would teach the Hungarians how to exploit U.S. counterespionage investigative procedures. He put me on alert while he waited for their response to his proposal to conduct the course.

FRIENDSHIP VERSUS HONOR

He'd been meeting with the Hungarians, apparently answering some question about his OPLAN, which he was busy expanding. Although the Hungarians continued to encourage Clyde about the OPLAN, they had also begun to pressure him about delivering certain documents. One he characterized as a document describing certain war plans down south.

He showed me a letter from a friend he called a controller/courier, who had been in contact with two agents in Italy, civilians who worked for the U.S. military and delivered documents to the Hungarians. He covered the name of the controller/courier with his thumb while I read the letter, suggesting to me it was probably Szabo. I remembered that Szabo spoke Italian.

He explained that his friend intended to arrange a meeting with these two Italian agents so Clyde could talk them into quitting the Hungarians and working for him. This was a scheme to give Clyde access to the documents that would satisfy some of the Hungarians' requirements.

In the mean time, his main focus was his OPLAN. He scheduled a meeting with me at the Mainz Holiday Inn to go over his latest update before delivering it to the Hungarians.

I arrived first. I selected an outdoor table just to the right of a four-foot-wide aisle that led from the rear door of the restaurant to the banister at the edge of the veranda overlooking the Rhein River. There were several tables on each side of the aisle. Very few were occupied that morning.

As I waited for Clyde, I noticed an American gentleman sit down at a table across the aisle from me, order coffee, then raise a German newspaper rather high in front of his face. A short time later, he was joined by an American woman. She approached his table without comment, placed her purse next to her chair, and sat down.

The man did not rise and didn't lower his paper. He simply looked around the far side of his paper and said something to the woman. She immediately picked up her purse and placed it on the table. She rummaged in it without taking anything out, then adjusted the position, so one end of the purse pointed at my table. She then rested her right hand over the purse with one finger hanging over the far end of the purse, as if poised to press a button.

When Clyde arrived, he chose a chair with his back to the couple's table, so I chided him for not taking the chair I had left him, with the best view of the river. When he changed, he was practically facing the lady's purse. I began reading the OPLAN update in a low voice, in order to record it, while he ordered coffee.

I finally looked up from the printout and noticed the couple was gone. After a short conversation with Clyde about his additions, I noticed the couple walk past our table. The lady followed the man and maneuvered her purse, which hung from her right shoulder, so that same end faced out toward our table. I saw her press her finger down on the other end as she passed our table. When they reached the banister, the lady's purse and hand stayed in the same position for several seconds before they left the veranda.

Clyde was pleased with my critique of the changes, and he hurried off to deliver his printout. I had driven several hours for this meeting, and I was glad Clyde felt the need for my input. I was also glad he had been in too much of a hurry to make the same observations I had made. I hoped the pictures USAI got were good ones.

FRIENDSHIP VERSUS HONOR

I never made any comments to Grant or anyone else about these or several other observations I'd made. Having personally conducted team surveillance in Germany and the States, taught the principles, and conducted practical exercises, I considered this incident evidence of long hours and extensive manpower supporting this operation. Grant introduced me to some of the support and coordination difficulties when he called me to a special meeting one evening.

In a hotel room in Stuttgart, I met two gentlemen from the States, one of whom introduced himself as an INSCOM attorney. He spoke first.

"Danny, I want you to know what a terrific job everyone thinks you are doing. We're getting some very important evidence on Clyde. Thank you."

"You're welcome, Sir."

"One thing I would like to ask you: we need for you to let Clyde do as much of the talking as possible. We need for him to admit his activities on tape."

The other gentleman added, "It will help us in our prosecution of him."

The attorney and his companion were sitting next to each other on the edge of the bed, and Grant was in a chair behind me. I couldn't see Grant's reaction, but he didn't have to wait long for mine. "Sir, why would you say that?"

They looked at each other as if to say, "How could this be any clearer?"

I asked the companion, "Sir, what organization are you with?"

"I'm connected with the investigation."

He obviously didn't realize he had already told me he was

with the Justice Department when he said "our prosecution." I accepted his answer, then I said, "Good, then you should be able to understand how much occurs between me and Clyde that can't be observed by listening to the tapes. You can't see the looks of suspicion or the rolling of his eyes when he is fabricating a story he thinks I will buy."

Grant stood up and curtly interrupted with, 'I think they understand, Danny. Unless anyone has any other questions, we probably should be going. I have to get Danny's signature on some documents."

The attorney offered, "No, I think we're done. Danny, I want to say again, you're doing a great job."

"Thanks again, Sir."

When they had left, and I had finished signing the electronic surveillance order, Grant apologized to me. "I'm sorry that happened, Danny. We stated explicitly that subject was not to be addressed. I was as surprised as you were."

"I'm glad to hear that. I have to say though, Grant, this meeting makes about as much sense to me as the one we had in Houston. What was the purpose of that meeting, or this one for that matter?"

"Danny, don't you remember what Clyde said about some people needing to be able to say, 'Yeah, I've met him?'"

I feared Romski's concession that I could continue just as I had been was not well received by his superiors. I was soon to learn that, in spite of Grant's continued support, this attack was only a prelude to a major battle.

9

NEW BLOOD

Late one afternoon Clyde called my office and asked me to meet him at the Stuttgart Bahnhof that evening to discuss the OPLAN before he left for Austria to meet a controller he called Mike. I knew about his trip but was surprised he wanted to stop off in Stuttgart on his way to talk to me. I agreed to meet him, although the timing was very bad.

I already had a meeting scheduled that afternoon with Grant, which I couldn't call off.

My recording device was at home, an hour from my office in afternoon traffic. I would barely have time to retrieve it before meeting Grant and no time to spend with Grant before meeting Clyde.

I raced to Steinenbronn and picked up the recorder, then

proceeded to a small lake in Sindelfingen for my initial contact with Grant. I informed him of the unscheduled meeting with Clyde, and he quickly directed me to a hotel to sign release papers.

At the hotel, I signed the required paperwork and collected copies of my personnel records, which USAI had approved for me to give Clyde to give the Hungarians. Then Grant directed me to return to the hotel after my meeting with Clyde.

I explained to Grant that I hadn't had time to conceal the recorder and microphone in the prescribed manner and had simply stuck it into the vest pocket of my sport jacket with the microphone sitting just above it in the cloth case. He questioned how I would be able to turn it on when I reached Clyde. I demonstrated, and he approved the new arrangement.

Just before I left the hotel room, a new agent entered the room. He introduced himself as Roland Nugent, then he said he would be joining us when I returned that evening. I drove to the Bahnhof, parked in the usual parking garage, and walked through the tunnel and shopping mall under the Bahnhof to the restaurant where Clyde was waiting. I reached in my coat and flipped the recorder switch, vigorously scratched my shoulder, then greeted Clyde with my usual "How are you, young man?"

He led me into the underground restaurant, where we discussed corrections he had made to the OPLAN. Then we left the restaurant to stroll along the pedestrian walkway lined with shops. He told me Mike had been sent to get a complete understanding of the OPLAN.

Clyde's aim was to get Mike enthusiastic enough about the plan to sell it to his Hungarians superiors, who could make the final decision. Following Grant's recent instruction to get Clyde to introduce me to someone in the foreign intelligence field, I suggested that Clyde take me along to help him sell the PLAN.

Clyde became very irritated at my suggestion, and he started quizzing me. I realized from the tone of his first question that he was pretending to be Mike, and I responded accordingly.

"Why do you want to do this?"

"Because I understand how you work?"

"How do you know how we work?"

"My friend, Clyde, told me how you work."

"How do you think we work?"

"As I understand it, you want me to take only those things I can take safely, and procedures will be implemented to minimize my time at risk and allow me the greatest opportunity for production. I understand I can be guaranteed an income plus bonuses for exceptional merchandise. To protect me from unwanted attention, an account can be set up for me to make the money available to me whenever I decide to retire.

"I can be provided information to help me in acquiring military assignments with increased access to critical information. Information I provide will be sanitized to protect my identity, and my services will be voluntary. I can take a vacation or quit anytime I like, and I can continue to work with my good friend, Clyde Conrad, whom I trust.

"I have made an irreversible commitment to you based on that understanding, and I would appreciate some kind of commitment from you and some assurance that I understand your procedures correctly."

"Plan on going with me on the nineteenth, Danny. You talk to the MF. You talk better than I do. I'm serious. Damn, Danny, when you read something, you know it!"

"Well, if you'd bring me an updated disk, I'd include everything you want about the OPLAN."

"You have everything." He assured me he would arrange with Mike for me to attend their next meeting.

As we left the walking street, he took me through a back entrance to the underground restaurant, which was built on two levels. We passed some large train schedules on the walls of the hallway entrance. On one of the schedules he marked with a pen the arrival time of the train he would use on his return from Austria, and he asked me to meet him when he stopped over in Stuttgart.

Later he went aboard his train to secure a sleeping compartment with the conductor, then he walked with me to get him some cigarettes. As we walked, Clyde threw his ticket stub on the station platform, claiming it was of no further use. On an impulse, I picked it up, scolded him for being careless about such identifying items, and walked back a few yards to a refuse can. I palmed the ticket stub as I pretended to throw it in the trash. When Clyde turned his back to me, I put it in the side pocket of my coat to save for Grant.

Clyde soon departed, and I returned to the hotel in Sindelfingen where I was debriefed by Grant and Roland. When I'd handed over the tapes and signed the necessary papers for my next meeting with Clyde, Roland explained that he would be the new chief of the operation in Germany because Romski would be taking a little vacation. He very calmly and courteously described some of the reasons he had been selected.

NEW BLOOD

"Danny, I have been asked to take over this operation because I have a great deal of experience in running counterespionage operations. I understand the procedures used by the Hungarians, the Czechs, and the Russians. I know what they will allow and what they won't.

"I know Clyde is your friend, but I don't want you to let that friendship cause you to be taken in by him. Most of what he's telling you is not true. Oh, he may even think some of the things he tells you are true. They would allow him to think they are to stroke his ego. They would let him think he is much more important to them than he really is.

"Most of what he tells you is fabricated just to impress you and because he has an inflated image of himself. He isn't making the kind of money he says he is, and they wouldn't allow him to control any agents himself. Believe me, I've had enough experience with them.

"You've done a great job, Danny. I'm only telling you this so you won't let him fool you."

Roland had stated his case with confidence, but for a change, he hadn't addressed my personal technique with Clyde. Based on his overall demeanor, I sensed he would at least listen to my rebuttal, but I proceeded cautiously.

"Roland, I have no doubt your experience gives you better insight into these matters. I assure you I am aware that Clyde is capable of fabricating everything he's told me. I keep reminding him of that. I've challenged him, and I will continue to challenge him, to prove his claims to me. I realize they could all be lies, although there are some consistencies in his stories, but being impressed with what he's telling me is part of my role and part

241

of the reason I've been able to get as much out of him as I have. I promise you I won't be taken in by him, but I would like to ask a favor of you, Roland."

"Sure, anything I can do for you, Danny."

"Consider the possibility, remote though it may be, that Clyde may not be like other people, like your average soldier-turned-spy. Consider the possibility that Clyde knows what you know about these intelligence agencies and he has learned to exploit them, the same as he has exploited our security measures and at least one of our own intelligence agencies.

"You don't have to believe him, but what would it hurt to act like what he's told me may in fact be true, at least until your investigation proves otherwise. I'll keep demanding proof from him, but if he doesn't provide it, or you prove his stories are all fabrications, great. Just don't tell me what you've proved so I can continue to be impressed by what he's telling me. Is that an unreasonable request?"

"No, Danny, I don't think it is."

His expression suggested almost pleasant surprise, even agreement with me. Or at least he wasn't threatened by it. When I left this debriefing I was a little more optimistic about my relationship with USAI, even though they had demonstrated again that someone was still completely at odds with my perception of Clyde Conrad and his espionage activities, and obviously at odds with Romski's.

Clyde returned from Austria very optimistic about Mike's reception of the OPLAN in general and his answers to the Hungarians' latest questions. I was waiting for him at the Stuttgart Bahnhof. An hour after he left me, I met Grant in Sindelfingen.

NEW BLOOD

My optimism about my relationship with USAI waned slightly when Grant met me just inside the hotel room. He handed me a recorder with one of the tapes I'd delivered from my meeting with Clyde at the Bahnhof the day he left for Austria.

Grant played the first few minutes of the tape for me. I heard Grant's voice, Roland's voice, and then voices from my car radio. It was immediately clear to me that I had left the recorder on during my demonstration of it for Grant, then unwittingly turned it off when I approached Clyde in the mall under the Bahnhof.

I remembered noticing that the tape seemed to have cut off before reaching the end, when I changed it for a new one, so I had changed the batteries at the same time. I explained that to Grant, but he refused to proceed until I agreed to a polygraph examination. There was an examiner waiting in the hall.

After the exam by the European chief of polygraph, I waited alone in the hotel room until he returned with the results. He gave me a complete bill of health, then he joked that I was a lousy liar. He was referring to the questions I had been told to purposely answer falsely. Grant and Roland expressed their confidence in me and proceeded with the debriefing.

Clyde's meeting in Austria with Mike had included some demonstrations by Clyde of some of the concepts in his OPLAN. One of the areas Mike's superiors had difficulty understanding was Clyde's claim that a stranger could learn everything he needed to know about a unit's document custodian with a simple telephone call. He had described to Mike a typical call to a U.S. unit.

"Fifth Corps, G-3, Sergeant Jones speaking. How may I help you, Sir?"

"Hello, this is Sergeant Smith. Can I reach your document custodian at this number?"

"No, but I would be glad to transfer you, except I believe he's on leave until Monday."

"Could you please give me his number so I can call him Monday?"

"Certainly! His extension is 7540."

"Thanks. Could you do me one more favor?"

"I'll try."

"I talked to him a while back, but I've forgotten his name."

"Oh, it's Sergeant Black."

"That doesn't sound familiar. How long has he been your custodian?"

"At least a year."

"Are you talking about the NATO document custodian or your U.S. document custodian?"

"U.S. Our NATO custodian is Staff Sergeant Brinks. His number is 7549."

Clyde told Mike he could have called either one of those sergeants direct and gotten the same information with a different story. Mike was incredulous, because the Hungarians are much more suspicious of strangers on the telephone.

He made Clyde write out some questions and give him the phone number of a U.S. unit. He left the table and went to the pay phone. When he returned, he was elated. He said, "It works! It works!"

When Mike said the decision would take some time while the Hungarians continued to translate Clyde's updates, Clyde considered that delay standard procedure. USAI was not so patient about the Hungarians' delay in paying me for documents already delivered and about my failure to meet any of Clyde's associates. Fortunately, both problems were about to be solved.

10

SHOWTIME

I increased my pressure on Clyde about the pay I hadn't received for my initial deliveries, hoping my frustration would justify my own delay in providing him the documents he really wanted. I also demanded some proof that Clyde wasn't the one jacking me around.

When he assured me he was about to introduce me to someone who could verify some of the escalated activities he claimed to have orchestrated, I let him know I was aware of how easily he could arrange for me to meet someone who would say what he had taught him to say. He assured me I could ask any questions I needed to satisfy my doubts.

He arranged for me to join him in Mainz when he met with Imre to deliver the additional classified lesson plans I had provided him. Either his proposal for teaching the special operation lessons to Hungarian agents had been turned down or he was now focused on the OPLAN, but he was ready to deliver my documents.

He told me I would have to wait somewhere in Mainz until he asked Imre if he was willing to meet me. USAI prepared for this meeting with the kind of sophisticated electronic surveillance I welcomed. It required no action on my part. It wasn't even fully described to me.

In the middle of Mainz's annual Rosen Montag celebration, Clyde left me sitting in a McDonald's restaurant in front of a row of windows facing the street, while he walked to the Bahnhof to meet Imre.

He said he would bring Imre by the window for me to see, even if Imre had not agreed to meet me. If Imre had agreed, Clyde would switch his leather shoulder bag full of documents from his right to his left shoulder.

After two hours, USAI must have become worried about how long Clyde was taking. Apparently, they sent someone to check on me. I noticed a nervous American among the revelers hurry down the middle of the street, take photos of an innocuous building across the street, then turn to face the McDonald's windows and search the tables from side to side. As soon as he spotted me, sitting alone, he raced back in the direction from which he'd come. His actions matched some of those I'd observed before.

One evening, while waiting on a bench for a meeting with Grant at the park in Wiesbaden, an American girl walking her dog about twenty-five yards from me picked up her pace as soon as she glanced in my direction and saw that I was observing her.

DAMIAN and MONGOOSE

The girl would have been checking before Grant approached me to see that I hadn't been followed to the meeting site. The guy in the middle of the street in Mainz was just checking to see if I was still there. I usually tried not to observe my surroundings all that much, for fear of drawing Clyde's attention to something or someone I didn't want him to notice, but sometimes it was too obvious to miss.

Clyde returned a short time later to say that he had received a message that Imre would be late. He left again in only a few minutes. He returned an hour or so later, walked past the window, and moved his bag to his left shoulder.

The man walking with him stopped and looked through the window, glancing from table to table. He was about six feet tall, appeared to be in his thirties, and weighed about one hundred eighty-five pounds. He had bushy eyebrows and dark, straight hair, slightly over his ears, and was balding where he parted his hair. Two minutes after Clyde and his partner disappeared from sight, I proceeded to the Mainz Holiday Inn to wait for them in an upstairs lounge as arranged.

As I waited, I saw two American men hurrying through the hallway and around the corner by the chairs where I sat. They were both obviously startled when they saw me, as if they had lost track of me. As soon as I looked up and made eye contact with them, they both quickly looked away. I hoped they wouldn't return when Clyde and his friend joined me.

Clyde arrived a short time later, and we waited for Imre to park his rental car. To pass the time, Clyde described his plan to meet in some neutral country with Zolton Szabo and the two Italian agents employed by the U.S. military.

He intended to have Alex and Imre there with him and was still willing to have me there as well. He planned to steal the two agents from the Hungarians and later interrogate Szabo, then eliminate him, with the Kercsiks' assistance. Clyde warned me not to let Imre know I knew about these plans.

He had warned me at McDonald's to be sure my questions of Imre didn't reveal too much that Clyde had told me, especially about Imre. I was also not to let Imre know I knew about his brother, Alex, or the details of Clyde's schemes. He said, "His truth is not necessarily your truth, Danny." Clyde's mood became pensive and guarded as soon as Imre approached and Clyde greeted him.

"We've been waiting for you. This is Danny. Danny, Imre."

I extended my hand and said, "Hello, Imre." He shook my hand as Clyde and I rose, and I repeated his name to confirm the pronunciation. "Imre?"

He answered with a smile. "Yes."

"My pleasure, Imre."

"Nice to meet you, Danny. Well I think this old man, I must give him time to come here."

"That's true," I agreed with a smile. Clyde laughed at our remarks as I continued. "I waited for him a pretty long time as well."

Imre enjoyed the banter. In his broken English he added, "You know it's—it's his age. Forgets everything."

"Yeah, it's easy for him to get lost. I've had to find him several times. I don't know how old you are, Imre, but—"

"I'm near thirty-five."

Clyde was smiling when he said, "I told Danny you were fifty, Imre." Then he became serious. "If anything should ever come up,

249

this is a good meeting place, either here if it's open or in the lobby downstairs if it isn't, because the lobby is open three hundred sixty-five days a year."

As he finished that statement, he walked us downstairs through the lobby to the restaurant. The lobby was the termination point for the Rosen Montag parade, which had ended. It was very noisy and crowded with dignitaries in fancy costumes.

We sat at a table near the back door of the restaurant, which led to the veranda overhanging the Rhein River. Imre described a huge traffic jam that had delayed his arrival.

As I listened intently to his voice, I was reminded of Clyde's tape I'd heard ten years earlier, with the voice that sounded like Szabo. Not only did Imre sound exactly like Szabo, he looked a lot like him, except that he was taller and younger.

He was very pleasant, easygoing, and intelligent. He seemed to make friends with me right away, and he was an easy person to like. I started to ask him a question, but Clyde interrupted me, while Imre interjected comments when Clyde would let him.

"Well, before we go through everything else—well—Imre works as a courier. Safe pick up and delivery. Uh, I think I've known Danny about thirteen years. Imre, about ten.

Imre quickly commented, "Yes, and we have good—good times together."

Clyde continued, but searched for his words. "Yeah. To do business, we gotta be up front with each other. On Imre's side of the house, uh, everything he hears we hear.

"They say things to him they won't say to me or you. From our side, we tell him what's happening, what's going on, what's coming, as often as possible. And he takes trips as often as possible, runs a trip in. It's good for him, and it doesn't hurt us. Basically, good business."

Imre interrupted again. "And uh, that way I think for me it's a good way to work. I have contacts with them, and if there are troubles, if there is something, I can tell you so you know about it. How to say what you should say—"

Clyde took over again. "Yeah. If there's gonna be questions that are gonna be asked, normally he will hear them before you do, and you'll hear the questions, and that will give you a little time to think and say, 'Uh-huh. What do I want to say?' His direct contact allows an agreement on what people are going to say. So if they ask him, 'How was he?' he can say, 'Well, he looked like this.' Basically say what you said. And it works real well.

"Danny works with CI out of Stuttgart, Imre."

I added, "But I used to be in the infantry with him."

"But he's on the inside, Imre, in the military, who's access is just about everywhere, as far as travel—" The waitress interrupted him. She gave me time to think how I would explain to Grant this cryptic description of Clyde and Imre's association.

I knew they had vaguely confirmed several of Clyde's schemes. They had just alluded to the agent Clyde had invented and controlled, the reports he had received about the Hungarians' suspicion and investigation of him, Clyde's coaching of Imre before the Hungarians questioned him about their suspicions of Clyde, and the vacations Clyde had arranged for his couriers by not showing up for delivery of documents.

As soon as the waitress left, I decided to see how much Clyde would let me get by with. "So, Imre, how long ago did you become a Swedish citizen?"

"Twenty-seven years ago."

Clyde interrupted. "He's a butcher by occupation."

Imre quickly retorted, "No, a doctor, a doctor."

Laughingly I asked, "A butcher? A doctor? A surgeon?"

"No, not surgeon, internal medicine. We work with hyper-blood pressure, the circulation."

"You work in a clinic or have a private practice?"

"No, I work in a hospital."

Clyde ended that subject for us. "In Europe, Danny, titles are respected. And we have to have a lot of respect."

I continued my query. "How do you manage the time for travel, Imre?"

"When I work night times, we never take it out in money. We take it out in time. And there is always a conference somewhere, a medical conference somewhere in the world, weekends. Uh, this weekend there is something in Vienna. I go to conferences."

Clyde interrupted again. "For him, Imre, he doesn't work, so he's always—"

I objected. "Oh, that's not true, Clyde."

"Sometimes it is."

As we laughed, I discovered Imre wasn't easily distracted. He said, "My wife has told me, 'Go, and I take care of things.'"

I asked, "Does she know what you do, Imre?"

"She knows what I do. It is the only possibility. You know it's very tough to work if you travel a lot, explaining to your wife."

I responded, "Well, maybe generally, but since I work for CI, my wife has always known I can't discuss my job or where I'm going. So now she thinks I'm on official business instead of seeing Clyde. I've chosen not to tell my wife because it works."

"Yes, it works for you. I must have it my way because she knows what kind of business, but she doesn't know the details. She doesn't know where I am, who I meet."

Clyde interrupted again. "Do you have a pen, Danny?"

"No. I gave it to you."

"I lost it. I lose everything. You know that." Imre handed him a pen, and Clyde asked, "You have a piece of paper? Anybody have a piece of paper?" I handed him a piece of paper, then he asked for my phone number.

Imre anticipated Clyde's reason for wanting the number and said, "If you don't mind, Danny."

I answered, "No, I don't mind."

Clyde said, "Now let me give you Imre's. Danny keeps his stuff in an electronic data bank, Imre."

As I handed Clyde my diary, I said, "Okay, here, Clyde. You know my secret code."

Following Grant's instruction, I had purchased the Casio electronic diary that Clyde had been insisting I buy. He had trouble getting mine to work because he wasn't pushing the buttons in the proper sequence, so I talked him through it.

I didn't have to tell him MONGOOSE was my code, because he asked me for it the day I bought the dairy, saying to me, "You know mine." I truly thought he had been too drunk to realize I was watching that day he typed DAMIAN into his diary.

Imre began to explain, with Clyde's assistance, that it would be safe for me to call him because telephones are not monitored in western or neutral countries like they are in the East, with all conversations recorded. I took a big chance with my next question. "I work in CI, and I work with Clyde for the same

253

reason: I like to do what I do best. How did you get started, Imre?"

Clyde was almost frantic when he interrupted, "You got to watch him, Imre. He's a real animal. Watch out!"

I laughed but expanded my question. "Why them, Imre? What connection did you have with them originally?"

Clyde was still nervous and repeated, "You gotta watch him. You gotta watch him." He seemed to be desperately trying to get Imre to look his way, but Imre set his jaw and looked straight at me as he answered in slightly broken English.

"I'm studying medicine in Budapest with a group of Swedish citizens, and they watch me from the beginning. They watch all the western students who come there. Then they pitch who they want, the smart ones."

"How, Imre?"

"After, I think, one year, two different men come to me. One is civilian. He is interested in industries and so on. The other is military."

"Were you in the Swedish military?"

"No. They said they would train me. I told them, 'Why not!' I took the military. Uh, there's a lot of reasons. I think I'm good at what I do. Okay, I'm only a courier, but I think I'm good."

"Well, if you work with Clyde, you're not only a courier; I can tell that."

As we laughed, Imre said, "In their eyes, in their eyes. I tried it, and I liked it. When I don't work for a long time, I miss it and the money."

I couldn't pass up the opportunity to say, "My problem is I've never been paid, Imre."

Clyde explained, "Danny gave something and never got paid for it, Imre. We're gonna try again. They may say, 'I don't like that,' but you don't have to worry about them calling the police."

Imre became thoughtful, then responded, "Uh-huh. I think that's the type we are. We all are a little crazy. My work bores me sometime. I like this for a change."

"I see, and I get the impression you also like the risk."

With a smile, he answered, "It's part of my life."

Clyde added, "Well, I don't think it's just the risk. You have to understand, when you walk into a place like this and look around, you know you're the only one of this species here. There's nobody else in this room who does what you do for a living. And an inside knowledge, I think, is also a big part. To know the things you know. Very seldom will there be anybody else that really knows what you know."

Imre seemed to agree with Clyde's general characterization when he responded with, "Uh-huh. This is sort of a success." He had reflected for a few seconds before responding and Clyde had stopped the cigarette girl to purchase a pack of Marlboro menthols. He made a big deal of it, talking very loud, as if he didn't want Imre saying any more while he wasn't listening. I decided to press Imre when I thought Clyde had become preoccupied.

"Imre, what I want is for someone to say, 'We need you for what you're good at.' I haven't seen any commitment from anyone. Trust and loyalty are a two-way street. I made the first commitment. What is it about those people?"

Before Imre could answer, Clyde interjected, "Let—lemme— He gave something, Imre, from intelligence. You know what went

255

on. They said, 'No, don't want to meet; don't want to talk; don't wanna pay nothing, absolutely nothing."

Imre looked at me and said, "You give them something, Danny; the answer is, 'We will think about that.' Or, 'We have no money.' It happens lots of times. 'Wait, we will think about it.' After years you ask them, 'Have you think about it?' 'We think about it.'"

Having a little trouble with his English, Imre seemed to be giving a general description of the Hungarians' exasperating attitude toward ideas instead of payment for documents. That impression was confirmed as he and Clyde began to recall how the Hungarians' view of security had caused them to reject some of Clyde's ideas because they didn't want people to have too much knowledge.

This led to a discussion about Clyde and Imre's having to hide their friendship from the Hungarians. Their recollections were so vague, I eventually changed the subject back to why I hadn't been paid for the documents I had sent, and Imre's answer surprised me.

"They don't know what they got. They don't recognize it. I don't know if there is, before, information like this . . . ."

"Oh, so they can't verify it?"

"Yeah, I think it can be worrisome"

"Clyde thought it was because they already had it all and didn't need anymore. You say it may be the opposite?"

Imre's answer had surprised even Clyde and prompted him to counter with, "No, I'm—You may be right, Imre, but I think somewhere in all the years of intelligence service they must have picked up somebody from intelligence."

Imre seemed unconvinced when he answered, "Uh-huh. A possibility, Clyde. I don't know."

Sensing Clyde's discomfort, I changed the subject again. Let me ask you this, Imre. All the books and all the movies recognize what we do."

"Uh-huh."

"They call it spying."

"Uh-huh."

"Clyde hates that word."

"Uh-huh."

Clyde had his head down as he leaned over the table to listen intently. He cringed as if he was afraid someone would hear us, then he lowered his voice and whispered contemptuously, "Okay, if that's what you like, we're spies."

"He thinks that's not a good word, Imre"

Clyde raised his head and confirmed, "That's not a good word."

"Isn't that what we do, Clyde?" I was smiling, and so was Clyde when he answered.

"No."

"What do we do, Clyde?"

"We are just an information service."

I asked Imre, "What do you think? What do we do?"

"We are businessmen. We sell information."

Clyde was grinning when he said, "Take that! Didn't I tell you, Danny?"

"Do you sell information, Imre?"

"No, but I help other people do it in a safe way. I take away a bit of the risk."

"Do you take it directly to the Hungarians?"

"I go and give it to the Hungarians."

"How long have you been doing it, Imre?"

"They contact me 1978. I have done it nearly ten years."

Clyde became nervous again and issued another warning. "Should we bring the spotlight out now? Watch him, Imre. You gotta watch him."

Imre ignored Clyde's warning. "Border officials in Germany, France, and Austria love titles. They never question my papers when they see 'doctor.'"

I took a big chance with Clyde when I asked, "What would you do if you got caught, Imre?"

"I would say, 'Let's make a deal. The maximum sentence in Sweden would be two years, and I would return right to my profession as a doctor. But I wouldn't go to jail if I didn't have to. If I did work for them, I would tell them nothing of importance and identify no one. Couriers aren't allowed to know anyone. I would give them locations of meeting places we don't use."

"What would you expect me to do under the same circumstances?"

"Do the same. I would give them only useless information."

Imre began to reflect on the difficulty he would have actually working against the Hungarians because of their security procedures. He said that such measures as photographing everyone who enters the country and categorizing them, then watching for the next time they enter, would make working against them virtually impossible. Clyde issued his final warning, the reason he'd been so nervous about my questions.

"Don't tell him things he shouldn't know, Imre. That knowledge could cause him trouble later. He could let it slip."

Our conversation was interrupted by one of the hundreds of costumed revelers, a palm reader who offered to tell everyone's fortune. Clyde engaged her in a lengthy conversation in German and English. We all joked with her, but Clyde decided to have his palm read and eventually took down her name and phone number.

I caught a glimpse of an American on the veranda, who had walked up and placed both hands and pressed his face to the picture window to search inside the restaurant. He stared at our table and the palm reader, then he quickly departed. I was facing the window, and so was Imre, but Clyde was busy with the palm reader.

While he was distracted, Imre leaned over the corner of the table and confided to me that Clyde was wrong not to let him explain as much as possible about the Hungarian and other East Block intelligence systems to help me protect myself. He even offered to take me aside for further explanations the first chance he got during future meetings.

When the palm reader left, Clyde took Imre and me back to the second floor and through the enclosed bridge across Rhine Alley, the street that divided the Holiday Inn into two buildings. We went down stairs to a huge hotel bar that was completely full, and the noise was deafening. We sat on overstuffed chairs with a coffee table between us, and Clyde and Imre left to go to the men's room. Clyde left his bag of documents with me, telling me to keep it safe.

When they were out of sight, I unzipped the leather bag and confirmed that the documents I had given Clyde were actually in the bag. I made a mental note to ask Clyde where he kept his copies and where he had copies made. He had told me he had safe-deposit boxes full of documents for future use.

259

When they returned, I asked Imre, practically shouting over the din, to describe Clyde's reputation with the Hungarians. Imre's eyes opened wide, and he turned his head to address Clyde personally.

"Clyde, I was going to tell you. I talk to couriers and other people from all the countries. There is no one like you. No one remembers anyone for a long time. You are a legend, the best."

Imre finished his drink quickly and rose to leave, and Clyde handed him the leather bag, which he hung from his shoulder. I asked him if he was staying the night in Mainz. He said he was leaving immediately and driving straight through to Hungary.

Clyde and I stayed to finish our drinks, and I informed him that I had looked at the documents in the bag and they appeared to be copies of my copies. I asked him where he had copies made. He said he had read my documents but did not have time to copy them. He would only say, "I have several places I can copy documents." After another beer, we walked to our cars, and Clyde explained the value of a courier using a rental car.

"They never take classified information on airplanes. They always keep the documents in the trunk of the rental car. If they are stopped, they can claim they were already in the trunk when they picked up the car."

We parted company a short time later. The next week, Clyde informed me he'd been told to meet the Hungarians to pick up my money. He arranged to meet me in Heidelberg the following week to pay me. A few days before my scheduled meeting with Clyde in Heidelberg, Grant informed me it had been decided that I had failed my last polygraph exam after all and I would have to take another examination in Munich, at 66th MI Brigade headquarters.

The chief of quality control for polygraph examinations flew in from the States to administer my exam. He had determined that my previous exam, given in Stuttgart because I had recorded Grant and Roland, had been adjudicated incorrectly by the chief in Europe. He had missed indications that I had deceived them.

I didn't waste my breath questioning the decision, but I commented to Grant that a controversy over the outcome of this new exam could jeopardize my receipt of the money everyone was waiting for. Grant said he was aware of that, then he told me to make my own excuses to my commander for being away the entire day.

I wasn't surprised to see a half dozen agents and supervisors congregated like vultures when I walked through the rear door of brigade headquarters and was quickly ushered to the interrogation room known as the fish bowl, a tiny room with one-way glass. What did surprise me was the identity of the chief of quality control for polygraph. My only other experience with this agent, several years back, had been a disaster, in which he eventually ruined an espionage/terrorism investigation by my office in Giessen, Germany.

I decided immediately I would have to at least try to clear that experience from my mind, as well as my total lack of respect for this man as an agent or examiner. The chief didn't make that easy for me.

He explained that he had detected some physical manipulations by me during the previous exam. He bragged that he was the only polygraph examiner who recognized these abnormalities and knew how to adjudicate them. When I asked what particular questions he had a problem with, he told me his only problem was with the controlled questions, to which I had been directed to lie.

With extreme difficulty, I stayed fairly calm when I stated, "Maybe I just don't like to lie." He quickly replied, "Don't worry. You'll only be asked questions we expect you to answer truthfully." Recognizing the chief's superior tone, I just said, "Good."

The exam lasted several hours. The subject matter was expanded beyond the inadvertent recording of Grant and Roland. I was asked whether I wished I were running the operation, if I'd lied about any of my past investigative experience, and if I'd discussed the operation with anyone.

When it was over, the chief seemed exhausted but could only conclude that I had been completely truthful, with no attempted deception. The exam was followed by a short meeting in the fish bowl with Grant and one of his superiors who had apparently flown in from the States.

With only a slight, somewhat reluctant admission that the results of the polygraph exam were in my favor, this supervisor issued my marching orders. He told me I would have to change my approach and start letting Clyde do all the talking. He spoke as if his special knowledge and superior authority made any explanation for his proclamation totally unnecessary.

I thought he ought to at least apologize for their unwarranted suspicion of me. I began wondering if the whole episode hadn't been calculated just to let me know how miserable they could make my life if I didn't start doing and saying exactly what they told me from now on.

I leaned back in my chair and asked, "Sir, why do you say that?" He turned his head slowly and deliberately toward Grant and gave him a look that asked, *Who the hell does he think he's talking to?*

I continued. "That unspoken communication just now between

you and Grant is similar to many of the communications between Clyde and me that can't be seen by the recorder. They tell me when he's not telling the truth and needs to be interrupted." The supervisor's expression told me he wasn't listening, so I surrendered. "But I will do my best, Sir, to change my approach and let Clyde do all the talking."

Grant jumped in quickly and said I could keep my planned rendezvous with Clyde. Then he stood and led me out of the fish bowl. I proceeded through the gauntlet of vultures, some of whom didn't try to hide their disappointment that I had passed the polygraph. I left by the back door and started my long ride home.

I reached Stuttgart too late to go to the office, so I went home to Steinenbronn. Shirley was home from her school in Heilbronn and glad to see me home at a reasonable hour. She stood beside me in the bedroom while I changed clothes. When I took my shirt off, Shirley turned around and started for the bedroom door, asking a question as she left.

"Was that the bad guys or the good guys who did that to you?"

"What do you mean, sweetheart?"

"Your arm! Who's been trying to get information out of you?"

I looked down at my arms. I was shocked to see my right arm was covered with little red specks. It looked like a strawberry. I answered, "Damn! I didn't realize how long they left that polygraph equipment on my arm, honey. I guess it was about twice as long as usual."

I turned toward her, realizing why she had left the room. She had asked her question jokingly, but I could see now that she hadn't been able to hold back the tears.

I hugged her and said softly, "As bad as this looks, honey, it was only routine. We often have to go through polygraph exams when we do CI investigative work. I admit this one was totally unnecessary and could even have jeopardized the mission, but it was the good guys. I didn't even realize the rash was there. It doesn't hurt. I just hope to hell it goes away by tomorrow."

Payday was just around the corner. I didn't know what to expect in payment, but I half expected a continued battle between Clyde and me over the future documents he would expect.

11

PAYDAY

On the evening of 26 February 1988, ten months after my meeting with Clyde at his home in Bosenheim, I met him at the Heidelberg Bahnhof. We ate dinner there and talked for a couple of hours. Clyde and his wife, Gitta, had returned from a long visit with relatives in Holland. He had also met with the Hungarians to further discuss his OPLAN, establish my future status, and collect my money.

He said he had collected ten thousand Marks for me and had reached an agreement with the Hungarians to pay me fifty thousand Marks annually for anything I could deliver, even if it was junk. He added, "For documents of real value, they will pay you whatever's right, whatever that means."

He said he had convinced them of my importance to him and

to his OPLAN, then he explained the Hungarians' reaction to the documents I had sent.

"Danny, the ten thousand Marks covers your earlier documents about communication security violations. They did say such information would have been much better if you could have identified those security weaknesses in the system before they were investigated. But everything else you sent was not acceptable."

I knew he was referring to all the CI documents and lesson plans, and I expected that answer, but I still wondered if it had really been the Hungarians' response or just his. I asked, "Why is that, Clyde?" His answer was less than convincing. He was irritated at having to repeat his previous argument.

"It was common sense, Danny. Everyone does those things the same way."

"I assume they sent those worthless documents back, Clyde."

He ignored my sarcasm, insisting again that war plans and related documents were what the Hungarians wanted. To remind me of the value of my position as a CI agent in gaining access to acceptable classified documents, he spent the next hour describing the scope of access he had managed during his military career.

He assumed I would recognize all the acronyms when he said, "Danny, I've worked with every Air force document, nuclear document, the ACE program in Belgium, IFF, SIF, INTEL, NATO, and classified area studies on all the countries of the world."

"Clyde, please let me assure you, I'm getting closer to clarifying exactly what documents are available to me in my area of operation. I'm steadily establishing a routine that will soon afford me some safety in collecting what is available to me."

He was clearly disappointed but chose not to press the issue. He changed the subject entirely, starting to discuss again his family's Holland trip. His youngest stepdaughter, Sabine, was visiting from California with her husband.

He expressed contempt for the fact that they had become Christians, saying, "They go to church and everything." His disappointment in Sabine reminded him of an incident for which he had never forgiven her.

"I visited her in California before she married. We made an agreement for me to build a vault in her apartment to which only I would have access. Once I arranged with a contractor to build the vault, I discovered she had moved to another location. I had to give up on that idea. I have to admit, they've made a success with their marriage and built a nice life for themselves."

Clyde rose from the table and led me toward the Bahnhof parking lot. He stopped beside his car, where almost no light shined on us, and bent over to raise both pants legs, where he had two ankle wallets. He removed ten thousand Marks in one hundred Mark bills. He said he had exchanged the ten one thousand Mark bills they had given him.

It was a sizable stack of bills, which I stuffed into several pockets of my sport jacket. I told him with a smile, "I'll count it later, and I'd like to get your suggestion later as to where best to store this and future payments." He departed immediately, and I proceeded to my car.

Grateful that the payoff had not prompted an arrest, I hoped USAI was waiting for more information, possibly even where Clyde stored his money. At that point, I wasn't sure how the investigation would proceed.

As I returned to Steinenbronn early that morning, I was glad

I'd prepared Shirley for another late arrival. Before departing for Heidelberg, I had managed to call her on a telephone in a building next to my company headquarters, where I wouldn't be overheard. She started crying as soon as I said I couldn't tell her how late I would be. She'd been doing that much more lately. This time she stopped crying and vented her frustration over the phone.

"Danny, when are you going to tell them to let someone else work late for a change?"

"Honey, there are others working late, but I'm sorry; I'm the only one who can do what I have to do this evening."

"Can't you tell them you need some rest? You know you're going to make yourself sick."

"I probably should, honey, but it would only delay the completion of these investigations. I know I've said it before, but this late stuff will be over soon."

"How soon?"

"Soon, honey. Sweetheart, I have a lot of driving to do. I'm sorry; I have to go."

"You know I just worry about you, Danny."

"I know, honey, but I'll be fine, really. I love you."

"I love you too."

When I finally reached Steinenbronn around three that morning, I realized I had a unique problem that I hoped I wouldn't have to explain to Shirley. The laws of evidence required that I maintain a strict chain-of-custody of the money Clyde had given me. I would have to keep possession of it until I could turn it over to Grant. I didn't even turn on the light when I walked into the bedroom. I knew Shirley would let me sleep until five, so I lay down beside her in my suit and said softly, "Goodnight, honey."

268

PAYDAY

Lately, I had found Shirley awake crying, but she must have gotten all that out of her system over the phone. She even had a little sarcasm ready, which she shared with the cats. "Boys, don't bother your mysterious daddy this morning. He's sleeping in his clothes."

I chuckled, then said, "I'll explain that when I wake up, honey. Goodnight."

She had the last word. "We don't need an explanation, do we, boys?"

She really didn't require an explanation when she woke me at five. After my two hours of sleep, I skipped my usual workout and showered with the bathroom door locked and my suit folded on a chair. At my headquarters in Stuttgart, I spoke to 1SG Frey in his office.

Charlie, does anyone other than you have the combination to your office safe?"

"No. Why? Do you want to use it?"

"Just while I help you with the painting you have scheduled for this morning."

"I can excuse you from that activity, Danny, but I may need some explanation of what you need to be doing."

"I don't want to be excused, Charlie. Just let me fold my coat and lock it in your safe until this afternoon when I have to attend a meeting on the other side of town. I'll be glad to explain in general what I'm doing."

I sensed from his glances at my sport coat that he thought I was carrying a weapon under my coat and needed to secure it, which would rate him an explanation. I slipped off my shoulder wallet and my coat in one motion and folded them together to create

269

the impression it was a weapon I was placing in his safe, then I proceeded to explain an activity which would justify a weapon.

"In my last assignment in the States, I worked with Colonel Cameron, before he became your battalion commander. On several special-access programs (SAPs), I provided CI support to a number of tactical units. I would monitor their activities and investigate any undue interest I detected. This sometimes led to arrests, but not often.

"Some of these SAPs are located in Europe and still require the same CI support. The Colonel decided not to have a new person read-on to these SAPs when he heard I was coming to his command. The program managers demand that the identity of anyone supporting them be classified.

"I know several people around here think SAP refers to some special counterespionage operation, but they're mistaken. The only involvement CI has with these SAPs is the kind of support I'm providing."

"Well, Danny, I'll take your word for that. I don't have any personal experience with that activity. I'll give you the combination to the safe and the key to my door, and you can lock it until you leave. No one needs to use my office today. Give the key to me when you leave this afternoon."

"Thanks, Charlie. I appreciate that."

The chain-of-custody went smoothly, and I turned the money over to Grant that evening. I later opened an account at a German Bank in a town nearby and leased a safety deposit box. I showed Clyde my account book and told him I put the money there temporarily. He said he did the same thing.

"I have about two hundred thousand Marks in hands-on money

I can get at a moments notice. I once earned two hundred thousand Marks in one day. My personal goal is to earn one million dollars in one day." He couldn't tell me when to expect the first installment on my fifty thousand Marks annually, but he assured me it would depend on continued production.

Additional documents followed from Grant, some unclassified and some classified, including one war plan. I had already learned about the war plan from my battalion commander.

During one of my routine visits to battalion headquarters, the commander passed me in the hall and asked me to wait in his office for him. I was standing at attention in front of his desk when he returned to his office and closed the door behind him. He put me at ease, grabbed a handful of classified documents, and handed them to me.

"Those are documents I'm studying to decide if I want to let you release them, Danny. One is our battalion war plan. Even though it's been sanitized some, I'm very reluctant to release it. I'd like your opinion."

After scanning the documents, I gave the Colonel my assessment. "I appreciate your asking my opinion, Sir. I can only tell you one thing for sure. Our target can probably get these whether you release them to him or not. I still don't know who all his friends are, but I know he has at least one other acquaintance in CI. I'd prefer that we know what documents the other side gets from him. We can always change our war plans, Sir.

"The only thing that worries me is that this one has been sanitized. The other side will have to verify its authenticity."

"Your contact will let you know what my decision is, Danny. I appreciate your comments. Is there anything you need from me?"

"No, but thank you, Sir."

The colonel never had to assist me in any way to keep my three lives from colliding, not even when I took on the additional position of Company First Sergeant while 1SG Frey attended a school in Munich. There were times, however, when I didn't do as well as I would have liked keeping my three lives separated. One such lapse occurred when I was sitting in my operations office catching up on message traffic from several counterespionage cases throughout the company.

Specialist Richie, one of my junior agents, having just received a encrypted message from our battalion, stormed into my office and addressed me with a whine in her voice and an exasperated tone, "Seeergeant Wiiilliams."

She'd used that tone before, so I didn't look up. Greg Zientek, our new company operations officer, also deep in thought over counterespionage messages, mocked her with, "Seeergeant Wiiilliams. Here it comes, Danny!"

Specialist Richie, a mission-oriented, intuitive agent with rare investigative instincts, was mad about the message she had received. After angrily stuffing it into the safe, she turned to me and asked, "When is INSCOM ever going to approve the operational plan for that investigation in Munich?"

I finished the sentence I was reading before I looked up. My response was involuntary. "Leann, Iiii dooon't knooow!"

Everything seemed to get quiet, and I sat motionless. Only Clyde Conrad used that expression, and I had repeated it. I imagined some friend of Clyde's standing in the hall who might recognize his expression. I knew I was being excessive, but I still hoped no one would take notice. No such luck. Greg laughingly mocked me to Specialist Richie.

"He doesn't knooow. Don't ask hiiim."

She had calmed down, then said, "It's been three weeks already. Waiting for them to do something is 'toiture!'" As always, Greg couldn't resist mocking her New England accent.

But his next comment didn't allay any of my fear. He asked her, "You think it's torture? Iiii dooon't knooow." He adopted that expression for the next couple of weeks before, fortunately, going on leave to the States for a month.

Unfortunately, I had to take over his two jobs as company and detachment operations officer, while still serving as 1SG and operations NCO. Things got a little hectic shortly thereafter, causing yet another lapse in keeping my lives separate.

I'd just completed a phone conversation in my first sergeant office with my Neurnberg NCOIC and was expecting another call from him within the hour. I crossed the hall to my operations office to complete an earlier task, with two of my training NCOs following me to request assistance with projects of their own. Before I could take a seat, they started vying for first consideration. I chose the senior NCO.

Just as he finished explaining his problem, a third NCO interrupted to inform me I had a phone call on line two. Expecting a quick conversation with my Neurnberg NCOIC, I took the call with the two training NCOs standing their ground in front of me.

"Hello, First Sergeant Williams here. How may I help you, Sir"

"Hello. How are you?"

"Just fine." I recognized Grant's voice."

"How about letting me buy you a hamburger this afternoon?"

"Sure."

"How about seven o'clock?"

"That's fine."

"Good. See you then."

I hung up without further comment. Before I could give the waiting senior NCO my answer to his problem, he squinted his eyes, cocked his head, and said, "Now that was a cryptic conversation."

He waited for a reply, but I ignored him and gave him an answer to his training problem, then turned to the other NCO. While I assisted her with her problem, the senior NCO hung around, smirking, still expecting me to explain my phone call.

I continued to ignore him as I walked back to my 1SG office. Both NCOs followed me, and the curious one taunted me.

"Are you sure we don't need to open an investigation on you, First Sergeant?"

With a chuckle, I closed my door behind me and sat down at my desk. I suddenly realized I hadn't concentrated enough on that phone call. I couldn't remember whether Grant had said hamburger or ice cream. Each meant a different location. I wasn't even sure whether he said seven or eight o'clock.

I relaxed and placed myself mentally in my other office. Slowly the conversation came back to me. I decided it was hamburger at seven. That meant I was to meet him at 5:00 at a kiosk in Echterdingen. It turned out I was right, but I vowed never to let that happen again.

At that meeting, Grant gave me the war plan and other intelligence documents the colonel had released.

PAYDAY

I later informed Clyde they were available to me. He continued to show his disappointment in documents related to CI, even the 527th MI BN GDP, but he reluctantly requested I bring them to him.

A week or so later, Grant handed me a secret codeword message addressed to my battalion commander from the U.S. Army medical command, Europe. I expected quite a challenge gaining any interest from Clyde in information so far removed from wartime general deployment plans.

The codeword document addressed a conference to be held at U.S. Army Europe headquarters in Heidelberg and listed the names of high-ranking officers expected to attend, including my battalion commander. It also addressed topics to be discussed, related to a special access program involving the delivery of highly sensitive medical supplies to Europe. An attached note directed 527th MI BN to provide CI support to the shipment.

Clyde's reaction to the document surprised me. Although he had been less than enthusiastic when I described it to him, he became quietly reflective once he'd read it. A short time later, at a meeting in Heidelberg, he told me he had already delivered the document to the Hungarians. He relayed the conversation he'd had with the man who accepted it.

"I offered to monitor the shipment for him. I told him which airport it would come into, and I told him I could have that watched around the clock and then follow the shipment to its destination for a price. He asked me, 'You can do that? You have those resources?' I said, 'I have those resources.' Then he says, 'We have our own resources. Don't do anything. We'll check it out first.'"

I asked, "So you think this is promising, Clyde?" He wasn't pleased with the skepticism in my voice, so I explained. "The document requested CI support from the battalion, but the specific time and location for the shipment are supposed to come in a later message."

"Did you read that message, Danny? There is something very important about to be delivered. My guess is some sort of antivirus. That could be worth millions! Watch this.

"All I have to do is position someone along the autobahn with a high-powered rifle, have him take out the driver of the truck, then have someone there to grab a sample when it spills out onto the side of the autobahn. A chemist can analyze that and give us the formula."

I was surprised, not only at his rash plan, but his interpretation of the message. I had attended classified briefings by this medical branch of the U.S. Army even while I was in the infantry, and I remembered Clyde had as well.

There was continuous research into dangers soldiers might face in foreign countries and the medication and antidotes required. While the research was always classified, the resulting medication delivered to the field seldom was. Although I considered his assessment incredibly optimistic, even for him, I humored him.

"I see what you mean. You understand the shipment could come into A Company's area and might not require any support from B Company. I'll let you know as soon as that next message arrives."

Grant and Roland shook their heads in amazement when I reported Clyde's scheme, but they didn't seem worried about his threat to kill the truck driver taking the shipment from the airport to storage. That concerned me, but I reasoned that possibly they either doubted Clyde's ability to make good his threat or they had a back-up plan for delivery. A visit from my battalion commander a short time later led me to suspect a more dangerous reason for their lack of concern.

LTC Cameron was having a meeting with my company commander while I worked alone in my operations office next door. After that meeting, the colonel walked up beside me as I stood at my safe and handed me a document, saying quietly, "I have something for you, Danny, to give to your friend."

The document was another SECRET, CODEWORD message concerning the SAP and sensitive medical shipment. Attached to the document was an EYES ONLY handwritten note, addressed to the B Company commander, naming Greg Zientek and me as the only other persons to be briefed concerning the message. The message instructed B Company to stand by for an order to provide CI support to a second sensitive medical shipment. When I finished reading it, Colonel Cameron offered further explanation.

"The shipment will be in A Company's area, but they screwed up the last one, so I'm going to have B Company provide the support. I wasn't able to attend the conference, but I'll see that you get full instructions when they come. This is for real, Danny."

Damn! Why did you have to say that? You're not good at subterfuge are you, Colonel?

Somewhat startled at my own immediate suspicion, and hoping I was mistaken, I asked him, "So, the only other person who needs to see this is Greg Zientek, Sir?"

"No! No one is supposed to see it. They will give you further instructions before you see your friend again."

DAMIAN and MONGOOSE

I glanced at the message again. Now this one and the previous one looked like so many messages I'd seen passed through channels during field exercises in a feeble attempt at intelligence deception. A picture flashed in my mind of a group of second lieutenants, most of whom had probably majored in basket weaving, sitting around a table cooking up just such a message.

As Colonel Cameron was leaving, I folded the document and put it in my coat pocket. The fact that he let me put a SECRET CODEWORD message in my pocket was confirmation to me that it was bogus, and that made me angry.

On my way home that evening, I wondered how anyone could be so arrogant as to risk compromising this operation with bogus documents. *They could not have known Clyde would turn this into his own personal scheme, but even though he has, he's still delivering everything to the Hungarians. If they even suspect it's not authentic, they will warn Clyde, and the operation is over. My superiors like to talk concern for my safety, but they're acting more reckless than Clyde.*

Clyde had no comment when I handed him the second CODEWORD document, but when we met again, he explained that he had arranged another special meeting in Mainz to deliver the document to the Hungarians. He'd already learned that Imre had been tasked as courier, and he wanted me to join them.

He warned me that he would need some time alone with Imre to give him an assignment he would discuss with me after he got Imre's reaction. Before we parted company that evening, I was treated to another one of his shockers, which suggested his assignment for Imre might include providing him some special drugs.

Clyde had studied the original message, especially the discussion topics at the USAREUR conference. From various clues, including a mention of the use of sheep for medical testing, he was convinced the classified medication was an anti-virus and of great importance. He believed a pharmaceutical firm would pay millions of dollars for the formula.

If his plan to kill the truck driver and procure a sample failed, he planned to kidnap one of those high-ranking officials named as attendees and torture him for the formula. When he smiled, I suspected I hadn't managed to hide my trepidation. His statement confirmed that.

"Danny, I know this isn't your kind of solution. It goes against your moral principles. But I can take care of this myself, and you don't have to know anything about it."

"Clyde, that's not my problem at all. I know you've been looking for any old excuse to kill someone. My only concern with your plan is that the Army will know their formula has been stolen. If you take out the truck driver or kidnap one of the officers who attended the conference, the Army will know their formula has been compromised and will implement their contingency plan."

"What contingency plan?"

"Clyde, if the Army suspects this medical formula has been compromised, they will immediately register a patent worldwide. I'm sure they could do that with one phone call. This is like any other information stolen from the Army. It's only good if they don't know it's stolen. Am I wrong?"

"No, I think you may be right."

He seemed only partially convinced, so I started thinking of some way to prevent his going ahead with his plans without telling me. An alternate plan formulated in my mind as I spoke.

"I have an idea you might consider. I told you I've dealt with several SAPs in the past. CI has a special branch of people who support those programs. Their headquarters is in the DC area and all those assignments come from there. I've worked with that headquarters.

"I know you've experienced how easily people talk to you, even now that you're out of the service. These guys do the same with people who have worked SAPs with them before and can't wait to brag about the latest one they're supporting. I've been asked to go back there to report on the missile agreement we just made with the Russians.

"I'd guess the formula would not be known by anyone in Europe, but only by someone at the medical research branch headquarters. They have line-and-block charts with all their names on them like everyone else. I'm sure I could get someone to point out the name of the four-eyed chemical genius in charge of the formula. Once we know that, he's our target."

"That's not a bad idea, Danny. We could kidnap the guy and take him out on a boat someplace. Once we get the formula, we could kill him and make it look like it was done by some terrorist group. That way, no one would suspect the formula was compromised."

"Sounds like a plan, Clyde. I'll check into it right away. In the meantime, what's going on with your OPLAN?"

"I don't know. All I hear is, 'Everything's on hold. We'll get back to you.' This is normal. They still haven't translated everything. When they do, the highest authority has to chop off on it. They met me with more questions, which I answered. I'll know they've bought it when they come up with the money. I can't see them doing this themselves. They'll want me to demonstrate that it works."

He shrugged his shoulders like he usually did, then laid out the schedule for our meeting with Imre in Mainz to discuss finding a buyer for our drug formula. I passed the schedule on to Grant. I was sure they would want me to have another meeting with Imre, but I was unsure they would wait for something to develop with this new preoccupation of Clyde's, let alone wait for the Hungarian's decision about his OPLAN.

I could understand why they might decide to end the operation. I had accidently learned how long they had been working on this case.

One morning after attending a 527th counterespionage conference at Battalion, I met Mr. Beard who had transferred to 66th MI Brigade in Munich. His job as operations officer at B Company had been taken over by Greg Zientek. He took me aside at Battalion Headquarters to confide in me.

"Danny, I hear you're conducting an operation in Bad Kreuznach. I started that case years ago. I'm glad to see someone is finally taking it seriously."

"Mr. Beard, I haven't been in BK for some time. I thought you knew I'm in full swing as Operations NCO at B Company and acting First Sergeant while Charlie is at school in Munich. When I was in BK, I provided CI support to some V Corps special access programs while I coordinated with 527th battalion units who would be chopped to Company B in war time. If you're telling me I might have been interfering with some operation there, I wasn't aware of it. Has Colonel Cameron suggested something like that?"

"Oh, no. No. I just thought— It doesn't matter, Danny."

"Great! You had me worried for a second."

Two days later, one of my more capable counterespionage

agents, whom I had transferred from B Company headquarters to detachment A, down the hall, asked me to look over a case file Mr. Beard had just sent him from Brigade. He said Mr. Beard was certain the NCO described in the lead sheet by some confidential source of another agency was the NCO his detachment was currently investigating in Stuttgart. The detachment agent wanted my opinion.

I was thoroughly familiar with the Stuttgart investigation but only vaguely recognized the case from brigade titled "Poker Face," from my past assignments. The case, as I recalled, was almost ten years old. After carefully reading the file, I determined two things with certainty.

First, several parts of the description were glaringly different from what we knew about the Stuttgart NCO. Second, I recognized Clyde Conrad immediately. Of course that recognition was based on what I had learned about Clyde in the past year.

I pointed out to the detachment agent the differences between his suspect and the description of the Poker Face NCO, and he readily agreed, but I left the final decision up to him. A few days after I had notified Grant of the untimely resurrection of Poker Face, the agent looked me up again.

"First Sergeant, you were right about that case not being our Stuttgart guy. Mr. Beard called to tell us to stop investigating it and to shred our copies and all our notes."

"Really? Did he say why?"

"Not a word. That's the end of it."

"Wow. Well, at least you're not wasting your time on it."

With that important bit of inside knowledge, I could only hope my meeting with Imre would be encouraging to USAI. I was skeptical when they decided to return to the stone-age recording equipment for my meeting in Mainz. Some changes were made because the technical specialist wanted to ensure the device could not be detected by Imre.

They used surgical tape for a new, flatter microphone on my chest. They used a simple ace bandage to attach the recorder to my leg. When I voiced concerns about the ace bandage, they assured me they'd used this method many times before.

In Mainz, Clyde had his private meeting with Imre, then the three of us spent several hours walking the streets and stopping at Clyde's favorite restaurants and Gasthauses for food and drinks. We talked primarily about the money we were going to make on the medical formula. Our success in obtaining the formula seemed to Clyde and Imre to be a foregone conclusion.

As we were returning to the Holiday Inn, with Clyde and Imre walking a few feet ahead of me, I felt the ace bandage loosen and the recorder slide down my leg. I dropped back, but just as I reached down to stop the recorder from falling all the way, Clyde turned around and came back to me, asking me what was wrong.

"My Casio dairy. I just realized it's gone. I guess I left it back at the Holiday Inn restaurant when I was waiting for you guys. And my leg has started hurting again."

"I'll bet it slipped down your leg."

I kept patting my coat and pants, looking for the diary, which I realized I actually had lost, as I answered, "No, I'm sure I left it on the table."

Remembering this cord was much shorter, I took a chance the recorder wouldn't pull loose and just let it dangle under my pants as we continued walking. I was able to secure it again with the ace bandage in the toilet at the hotel restaurant, where I also changed the tape. I didn't find my diary at the table, so I reported it at the desk.

From the hotel, I drove us to Frankfurt Airport. We left Imre there to rent a car and drive the document to Budapest. On our return to Mainz, Clyde explained that in their private meeting, he had directed Imre to talk to Alex about the validity of Clyde's conclusion that the documents were in reference to an anti-virus. He also wanted them to explore the possibility of negotiating a deal for the formula with a pharmaceutical firm in Sweden. He then wanted all four of us to have a planning meeting.

Before returning to Stuttgart that evening, I went directly to Wiesbaden for a debriefing by Grant and Roland. I had two hours to kill before arriving at their hotel at the appointed time, so I parked several blocks away on a dark side street. It took most of those two hours to pry the surgical tape from my chest to free the microphone. The tape left red welts all over my chest and stomach, which continued to burn all night.

Roland, it seemed, had begun to have second thoughts about his original assessment of Clyde, and he expressed his bewilderment in a question. "Is this guy a genius, or just a clever SOB, Danny?"

"I'm not sure, Roland. Maybe both. One thing I finally know for sure: he's capable of anything. I only hope I can temper his thirst for blood."

Grant asked me what I thought about Clyde's interpretation of the documents addressing the medical project. He explained that he and Roland didn't know any details beyond what was in the messages. He was about as convincing as Colonel Cameron had been. I had finally learned to play the fool, so I answered carefully.

PAYDAY

"His assessment is logical, Grant. I personally would have thought he'd have assumed a new antidote for nerve gas or something like that, in light of what the Russians are currently doing with snake venom in Afghanistan. His explanation is feasible, although I doubt he's shared it with any Hungarians except his friends."

In subsequent meetings, Grant seemed to want to encourage Clyde's assumptions. He even provided me with a recent *Playboy* article about some U.S. Army installations and the medical research they were allegedly conducting. He suggested I share the article with Clyde.

At our next meeting, Clyde needed little encouragement from me or the article. He had already started arranging our planning meeting in Kiel, West Germany.

In the meantime, he had more meetings with his newest Hungarian controller, Mike, to discuss his OPLAN. He also collected fifteen thousand Marks for me for documents I had delivered, not including the two CODEWORD documents, because they were still assessing them. He expected they would be worth several thousand Marks on their own. The additional money provided me an opportunity to enlist his help in choosing a place to hide my money, so I suggested the idea to Grant.

USAI agreed to my asking Clyde to go to Switzerland with me to open an account and put the fifteen thousand Marks in a safe-deposit box. They arranged to copy the serial numbers, rather than exchange the money, in case Clyde had marked the bills and might want to look at them. They hoped this arrangement might prompt Clyde to reveal the location of his own accounts.

I drove us in Clyde's Audi to Zurich, where Clyde had

recommended a good bank. He said he needed to take care of some business there himself. He took advantage of the drive to pressure me to start delivering combat unit war plans. When I repeated my concern about special security measures and paranoid CI agents at my unit, he became frustrated.

"Danny, invite me to your office when we finish this trip. I'd like to look over your situation and make some recommendations for you to overcome the security measures. I might even come back some evening and do the job for you." He made the offer only partly in jest, and I acknowledged that.

"Clyde, I know you mean that. If it comes down to that, it might be an option, but I'm going to pass on that for now. It's not an impossible situation at my headquarters, but it's tricky. Beside the cipher lock on the door leading from the stairwell to my floor, there's also one on the door in the stairwell at the opposite end of the hall for which I don't even have the code, and it's changed several times per month by the detachment, the same as ours.

In addition, each office in both my headquarters and the detachment is locked at night. Each office has a safe, and currently I have the combinations to only the safe in my office and the First Sergeant's office. That's all pretty routine, Clyde, but the tricky part is the atmosphere after duty hours.

"Some of the rooms in the attic above my floor as well as a few rooms at the far end of my hall have been converted into quarters, showers, and latrines for some of the single soldiers, some who work in my headquarters and some who work in the detachment. They're often in their offices during off-duty hours to catch up on work. There's also the attitude among the agents to contend with, Clyde.

"For example, the last time I copied some of those documents I gave you, I was surprised by my operations officer. It was six in the morning. He never comes in before eight. The copy machine is located in the hallway. He said hello to me as soon as he entered the hall from the stairwell, then went into the operations office we share. I was at the end of copying, so there were still a few pages in the machine, and I couldn't stop.

"He turned around and came out into the hall and asked me what I was doing. I told him I was catching up on some of my war plan work that one of our agents didn't finish for me the night before.

"He warned me, 'I wouldn't do that if I were you, Danny. That kind of activity, before or after duty hours, causes a lot of suspicion. Before you know it, someone will start an investigation on you.' Fortunately I was finished, so I thanked him for the warning, and he went back into his office.

"I've already put your notebook to work, Clyde. I'm in the process of establishing some other controls that will give me the kind of safe access I need."

"Good!" He had been listening intently and seemed to have bought my excuse for not yet delivering the war plans, as well as my sincerity about intending to do so as soon as safely possible. I'd been careful to paint a truthful picture of my situation, because I still didn't know if he knew other agents.

He immediately launched a discourse on the various benefits of the notebook and gave a few examples of the uses he'd made of his notebook to overcome security barriers he'd encountered at 8ID. I explained that I would likely get more value out of the notebook once First Sergeant Frey returned from school. That statement prompted a strange question from Clyde.

DAMIAN and MONGOOSE

———————

"What happens if you lose your CI badge and credentials, Danny?"

"I don't know anyone who has, Clyde, but it's generally considered a career breaker."

"So if your First Sergeant lost his credentials, you would become the permanent First Sergeant?"

"Probably, Clyde, but for our purposes, I will probably have much better control of my time as Operations NCO than as First Sergeant." I could see the wheels turning behind the smirk on his face. Luckily, we were approaching Zurich and were passing the exit to Lucerne, which interrupted his train of thought.

"I was going to have you drive to Lucerne. I received a card from them telling me my ten years is about up on my safe deposit box, and I need to pay up again. I changed my mind, because I like to take Gitta with me when I go to a nice place like that. It's a great looking town. Shirley would like it. I'll come back later and bring Gitta. I still have a little time to take care of that."

We parked in an underground parking lot in Zurich, and Clyde took the keys from me to open his trunk. He opened one of his two packed suitcases, which he always kept at the ready in his trunk, and pulled out four or five keys. He laughingly commented, "I can't always remember which key goes to which safety deposit box, so I have to bring several of them." From there he led me to a restaurant on Bahnhof Strasse, where we ordered coffee. We sat by a window from which we could see the walking bridge over the main autobahn into Zurich. Staring at the bridge, Clyde began reminiscing.

"That's where Imre met with the guy from the embassy. I sat

right here so I could see it go down. The guy walked up to Imre with a prearranged signal, and Imre instructed him to take the money to a little town just down the autobahn. We'd already told him exactly what kind of bag to bring the money in.

"We said, 'No metal. If we detect any metal, we don't touch it.' We'd even told him the hotel where he had to stay in Zurich. Watch this, Danny: This guy says to Imre, 'Next time instruct me to stay in a different hotel.' He picked the most expensive hotel in Zurich. Can you believe that? What a dick!

"Imre told him exactly where to go in this little town outside of Zurich and where to park his car, then start walking. He told him, 'When you pass by this trash can, drop the money in there and keep walking right over this little hill. Don't stop walking until you're out of sight at the bottom of the hill, then you can turn around and walk back and pick up your merchandise.'

"Excerpts, Danny. All they wanted were excerpts. We told him, 'If anything goes wrong, there will be someone back in those woods with a high-powered rifle and scope.'

"It worked like a charm. I was sitting in a Gasthaus right in front of the trash can. When he disappeared over the hill, I jumped on a bicycle parked outside, drove past the trash can, grabbed the money and dropped the merchandise, then headed off through a field down the hill the opposite way and into the woods, where my car was parked on a back road. I threw the bike into the car and took off. Imre couldn't believe how well it worked."

"Sounds like a well-thought-out plan to me, Clyde. Did you do it again?"

"We did some other things, Danny. They knew everything I gave them was good, but all they wanted were excerpts, and they didn't want to pay. The Americans pay the worst of anyone. My associates couldn't understand. 'Let's do it again! Let's do it again!' I didn't know what to tell them. I don't know, Danny. I just don't know. I had to stop it. I thought they were starting to try to identify me."

"Who got the stationery with the intelligence heading on it and translated the excerpts?"

"Imre, from Budapest. He did the translation too, because he could do it in the Budapest dialect."

"Clyde, I really appreciate you sharing with me some of the details about your successful schemes, and I'm looking forward to being involved in some myself and in implementing your OPLAN, whether the Hungarians do it or we do it ourselves. And I'm willing to invest in the plan, but I'd like to make those decisions myself, so I have to ask you a question. Did you keep some of the money the Hungarians gave you for me?"

"Danny, I hope you're willing to invest in the OPLAN, but I gave you exactly what they gave me for you. I always intend to do that."

"I had to ask, Clyde."

He grinned as he responded, "I'd be disappointed if you didn't, Danny."

"Well, it's that same problem I mentioned before, Clyde. I want you to know I understand the importance of delivering product, acceptable product, and I hope you know I'm working at doing that as quickly and as safely as I can, but I keep wondering if you trust me enough to include me in the things I would really find challenging."

"Danny, let me say something." He leaned back against the booth and gathered his thoughts. "You remember me telling you the hardest thing for me to find is someone I could really trust? I can't tell you how much you've done for me. Until you came along, I was shut down completely. Now, I'm out there again, thrusting like old times. You did that for me."

"Really?"

"I mean it, Danny. I owe you a lot."

"Okay. I'm glad to hear that."

The waitress came by and Clyde paid the bill. He stood and said, "Come on. I'll show you the best bank in Zurich."

The Union Bank of Zurich was located across the autobahn from the restaurant. Clyde watched as I opened an account, then he walked with me to the lower floor where I leased a safety deposit box and signed for my key. I was glad when he followed me into the vault where the boxes were, because I assumed he would be servicing some of his accounts. No such luck.

As I followed the attendant toward the boxes, Clyde started for the stairs saying, "I'll meet you in the lobby when you're through. Just wait for me. I have a few things of my own to take care of."

Realizing his accounts must be in a nearby bank, I changed my plan, in hopes of at least seeing which direction he took. I quickly took my box to the table and opened it, in case Clyde turned around before reaching the top of the stairs, then I closed it and put it back without putting the money in it. I rushed up the stairs to the lobby, but Clyde was gone.

I went out the front door and looked up both sides of the street, then I returned to the lobby to double-check. I sat in the lobby and waited nearly two hours for Clyde to return. When he did, we walked to the underground garage where the car was still parked in the same spot, then we started home.

DAMIAN and MONGOOSE

During the trip back to Stuttgart, Clyde began to reflect again on having someone he could trust. "Danny, I thought about having someone step in and make sure that my son knows everything he needs to know. I need someone to make sure Gitta knows where everything is so she can take care of Jeurgen. I thought about putting together a package so someone can walk in and say, 'Here's what you need to do. Here's where this is. Here's where you need to go.'

"I gave Jeurgen a code when he was very young so he would recognize any friend of mine. If someone comes up to Jeurgen and says, 'Your dad sent me,' or 'I'm a friend of your dad's,' Jeurgen will say, 'What's your code?' If you don't know that code, he knows not to talk to you no matter what you say." Clyde had made reference to the code before, but this was his first mention of a package.

"Everyone should do that with their kids, Clyde. If you're asking me if I would be willing to take care of that for you, I would in a heartbeat."

"Yes, I would like you to do that."

"Whenever you put together that package, that will be fine with me, Clyde."

"Good!" Clyde continued his reflection on plans for his son's future. He expanded previous explanations of training he had given his son over the years, by describing the games he played with him. One he called, "Shoes."

He would force Jeurgen to put himself in another person's shoes by assuming the role of the person Clyde would describe. Clyde would invent situations and require Jeurgen to make decisions as if he were that person.

PAYDAY

Another game Clyde called, "Tipping," required Jeurgen to list from memory as many characteristics as possible of a stranger he had observed for a short time while sitting in a restaurant or walking along a path near a person. At first it appeared that Clyde wanted Jeurgen to be able to read people, but he soon made it clear that he wanted him to see life from other points of view, see the relativity of what he referred to as principles and rules. He called it teaching him philosophy, but I saw it as trying to instill in Jeurgen his amoral, apolitical viewpoint.

Clyde went beyond philosophy and started teaching him surveillance and surveillance detection, with practical exercises requiring Jeurgen to follow him without being detected and catching his father following him without revealing that he had seen him. Clyde even took advantage of a situation that occurred at Jeurgen's school to try to interest him in specialized training in the art of killing. He described the incident with enthusiasm.

"Jeurgen came home from his German school with bruises given to him by a bully at school. When I asked him what his reaction was to the bully, he said, 'Nothing.' I offered to send him for specialized training in the art of killing. He didn't seem interested, so I gave him my own remedy.

"I said, 'The only way to stop that bully from bothering you again is to put his eye out. Just push your thumb right in his eye the next time you see him and he'll leave you alone, and so will everyone else. And I'll stand by you if anyone at the school tries to give you trouble.' When he's ready, I'll send him to Hungary for that training."

I couldn't avoid my sadness for Jeurgen. I had no doubt Clyde's pressure was having an adverse effect on his emotional stability.

However, from vague admissions by Clyde, I got the impression Jeurgen might be resisting this philosophy training, merely giving lip service out of respect for his dad.

The evening after we returned from Zurich, I returned the fifteen thousand Marks to Grant and reminded him of the pending meeting with Imre and his brother, Alexander, hoping they would consider it worth their patience. They didn't have to wait long, but other problems arose.

12

SANDOR

While 1SG Frey attended his school in Munich, a situation occurred that I feared would attract Clyde's attention. The suspect in an espionage investigation by B Company's Munich detachment was about to be arrested. While the Germans would make the arrest under the U.S. Army's Status of Forces Agreement, I was sure that the *Stars and Stripes* newspaper would mention B Company in connection with the investigation.

If Clyde read the article, he might wonder why I didn't warn him of the investigation. I mentioned my concerns to Grant. He wasn't aware of the pending arrest, but he surprised me with the revelation that USAI might be willing to provide Clyde some information related to CE investigations.

I knew I would rather not provide that type of information to

Clyde because I had already told him my position focused on administrative matters, and I seldom had access to that type of information. However, a call I'd made to Clyde the day before, while it greatly angered Grant, also provided me a chance to pretend to give Clyde information about an ongoing case, without actually compromising the investigation or admitting to Clyde that I monitored all espionage investigations and participated in some.

Clyde had told me that Mike had warned him to be prepared to go to Hungary. He said he would call me after his next meeting with Mike to let me know if he was going right away. I told Grant and Roland and asked if they wanted me to call him if he didn't call me so they would know when he was going. Roland answered with a textbook question. "What would you normally do, Danny?" I answered, "I would let my friend know I was worried about him."

Nothing more was said, but I understood Roland's question to mean that, as their source, I should do what was normal for me. I was relieved that someone else followed that concept, which I had taught from the platform many times.

When Clyde didn't call me, I phoned his home and talked to Gitta. She said he was on a trip, and she expected him to return in a day or so. I asked her to have him call me when he returned so I could ask another favor of him in connection with the jeweler in BK. Grant became angry when I reported my call at our next meeting, to which he had come alone. He asked, "Why did you call him?"

I repeated what Roland had said, but Grant's lack of response suggested he hadn't heard Roland's statement to me. That's when

I voiced my concern about the pending arrest in Munich. I tried to smooth things over by suggesting a way to capitalize on the phone call. The Munich arrest was taking place that day, and Clyde likely wouldn't call until the next day. I offered a plan:

"When he calls to arrange a meeting, I could say I called him on Saturday to notify him of the arrest on Monday. I could say I overheard two agents from my Munich detachment talking about the arrest as they stood in the hall outside my office. I can tell Clyde I didn't know if he could pass the information to the Russians in time to save their agent, but I tried."

Grant approved my suggestion, and I told Clyde a few days later. He was certain that neither the Russians nor the Hungarians would be interested in the information, but he would contact them and let me know. He also expressed concern that I had talked to Gitta.

He gave me the number of a pay phone near his house and told me to buy a small cassette player and put a music tape in it. In an emergency, I could call his home. If he answered, he would tell me to call back in 30 minutes, then wait at the pay phone for my call. If Gitta answered, I was to say nothing and play a few seconds of music over the phone, then hang up and call him in 30 minutes on the pay phone. At our next meeting he changed the phone number to his stepdaughter, Hanelore's, apartment phone.

Clyde later relayed the Hungarians' reaction to any warnings of pending arrests of suspected agents. "They said they would be very interested, and the Russians would be especially interested." I said I would keep my eyes and ears open.

Of course there were other investigations with arrests imminent, and I hoped we could keep our company's name out of the press.

DAMIAN and MONGOOSE

Another one of our company's ongoing espionage investigations caused me concern for an entirely different and more personal reason.

I was at my operations desk reading the message traffic when I came across a message from our brigade commander to our battalion, with info to Company B that made my blood boil. It contained an ultimatum from the brigade commander concerning a civilian employee who had volunteered, at our request, to accept an invitation from two East German intelligence officers to come to East Berlin to discuss selling them U.S. Army classified documents. She was the secretary of a U.S. Army officer.

As our undercover source, she had reported her meeting with the two agents, which included an account of the conversation in which she had to ward off sexual advances while convincing these intelligence officers that she was willing to cooperate with them in the delivery of classified documents. When one of them asked her for the name of her supervisor, saying he would be checking on her, she gave him her boss's name.

The brigade commander's message stated that he intended to prosecute her or get her fired after the operation was over for giving the name of a U.S. Army officer to East German agents without first getting permission. I reacted angrily to such an injustice against an undercover source doing such a brilliant job. I lashed out at Greg, who was reading messages at his desk.

"Greg, have you read this message from the brigade commander about the source in that East German case?"

"Yes, I've read it. It's typical, isn't it?"

"Greg, I know how you are. You'll just let them dig their own hole, and you won't fight them over this. I'm not going to sit here and let them do or even say anything to upset that incredible lady, let alone get her fired or worse. I'm serious, Greg. If you don't do something to head this off, I will sit down and write a message to INSCOM naming names and revealing just how irrational this kind of injustice is and how easily it could jeopardize an important operation."

"I've never heard you get this excited about anything before, Danny." Greg was standing. I realized he was surprised and a little insulted by my insubordinate tone. I apologized but insisted that he do something before anyone said something to the young lady.

He left the room, and I calmed down. We never talked about it again. I never asked him if he did anything, but the threats weren't carried out, and the operation resulted in arrests.

The next weekend I drove Clyde to a small town outside of Kiel, where we spent the night. Bragging about having reached his target weight, he insisted on one stop along the way to buy himself two beers, announcing that this marked the end of his dieting and abstinence. Imre and Alex took the overnight ferry from Goeteborg, Sweden, and met us the next morning in Kiel.

After introductions, Imre explained to Clyde that he and Alex had made some inquiries and were ready to start negotiations with a pharmaceutical firm in Sweden. Imre seemed excited, a bit too excited for Clyde, saying, "This will be worth a hundred million at least."

Alex kept his head down as we stood around a small table in a coffee shop, and he didn't lift it when he interrupted Imre with a comment. "We need to get started as soon as possible."

Imre answered, "Yes, we must get started."

Clyde took over. "That's great, but we need to discuss a few things so we're all in agreement, then thrust on. I have a few questions about how to protect ourselves. Let's go somewhere and sit down."

Imre was eager to go with Clyde, but Alex seemed slightly offended. Either he resented Clyde's condescending tone, or he saw no need for any additional planning. He suppressed a response, wrinkling his forehead as he looked down again, and reluctantly followed, deep in thought.

Alex was clearly older than Imre, graying slightly around one temple. He was shorter and a little heavier. He wore his dark hair the way Imre did. He had the same dark, bushy eyebrows, but smaller ears, a squarer chin, and a flatter nose. His dark eyes were also smaller.

Alex's English was not as good as his brother's, but Imre assisted him when he looked to him for a translation. He didn't talk much and smiled even less. From what Clyde had told me about Alex, I expected him to be very serious and very cautious. He was that. He was even more restrained than Clyde, and considerably colder.

Clyde led us to a restaurant. While we waited for our meals, Clyde started a conversation with Imre. "What can I use, so I can be absolutely certain that what a person says is the truth?"

Imre answered, "Scopolamine," then translated the question for Alex, who agreed emphatically. "Scopolamine is best. You can be sure."

Imre explained, "When you kill him, you can be sure he told you the truth."

Imre and I were sitting across from Alex and Clyde. I turned to Imre with a smile and said, "Clyde has told me a little about Alexander, and I already know Clyde is anxious to torture and kill someone, but I'm a little surprised, Imre, to learn that you're so cold blooded."

Imre didn't hesitate. "For this kind of money, I'd kill a whole city full of people."

I glanced quickly at Alex to catch his expression, but he was looking down. I smiled again and asked Imre another question. "So tell me again. How much money can we make?"

"Maybe a hundred million. Maybe more."

Clyde took over the conversation. "We need to talk about that, about how to protect ourselves from a big pharmaceutical firm, who has a dozen high-powered lawyers."

Imre started to translate, but Alex was already answering. "That's not a problem. We can take care of that. We let you know, very soon, how it should go."

Imre was looking down when he added, "It is very easy."

Both Alex and Imre were using a tone of finality, dismissing Clyde's concerns as groundless. Imre to a lesser degree. Assuming an attitude of superiority, Clyde took back control and ended that discussion.

"I think the most important observation that's been made was a warning by Danny that the U.S. Army may have a contingency plan to patent the formula if they think it's been compromised. I'll be waiting for your report on your progress with the pharmaceutical firm. It's important that we all agree before we take the next step."

Imre nodded and said, "Yes, we should all agree." Imre seemed to be the buffer between two bulls. There was tension in the air, and no one was speaking. A little uneasy that Clyde had seen a need to justify my part in this scheme, I broke the silence. "Well, I'm agreeable with making money." As everyone nodded and smiled in approval, I casually asked Imre about their trip from Goeteborg.

He enthusiastically endorsed the gambling, drinking, and partying that he and Alex had enjoyed on the ferry most of the previous night. Alex nodded his agreement without smiling. I asked them about their medical fields, and Alex confirmed that they were both in internal medicine.

Eventually Clyde needed more cigarettes, so we left the restaurant to get him some, then we stopped in a local Gasthaus for another beer. As we drank, the Kercsiks and I spent several minutes in conversation about our families.

Clyde seemed uncomfortable with the subject and addressed Alexander. "Danny is the best joke teller I know," then he turned to me with an order, "Tell them a joke, Danny." Surprised, I answered, "Nah. You're the joke teller, Clyde.

He persisted. "Tell them the one about the toothbrush salesman." This time he looked away from me. I could see he was trying to convince Alex I was okay, but the joke he wanted required a little acting, the last thing I wanted Alex to see. I sidestepped Clyde's order.

"Let me tell you a doctor joke. You translate for me, Imre. Did you hear about the doctor who reached in his pocket for a pen to write a prescription?" Imre translated, then I continued. "He pulled out a rectal thermometer and said, 'Oh shit! Some asshole's got my pen!'" Imre laughed, then translated for Alex. His smile seemed genuine, as did his comment.

"That's really funny. I'll have to remember that."

Clyde was determined. He leaned forward and said, "Now tell them the one about the toothbrush salesman."

"I don't think they will understand that, Clyde. It's too hard to translate."

He narrowed his eyes and said, "Yes they will," then looked down at the table. It was definitely an order, so I had no choice but to make it good enough to satisfy Clyde and take my chances with Alex. I told it with my usual flair, with lots of gestures, but slowly, giving Imre a chance to translate.

"This guy has a speech impediment—trouble speaking. He gets a job selling toothbrushes. He goes through the training with two other guys and they're all sent out to sell. They have a meeting the next day, and the manager asks how many toothbrushes were sold.

"One guy has sold three hundred toothbrushes; the other has sold two hundred. Our friend with the speech problem says, 'I thonld one toonthbrunsh.' 'How many?' 'One toonthbrunsh.'"

I continued imitating the speech impediment as I finished the joke. But I was very concerned that Alex, who had lifted his head, was watching me far too intently.

"The manager calls our friend aside after the meeting and says, 'Tomorrow, you're going to have to catch up. Get yourself a gimmick and sell a lot of toothbrushes.' Our friend asks, 'Whant kind onf ginmminck?' The manager says, 'The kind that makes people want to buy toothbrushes.' Our friend says, 'Wenll, onkay.'

"After a weekend, one guy has sold a thousand toothbrushes, and the other, nine hundred toothbrushes. Our friend tells the manager, 'I thonld fornty-twon thounsand toonthbrunshes.' 'How

303

many?' 'Fornty-twon thounsand,' 'What did you do?' 'I gont me a ginmminck.' 'What kind of gimmick?'

"'I gont me a chainr and some chinps and dinp and sant ountside the grocery stonre. People can't resinst chinps and dinp. Monst woulnd sany, "Thins dinp taste linke shint!"

I'd sany, "It ins shint. Wanna buy a toonthbrunsh?"'

When Imre and Alex burst out laughing, Clyde said, "See! See!"

Alex leaned forward with one elbow on the table. Focusing on my eyes, he said very slowly and deliberately, "You'd make a very good actor, Danny."

It was just what I didn't want to hear. I shook my head as I replied, "Only if all I have to do is tell jokes."

Alex leaned back and became contemplative again until we left the guest house and walked toward the ferry. When we passed a toilet next to the sidewalk, Alex and I needed to use it, while Clyde and Imre stayed outside and talked. It amazed me that Clyde would leave me alone with either of them because he was always afraid I would say something that revealed a truth that wasn't their truth. I was more amazed, standing at the urinal, at the question Alex asked me.

"Danny, why is Clyde so afraid to get going with this plan and make some money?"

I raised my eyebrows and thought for a few seconds. Then I answered, "I've known Clyde a long time, Alex. I don't think he's afraid of anything. I believe he is just trying to think of everything he can do to protect himself. I don't think anything will stop him from doing this."

Alex seemed to be enlisting me as an advocate when he said, "I hope not. There's plenty of money in this."

Alex and Imre boarded the ferry, and Clyde and I headed back to BK. On the way I told Clyde about my conversation with Alex. Clyde explained that he always had to keep a tight reign on them when they did anything together, describing their usual attitude: "Let's do it again. That was great. It worked. It worked."

We also rehashed my plan to return to the States to identify CI agents who would have the name of the person with access to the formula. Clyde assured me he'd let me know as soon as the Kercsiks had anything concrete about negotiations with the Swedish pharmaceutical firm.

A week or so later, when Clyde arranged to meet me in downtown Stuttgart, I assumed he had heard from the Kercsiks. He hadn't, and he seemed very anxious about something as we talked about the money we could potentially make. He finally revealed the answer he had decided on about how to protect ourselves against a dozen pharmaceutical company lawyers.

"Danny, I've been giving the money a lot of thought. This is going to mean billions for the pharmaceutical firm that gets the formula. The best way to protect ourselves from a bunch of lawyers is to ask for an amount that is great for us but nothing for them. I say ten million."

"I certainly have no problem with that, Clyde. Do you think Imre and Alex will?"

"They'll do what I tell them. I'll let them gather information and talk to people, but the final decision will be mine. I want everyone to agree, but I'll do the final negotiating.

"Danny, I sat down and I thought, of all the names on that list of attendees at that USAEUR conference, who is most likely to know the formula? Colonel Cameron, Danny! He's the one in charge of providing security in Europe. Even if he doesn't have the formula himself, he knows who does, and he would be very easy to kidnap. Am I right?"

I didn't really have an answer. In fact, I was somewhat bewildered, so I started buying time as I replied, "You may be right. I just have the same concern I had before."

He was grinning when he interrupted my thoughts. "Danny, I know why you don't want to do this. He's a friend; isn't he?"

"Colonel Cameron? Well, I guess we're friends. We have been, but I don't think of him that way because he's my battalion commander, Clyde. You do know he never even attended the conference. He may know who has the formula, but it will probably be someone back in the States.

"Wouldn't it be much safer if we could identify the guy with the formula the way I suggested before? I'm very serious about being able to get information out of the CI people in the States with no suspicion whatever. They're already talking about sending me TDY to DC in connection with this Intermediate Range Missile Facility (IMF) Treaty we just signed with the Russians. I wouldn't even have to apply for leave."

"He's a friend!" Clyde was smiling, but I couldn't tell if he had completely dismissed my argument.

"That doesn't matter, Clyde. Let's do what you think best. Do you want me to make contact with those guys in DC or not? You could even go with me if you want to."

"I trust you to take care of that, Danny."

"Good. I'll let you know when they want to send me TDY. It should be soon, but let me ask you something, Clyde. While you're completing this deal with the formula, are you still planning for us to work your OPLAN with the Hungarians?"

SANDOR

"Absolutely! Danny, you should give that a try. Work the plan, I mean. Let me know what you think of it, if it works the way I know it does on some of those contacts you've made here in Stuttgart."

"You're right, Clyde, I'll have to do that."

When I reported Clyde's impatience to Grant and Roland, they weren't worried about his plan to kidnap Colonel Cameron, saying, "We'll warn the Colonel." Finally, Roland let the cat out of the bag. "Danny, there may be a problem with those code word documents."

"What problem?"

"I'm thinking they may be bogus."

"You think?"

"Some things have been said."

"I see. I thought about that myself, Roland, but I decided no one could be that stupid, not even a general. Not only could they jeopardize the mission and risk their source's life with a guy who has promised to put a bullet between his eyes, but it also makes no sense. Purposely giving the Hungarians bogus information would only be worthwhile if you never plan to arrest Clyde. I seriously doubt if anyone is ready to spend the money to extend this operation much further."

"We've already spent a million dollars, Danny. But I can tell you they are bogus documents."

"I was afraid you were going to say that, Roland. Well, nothing can be done about it now, but I have just one request, and I'm serious. When this is over, I want the name of the guy who made that stupid decision."

"I hear you, Danny. Let me ask you something. Do you think this operation is an OFCO?"

"That depends on your objective, Roland. By the strictest definition, an offensive counterintelligence operation (OFCO) is designed to penetrate to the highest echelon of any foreign intelligence collection apparatus for the purpose of influencing their decisions while maintaining plausible denial that you were ever there. A defensive counterintelligence operation (DCE) is designed to collect evidence for the purpose of arresting the suspect. This has the potential to become an OFCO, and you're already using some offensive procedures to collect evidence, but the objective seems to be DCE."

"What would you do, Danny?" Roland's question was refreshing but seemed a bit too late.

"I'm sure Grant has told you what I'm willing to do, Roland. I'd be glad to help Clyde establish his OPLAN and even help you train people for him to recruit so you could control every recruitment he makes and every document he collects, at least until every other associate of his is identified and can be neutralized. However, that would require a tremendous commitment of resources."

"That will never happen, Danny."

"Yeah, I know. Then it's just a question of whom you want to arrest, where, and when? If you want, I could persuade Clyde to arrange that meeting in Austria between him and Szabo and the two Italian agents, with Imre and Alex there too. You could arrest everyone at once.

You could even arrest me, in case Clyde might reveal more information to me after the arrest. Of course, that would depend on whether you've coordinated with the Austrians and the Italians."

"There's been no coordination, Danny, except with the Swedes."

"Yeah, I was afraid of that. So do you want to arrest Clyde in the States?"

"You could get him to the States?"

"I don't see why not."

Grant was more skeptical, asking, "How would you do that, Danny?"

"Well, I've given that some thought. I've been selected for the IMF team, and I've been touring the missile facilities the Russians will be sending their teams to inspect. There's going to be some special training in the States for the CI agents who will accompany those Russian inspectors. I intended to send detachment agents who already support those missile facilities, but I could also send myself.

"I've already told Clyde I would probably be sent to the States for training, and I could identify someone who would know the medical formula he's after. I could tell him I want him to be there with me so he can arrange for the kidnapping he has planned for the guy I identify. You could arrest him right in the airport when he arrives."

Roland and Grant both agreed, and Roland said, "You see if he will accept that, Danny. You can do just about anything you want to with him, can't you?"

"Maybe, as long as I don't forget that I can never take him for granted."

Grant wanted me to get additional information while I was arranging a trip with Clyde to the States. He explained it as an afterthought.

"I intended to tell you this, Danny. There are people who want to know if he shows any interest in the IMF Treaty."

DAMIAN and MONGOOSE

"Okay. I'll see what I can do. By the way, I know I've already told you about Clyde wanting me to test out his preparation technique for a field man, but he will actually be expecting me to make friends with someone connected with document control and prepare him for recruitment."

Grant responded with one of his unit's canned responses, suggesting they had little or no confidence in any of Clyde's ideas. "You should do that, Danny."

I suspected Clyde would be contacting me soon, and I thought an early test and enthusiastic report on his field man techniques might produce more confidence in me and my plan for going to the States and distract him from putting his kidnapping plans into action in Germany. I decided to run the test that next week.

I arranged a day of liaison with VII Corps units in Stuttgart concerning my company's war plan. I returned to their local headquarters to visit a G-3 major who had promised me a copy of his draft war plan. When I discovered at the front desk that the Stuttgart detachment's access roster had been updated and my name had been inadvertently left off, I requested an escort.

I was met by SFC Wayne, who escorted me to his office upstairs, then checked to see if the major had returned from a staff meeting. The staff meeting was still going, so SFC Wayne offered me a seat next to his desk. As soon as I learned he was the document custodian for his unit, I engaged him in conversation, thinking up a story as I spoke.

"Sergeant Wayne, if you have the time, you could do me a great service. I'm the operations sergeant at B Company, 527th MI Bn. Strategic CI used to be responsible for all documents security inspections. Now that your tactical CI has that responsibility, they often request assistance and suggestions from my headquarters.

"I'm going to put together a training team to provide training in the annual inspection of the handling and storage of classified documents. I believe in teaching to weakness and not wasting people's time on things that aren't problems.

"Could I make an appointment with you to discuss any issues, get your suggestions, and address some techniques you've developed to avoid problems in running a classified document section like this one?"

"My only problem is keeping people on the job. You see, I'm having to run the shop myself today. Both clerks are out with female problems. One is pregnant; the other is having cramps. I tried to talk some sense into the one clerk. She's single. I told her she was going to get into trouble, but she wouldn't listen. I finally got her to talk to someone about whether she should have this baby. She's there now. I still don't know what her decision will be.

"Other than being behind on paperwork and filing, I don't have any real problems, but I certainly did at first. Officers were taking documents to their office and keeping them as long as they wanted. They used them to create updates and other documents. You know, cut and paste. Some documents started coming up missing.

"I told my boss, the colonel whose holding the staff meeting, I needed the authority to take complete control of all documents and have them returned before close of business every day. I got a lot of static from the other sections, especially the officers, but my boss backed me up. Now I have complete control of all documents except NATO documents. I helped the NATO document custodian get the same kind of control.

"My boss has been selected for his first star, and he's taking me with him to his next assignment. I don't take anything off anybody. I handle his schedule, and no one sees him without going through me. He should be out of the staff meeting in a few minutes. Damn! They're getting out now. I'll have to get his coffee ready. I'll be right back."

SFC Wayne carried a cup of coffee into the colonel's office. When he came out, the colonel met him in front of his desk. I was standing, so the sergeant introduced me to his colonel and told him my business. The colonel shook my hand and informed me the G-3 major had left for the day. A few minutes later, the colonel left for the day.

SFC Wayne invited me to join him for lunch. I accepted on condition that I pay. We walked to the local fast food restaurant on post. During the walk and about a two hour lunch, he continued his description of his job, explaining some procedures he'd adopted and some difficulties he'd eliminated. Eventually he focused on the control he'd assumed.

"The key is respect, not just in the office, but in my social life too. I socialize with the senior officers. I play golf with them, and I'm invited to their poker games. And I mean nothing but high-stakes poker games. Everyone knows I play to win. I've taken a lot of their money and they respect me for it.

"I was raised in a family with older brothers. Until I was in high school, they beat me up regularly. They got mad about almost anything, and they took it out on me. One day, I got tired of it and bought myself a gun.

SANDOR

"The next time one of my brothers decided he was going to beat the crap out of me, I pulled that gun and said, 'You've beat me for the last time. I'll shoot the next one who tries.' I carried that gun all through high school. My brothers never bothered me again. They had respect for me."

"I can see why they would. I used to know a few people in the infantry who were into high-stakes poker. In fact, I have a friend right now who still is. I don't gamble myself, but I know my friend is always looking for a challenging game of poker. Do you guys ever accept new players?"

"As long as he knows he has to bring a lot of money. These guys are mostly senior officers."

"Actually, he wouldn't play in any other game. If I gave him your name and number could he call you sometime to find out when and where the next game will be?"

"Sure. Have him call me at my office."

He invited me to visit him again. He said he would walk me through his classified document control operation. We parted company, and I drove to my office, trying to relate these last few hours to the OPLAN. I knew Clyde's technique for identifying, befriending, and preparing document custodians for eventual recruitment was expected to require several encounters. I thought through the process.

Clyde would first identify soldiers with access to critical documents, preferably a soldier in a vulnerable stage of his career, in a foreign country without his spouse, needing a place for his family to live, overdue for a promotion, financially strapped, underutilized in his military job, or otherwise exploitable.

Clyde knows how to introduce fears and frustrations and create an attitude of resentment, even rebellion, against authority. His next stage would involve tempting him with the good life and taking advantage of the inherent need of a good soldier to have his actions count for him.

What about a senior document custodian with an attitude similar to his own, an arrogant thirst for power and respect, or fear, as Clyde would put it? Could Clyde take advantage of a soldier's addiction to poker and use some of his sleight of hand with cards to put someone like that in debt to him?

I remembered Clyde telling me about a female soldier he was attempting to persuade to do some work for him. He had instructed a friend to ply her with sex. Then, when his friend failed to follow through, he instructed his stepdaughter, Hanelore, to date his friend to find out if he was straight.

Clyde also showed me telephone numbers in his electronic diary of madams whose services he had used to guarantee cooperation from other friends. He had offered me these same services, saying we should get together sometime just to have some fun instead of talking operation all the time.

I sidestepped his offer, saying I had to avoid any questionable activity in order to protect my status as a counterintelligence agent. He never stopped trying.

Clyde had already employed every trick he knew to prepare and recruit agents. The one trick he said he had for at least one field man was one of those he had kept from the Hungarians.

To help a field man gain more legitimate access to soldiers, he planned for him to marry a female soldier. Once the field man obtained a military ID card, with access to all military facilities, Clyde intended to have the military wife meet with a fatal accident. One thing I knew for sure, I did not intend to report any personal details about the SFC on whom I had tested his OPLAN techniques.

I told Grant a little about him and commented that the techniques worked so well, they scared me. Grant was unimpressed and showed no interest in details, so I told him I had no intention of giving Clyde any details about the SFC.

When I reported to Clyde that I had tested the techniques, he was already excited about something else. He quickly acknowledged my comment with, "They're great, aren't they! They work every time." Then he told me his latest news.

"I talked to Mike, Danny. He says the OPLAN is getting a favorable reception. They want me to pay them a visit to hash out the details."

"Are you going?"

"Yes, but not right away. The people who need to make the decisions are off on another assignment. The tentative date is 17 July. This is normal, asking me to come to Hungary. They consider it a gesture of good faith on my part. They expect it to make sure nothing is wrong."

"How long will you be there?"

"Usually a week. They treat me like a king, Danny. I'll stay in a private villa. I can go anywhere I want, have anything I want, and pay for nothing. I get a driver, and someone will go along with me to take care of everything. All I have to do is be available for any meetings they have."

"That's good. Clyde, I've been asked to pick a time to return to the States for some training for that IMF treaty. Have you been reading in the German paper or *Stars and Stripes* about the inspection teams the Russians have been sending?"

"Just a little."

"There has been considerable news coverage because of demonstrations outside several of the medium-range missile storage
facilities throughout Germany. Clyde, I would like to make a
request of you. I appreciate the fact that you trust me to handle
identifying the agents who are supporting that CODEWORD
medical program."

"I do, Danny!"

"And I'm going to do that, but I'd like you to be there when I
identify the guy with the formula so we can get the formula right
away. You could stay in a hotel near mine and have the arrangements made for taking the guy for a boat ride."

"You identify him, and we can pick him up later."

"I know we can, but I can't imagine another opportunity as
good as this one to get everything taken care of with the least
suspicion. Some of the agents involved with the IMF treaty will
be the same ones working with the CODEWORD program. That
will cover my actions completely, and a kidnapping of this guy by
terrorists would be more likely identified with IMF."

"That may be true. If you want me to be there, I'll be there."
His gesture seemed genuine, so I answered quickly, "Great. When
would be the best time for you?" He continued to surprise me
when he said, "You know my schedule. I have at least a couple of
months before I go to Budapest. You pick the time."

13

<u>ARREST</u>

At my next debriefing I reported, "Roland, Clyde has agreed to go to the States with me."

"What? No! We're not ready for that, Danny!" He had jumped out of his chair.

"Oh, he told me to pick the time. So not until you guys are ready."

"We can't do that, Danny."

"I thought you told me to see if he would go for that."

"Well, the Justice department won't go for it. They're afraid if we trick him into going to the States, the defense can claim we were circumventing the extradition laws because there is no extradition agreement between the United States and Germany for espionage."

"Yes, I know. So what's the plan?"

"Right now, there isn't one. We're still negotiating. The Justice Department may not want to prosecute him at all."

"How is that possible, Roland?"

"It has to do with those CODEWORD documents. The Army has refused to allow them to be used in court. The Justice Department says either they use all the documents or they don't prosecute."

"What are your alternatives?"

Grant took over and explained. "We're considering other possibilities, Danny. We're thinking about a military court-martial. We could have the Army reactivate him, then arrest him. We're even considering having the Germans arrest him and try him, since he's here under their work agreement. In the meantime, we proceed with this operation. You'll have to stall him on going to the States."

"Okay. Are you going to let him go to Hungary?"

"We haven't decided yet, Danny"

While the future of the operation was obviously uncertain, Clyde was preparing to go into high gear. The Kercsiks had told him they were still negotiating with some pharmaceutical firm, but Clyde's new controller, Mike, was ready for Clyde and me to deliver some specific classified material.

Mike had given Clyde two lists of critical documents the Hungarians wanted. One list was intended for me and the other for Clyde. His list included joint chief of staff documents, indicating to me that the Hungarians had reason to believe he would have access even to that level. Some of the documents were unknown to him or me. Since he had made copies of the lists, he gave both originals to me.

Another document, which the Hungarians had already asked him for, wasn't on either list. He described it only as an important document from down south. He had expected to get it from Szabo, who would get it from the Italian agents whom Clyde intended to steal from the Hungarians. However, Clyde hadn't heard from Szabo in some time, and he had become frustrated.

"Szabo has dropped off the face of the earth, Danny. I've tried to locate him. You know that Gasthaus on the road as you go out past Rose Barracks, next to the Nahe River? Szabo receives his mail there. They haven't seen him. His wife hasn't heard from him either. He sends her a check every month for her stay at a mental hospital. I have no idea where he is.

"If Szabo doesn't get it from the Italians, I'm sure I can get it from the sergeant major. They keep pushing me to press the sergeant major for that document, but I'm not going to do that. It's just a matter of time. He's on an FTX right now. He said he would think about it and get back to me when the exercise is over."

This was the first I'd heard of his attempted recruitment of the sergeant major. I had to bite my tongue to keep from blurting out how much it sounded like he was dealing with a controlled source. I asked, "Are you talking about the 8ID, G-3 sergeant major?"

Without hesitation, he answered, "Yeah."

With skepticism, I inquired, "What makes you think he is going to get this document for you?"

"The twenty thousand Marks I've promised him."

"Has he given you documents before?"

"We've done other things together. Even if he doesn't give me this document, there's a mutual trust there. I have plenty of stuff on him."

"Is he the guy you got those tools for to help him pass his inspection?"

"Right."

"I don't think I've met him, Clyde. What's his name?"

"Sergeant Major Rogers."

"I haven't met him."

"We've had some long talks, Danny. He's planning to retire soon. He's going to start a business in Germany when he gets out. We talked about how much he expects to make, including what he'll get from retirement. I told him what he could make in this business. With his access, he could clean up."

I listened intently as Clyde explained why he thought any sergeant major could justify demanding copies of all the classified documents in his unit. He based that assumption entirely on the fear he had garnered in less powerful positions. He said he had also described his procedures to SGM Rogers for using digital equipment to copy every document in his possession in one sitting. As I listened, doubts flooded my mind. On my trip home, I pondered my suspicions of SGM Roger.

His statement that he'll think about it and get back to Clyde is the exact instruction a person gets when he reports to a CI office that he's been asked to supply classified documents. Even if he isn't controlled by the same people controlling me, he might be working with some local CI office who doesn't know about this operation. That could be an even more dangerous situation.

Most likely, since USAI starts at the top in an investigation, they interviewed the G-3 sergeant major long before Clyde pitched espionage to him. Even if Clyde has dirt on him, the sergeant major would have guessed why USAI is investigating Clyde and would have had no choice but to cooperate with them.

Maybe USAIs vagueness about the direction of this operation means they're thinking of phasing me out in favor of someone they can control better. They haven't been too happy with me, especially my refusal to believe the Hungarians are just stringing Clyde along about his OPLAN.

As objectively as possible, I reported to Grant exactly what Clyde had told me about SGM Rogers. Roland was surprised that Clyde had told me the sergeant major's name. As I was relaying Clyde's comments about the SGM, Roland must have detected some suspicion in my voice and asked, "Danny, what do you think about the sergeant major?"

Damn, Roland! That question is a dead giveaway, but I can't tell you my doubts and take the chance you might worry that I would say anything to Clyde to make him suspicious of SGM Rogers.

"Well, Roland, there are sergeants major and there are sergeants major."

"Yeah, that's true, Danny. Sergeant Major Rogers is under our control." He hesitated a moment, and I nodded and smiled. Nothing more needed to be said, so he changed the subject.

"Let me ask you something, Danny. Do you think Clyde is a homosexual?"

"He's never indicated it to me, Roland. Why do you ask?"

"It was just something Sergeant Major Rogers said about Clyde being so friendly. Do you think he could be?"

"If you're asking if he would engage in homosexuality to further his business, I would no longer put anything past him."

"He's Machiavellian?"

"Absolutely."

Grant instructed me to continue meeting with Clyde, giving me no indication what direction the operation, now in the thirteenth month since I started, would take. I avoided any further discussion with Clyde about a trip to the States. He didn't seem to mind, because he was preoccupied with his trip to Hungary. He was still meeting with officials, and he was still optimistic, even though he knew they were still investigating him.

He had received a telephone warning from Imre before their last meeting. Imre said that he had been ordered to meet Clyde at a location which had always been reserved for Alexander. Imre suspected they would both be under surveillance by the Hungarian authorities. Clyde told Imre to meet him but to conduct himself as if he didn't know Clyde's true identity.

After Clyde had followed Imre to a restaurant in the prescribed manner, Imre handed him a message. Clyde pretended to be upset with the message and told Imre to get in touch with his superiors to let them know he was upset, then meet him again in two hours with a concession.

Clyde believed the Hungarians were satisfied with both of their performances. He was sure they were merely trying to convince themselves they should continue working with him because they wanted his OPLAN. A week or so later, Clyde asked me to meet him on Saturday at the Mainz Holiday Inn.

He was preparing to go to Hungary, and he used me as a sounding board for his ideas on selling the OPLAN to the officials in a position to make the decision and authorize the money. He expected them to provide him operating money to validate the OPLAN. He assumed his biggest obstacle would be that one million Marks they would have to pay for a document custodian's one-time delivery of his entire classified holdings.

He also expected some research by the Hungarians into his requirements for digital technology. He believed their technicians would design his special box for storing the digital video camera, which would have to look like a standard mail package. He didn't think I quite understood how that box was supposed to work, but I'd already thought of a way to show him I did.

At our next meeting, I showed him a six-inch by six-inch cardboard box about twelve inches long, wrapped and addressed like a mail package. I demonstrated how to slide the box apart just enough to reveal a few switches and the lens of a video camera mounted inside the box. The box was designed to rest on two upright, three-ring notebooks when opened and take pictures of documents placed on the desk between the notebooks.

In the event of an unscheduled interruption, the camera could be turned off and the box slid back together quickly. Cord glued around the box hid the seams formed when the parts of the box slid together, giving the appearance of an unopened mail package.

Clyde was speechless at first, opening and closing the box over and over. Then he said, "This is amazing, Danny. I'm taking this to Hungary with me."

"Great. I'm sure they will realize it has to be made of something much stronger, depending on the weight of the camera."

"This is great. I wasn't sure you understood."

"I've been paying attention."

Clyde left for Hungary in the middle of July as planned, and he was gone a full week. He called me immediately after returning from Budapest. He arranged to meet me in Heidelberg. He seemed a bit aloof. I imagined the worst, since the Hungarians had already warned him to be careful of his CI friend.

What if they persuaded him to make sure I'm not wired? I'd better leave the recorder in my car. I would almost welcome his asking me to prove I'm not carrying a recording device. I'll act indignant, but I'll insist on establishing my loyalty once and for all.

With the recorder in my briefcase in the car, parked on a street near the Bahnhof, I met Clyde at a Gasthaus a block away and greeted him with my usual "How are you, young man?"

He stood and said, "I'm doing great. How about you?"

I shook his hand and answered, "I'm fine. I'm just glad to see you're in one piece, considering where you've been."

He was pensive, and I was apprehensive, wondering if my earlier fears were about to be justified, so I said, "I have to admit, Clyde, I was worried about you."

"Everything went just great. I hope you're ready, Danny. We're both going to be very busy for the next few months." He ordered two beers. As we waited, he started reporting on his week in Budapest, as if nothing had changed between us.

"Mike met me at the border. He put me up in a nice villa, then he drove me to his house. He said he wanted me to know a little about him. He wanted to be up front with me and wanted me to trust him." Clyde suddenly noticed he was out of cigarettes and stood.

I realized our relationship had not changed, and my fears were needless. I decided it was very important to record Clyde's account of his visit to Hungary. I stood as well and said, "Damn, Clyde, for the last few minutes I've been trying to decide if I left my car lights on. I think I did. Why don't you get yourself some cigarettes and order me a schnitzel, and I'll run back and turn them off. I won't be long."

He didn't seem upset. I ran all the way to my car, stuffed the recorder and extra tapes in my coat, and ran back. Before entering the restaurant, I turned on the recorder. When I joined him at the table, I asked, "Did you order my schnitzel?" He nodded, and I asked, "So, Mike met you at the border and checked you into a villa, then he took you to his house?"

"Yeah. He said he wanted us to be able to trust each other. He wanted me to know where he lived, let me know he has a family just like I do. He said he wanted to be up front with me, and he wanted me to be comfortable with him. But he said, 'There will need to be a few changes.'"

Clyde laughed as he continued. "He says, 'I read your file. You've been paid upward of seven figures. We feel you could obey the rules a little better. You're never on time to meetings. Never! There are other things, but for that kind of money, you could make some changes.' He says, 'We've pulled a curtain over the past. We want to return to business as usual.

"'Eventually though, when we've worked together for a while, just for my own understanding, maybe you'll tell me what you did to get a career professional fired. No one knows how you did it. You took money from him like taking candy from a baby. Someday I'd like you to trust me enough to tell me how you did it.'"

"Was that when you invented an agent, Clyde?"

"Yeah, but he doesn't know that."

"You think you might tell him?"

"No, but I think we're going to get along just fine. He's right about me never being on time. I'll have to make some adjustments."

"What about the OPLAN, Clyde?"

"That's the best part. They paid me twenty-seven thousand Marks to start the plan. They want us to recruit three document custodians. They picked the ones they want. They said, 'No deadline.' They don't care if it takes a year for the first one. In fact, they still think that's better, even though I told them we could have all three in nine months."

"We, Clyde?"

"Absolutely. They said they understand completely why you are so important to the plan. They've authorized us to open a joint Swiss account. They will pay our monthly salaries into that account and whatever bonuses we make.

"Oh, and the general gave me this thousand Marks for you, just for that box you made. He said it would need a lot of work, but it showed you were industrious. He took the money from his pocket and said to make sure you get it as a bonus. They will have to do a lot of research into the availability of digital technology in video cameras, but they like the idea."

"Damn. Sounds good to me, Clyde. When we show them the plan works, are they going to implement it full scale?"

"They'll have to, Danny. It's the compartmentalization thing. They said three is the maximum number of recruits we will be allowed to handle.

"Watch this: Mike said, 'I predict this will be the best thing that's ever happened to our intelligence program. One day, little children will be reading about us in school.'"

"Really? Does everyone else understand it as well as Mike does?"

ARREST

"Well, they've had to make some changes because of the way their system works. For one thing, they aren't ready to invest in the video stores yet, for building the database, but they like the idea of making one big payment into a Swiss account for a custodian's entire classified holdings, then waiting until he moves to a better assignment.

"Another thing they want to change is communication. They gave me a new communication procedure. I'm just supposed to test it before they implement it. It's a burst-transmission device. When we go to my car, I'll show it to you.

"It has a QWERTY keyboard and a cradle for a normal pay phone receiver. It will encode all messages typed into it, even complete documents, then transmit it telephonically in a split-second. It can also be used to set up meeting times and locations. I was directed to test the effectiveness of the technology by sending short messages from various locations in Europe. I'll keep it in one of my suitcases in the trunk of my car. I'll show you how to work it."

"Clyde, I appreciate that the Hungarians believe I'm important to the plan—"

"I told them they had no choice."

"I appreciate that, too. And I appreciate your policy to never reveal the identity of any of your associates unless they agree, but I have a special request of you. I think it would be best to not reveal my identity to anyone who doesn't already know about me."

"Always, Danny"

"Oh, I know that, but I think I might be in a position to help in another way. One can never tell when one of your associates might come under investigation by CI. If I knew the names of

327

all of your associates, I could keep my ears open and start monitoring message traffic for clues to any such investigations. If you agree to that, we should sit down sometime and make a list of them and where they work."

"I'll do that, Danny"

We returned to the Bahnhof, where Clyde had his car, and Clyde showed me how to operate his new burst-transmission device. I kidded him about accepting one of their gadgets. He said he would have to keep this one because they plan to use it worldwide. He considered it an acceptable risk since they trusted him enough to test it for them, and they plan to integrate it into the OPLAN.

A short time after my debriefing of this conversation, Grant notified me that I would be meeting with German investigators who wanted to interview me before deciding whether to prosecute Clyde in German court. In the early evening, Grant left me in a hotel room in downtown Stuttgart with Inspector Mueller from Bundes Kriminal Amt (BKA), the German equivalent of the FBI. He was accompanied by a translator/stenographer.

Grant had already typed, and I had executed, a four-page statement summarizing my past fifteen months with Clyde Lee Conrad. Mueller had a copy of my sworn statement when he interviewed me for approximately five hours. He explained that German law would not permit recordings as evidence, or allow the BKA to rely on them or on any U.S. investigation. The BKA would have to launch their own investigation of Clyde.

The purpose of this interview was to clarify my sworn statement, which would be admissible in court. If they decided to prosecute Clyde, they would take a full deposition from me at a later date, and I would be required to provide only what I could remember. I would not be allowed to hear the recordings.

Following this interview, Roland explained that the Germans were so impressed with the information I provided them that evening, they would be more than happy to take the case. But they wanted to know why the United States would not prosecute Clyde themselves. Roland wasn't at all certain the Germans believed the answer USAI gave them, but he didn't clarify that for me. He also didn't tell me when the Germans would arrest Clyde or whether I would meet with him again.

I believed Clyde's time was very short. The atmosphere at my last few meetings with Grant and Roland had been electrified. I could see his and Grant's fatigue giving way to excitement and a sense of accomplishment, but I knew they would not include me if they were planning any celebration of their successful mission.

I don't think they knew how to include me without running the risk that I would learn details that I hadn't learned from Clyde, details that might corrupt my testimony at his trial. However, in his enthusiasm Roland confided in me.

"Danny, you know you're going to be a celebrity. Reporters will be knocking down your door. That will virtually eliminate you from use in counterintelligence operations in the future."

I was disappointed that Roland was hanging onto the philosophy that the only effective counterespionage investigators are the invisible ones, but I assumed he was right about the reporters.

He assured me that he thought I'd done a good job, then he reinforced that vote of confidence with an explanation of his selection as European supervisor of the operation.

"Danny, after my first meeting with you, I was asked if I had persuaded you that most of what Clyde was telling you was untrue. They asked if you were going to start doing things the way they wanted. I told them I thought you were doing the best job they could possibly expect. They said, 'In that case, we don't need you,' and they sent me back to my unit. I thought that was the end of it, but they called me back again."

I told him how much I appreciated his support. His demeanor suggested that he felt vindicated for his confidence in me. At another meeting, Grant hinted that the operation was close to the end and shared his own insight with me.

"You'd better start thinking about where you want to go from here. You can choose just about any assignment you want after this. You could go to the Farm."

"I'm sure you know I would rather serve in an operational capacity than any other, but if attending special operational classes at the Farm is a prerequisite, I would certainly be willing to do that."

"I mean as an instructor Danny. The operational team has received awards, and a Legion of Merit has been delivered for you, but the brigade commander is keeping it in his desk until after Clyde's conviction. INSCOM believes that any benefit to you, as a result of the investigation, could be used by Clyde's defense to discredit your testimony at his trial."

I was glad to stay in the background, because, although I was proud of our mission accomplishment, I wasn't anxious to celebrate the misery about to befall Clyde and his family. I also hoped I would have at least one more meeting with Clyde before the conclusion of the operation in order to get him to give me his package for Jeurgen and identify all his associates.

I knew the vague clues he had given me to identities of some of his associates would require some serious investigative work. However, I began to doubt the likelihood of another meeting with Clyde, when 1SG Frey walked into my office one morning with a message.

"Danny, I received a message instructing me to pick one agent to conduct a special investigation for several weeks. Read it and tell me what you think."

I read the message and knew immediately that USAI was preparing to launch a full-scale, overt investigation into possible associates of Clyde Conrad the moment he was arrested. Although the message didn't mention Clyde or an arrest, it called for all selected agents to meet in Wiesbaden. I knew that was the headquarters for the operation, but I responded carefully.

"Charlie, I'd love to do it myself, but I'm in a concentrated phase with that project I told you about. I know whom I would choose, though."

"Whom would you choose?"

"I'd choose you. The kind of investigation they're talking about here requires your kind of common sense. I know you haven't had a lot of investigative experience, but you and I are going to trade places soon, and you could use the experience before you take over as operations sergeant."

"That's funny you should say that, Danny. Company A was tasked to send someone too. 1SG Fin is sending himself."

"That's what I would do if I were you. I can handle the 1SG job while you're gone.

"Thanks, Danny. I might just do that."

The next evening he caught me alone in my office. Without

smiling he growled, "Danny, you lying SOB! You really had me believing every word you told me."

Realizing he must have attended the meeting, I leaned back with a smile and answered, "So you're doing the investigation yourself. That's good."

"Danny, you must know a lot about all that stuff you were telling me about SAPs to make it so convincing."

"I know everything about that stuff, and for all I knew, you might have known it too. The trick to being convincing is to stay as close to the truth as possible. I think you'll enjoy yourself, Charlie. Did anyone say when you'll start?"

"No. They'll let us know. I have to tell you one thing, Danny. As soon as I read the case file, I said to myself, *They don't understand Danny Williams.* They used the wrong approach with you."

"You mean treating me like Joe Shit the Rag Man? Yeah, I know, but the mission was accomplished. They offered me a job anywhere I want to go, even teaching at the Farm."

"Believe me, Danny. You don't want to be anywhere near any of those guys."

"Oh, I know that's true of some, but surely not all of them."

"I'm not so sure, Danny. They were all sitting around talking about how they could have done the whole thing without you. When the colonel got up to leave, he said, 'I think Danny Williams made this case.' When he was gone, I didn't hear anyone agree with him."

"You might be right, Charlie. I probably should forget all about any special assignment, if they even intend to offer me one. It's just hard to believe, after all the information I got for them, they still can't appreciate the methods I used."

ARREST

I knew the end was at hand when I met again with Inspector Mueller and his partner, Inspector Ripper. They wanted my input before they arrested Clyde. Ripper asked my opinion. "Can we knock on his door?"

"Only if you want to lose everything he has in his electronic diary. There's a button on the back which will clear the whole thing. He keeps it near him at all times. It will be on a night-stand right by his head. He also has two computers and numerous disks in the house, which are probably loaded with information you can use. If you give him a warning, he'll try to destroy everything."

"Does he have any guns?"

"I don't know, but I don't think he plans to shoot anyone. He says he plans to make you shoot him so he can't be questioned, but I know he won't endanger his family."

"Thanks, Danny. That's the kind of information we need."

Ripper later described the arrest, which occurred around 2:30 AM, 23 August 1989.

After picking the lock on his front door, Ripper quietly led several officers through the house to Clyde and Gitta's bedroom. Ripper placed his nine-millimeter pistol next to Clyde's head as the light was turned on and woke Clyde with his most colorful English command.

"Take your fingers out of your wife and put your hands where I can see them!"

Clyde responded nonchalantly, "What's this all about?"

As he retrieved Clyde's electronic diary from his night-stand, Ripper answered, "I think you know exactly what this is all about, Mr. Conrad."

As Clyde was being taken into custody, computers were

confiscated, and officers searched his home and car for evidence, including his burst-transmitter. The house suddenly filled with screams. Startled policemen found Jeurgen running from room to room, screaming incoherently. His mother tried to comfort him as Clyde was led to a police car.

At this description of the arrest, I was saddened and angry. I blamed Clyde for the emotional stress he had caused Jeurgen for so many years.

Ripper said the Kercsiks, who were arrested by the Swedes around the same time as Clyde, also became angry and very cooperative when they learned of Jeurgen's reaction and Clyde's lifetime indoctrination of his son.

Shirley learned of Clyde's arrest as she listened to the Armed Forces Network during her fifty mile trip home from Heilbronn after school the next day. She knew immediately what I'd been doing for the past fifteen months.

Zolton Szabo heard the same broadcast on his way to Bad Kreuznach to visit Clyde. He immediately drove to Hungary and stayed for a short time before returning to Austria, where he was arrested by the Austrians.

14

TRIAL

Clyde sat in prison in Koblenz while the Germans built a case against him for espionage. I had a couple of meetings with Grant and Roland to complete last minute administrative requirements. Roland presented me with two bottles of wine from Bad Kreuznach, and Grant and Lieutenant Colonel Storm, director of the operation for FCA, invited Shirley and me out to dinner. They presented Shirley a bouquet of roses and thanked her for her support and patience.

After LTC Storm had left, Grant expressed his own gratitude for Shirley's endurance of hundreds of late hours alone without knowing what I was doing. He assured her, "He was spending those hours on one of the most significant operations in U.S. Army intelligence history."

Shirley had no comment about Grant's apparent need to defend me. What she did say surprised both of us. "I have one question: was Danny right?"

Grant was hesitant when he asked in return, "What do you mean?"

"Was he right in his assessment of the investigation?"

With slight uneasiness and obviously hoping to end that discussion, Grant answered, "Most of the time." He glanced at me, and I kept quiet, happy to see that Shirley was satisfied with his reply, or at least content that she had gotten that off her chest. I feared Grant might get the wrong message, and I mentioned it to Shirley later.

"Honey, I appreciate your loyalty. I'm even glad to see you understood all those general complaints I shared with you about the continual battle I was fighting with superiors who insisted that my evaluation of the situation was all wrong and who did everything in their power to make our investigations more difficult. The only problem is that Grant is going to wonder if I told you anything about this particular operation."

Her sarcasm was so obvious I had to laugh. All she said was, "Sorry." I laughed even harder when she gave me her impression of Grant's assurance that I had spent those late hours in the service of my country. She asked me, "If I don't already trust my husband, why would I believe a bunch of guys telling me what you were doing all those late hours and weekends?"

I had no further contact with FCA for several weeks. News accounts of Clyde's arrest did not identify me by name. However, Roland's prediction about reporters came true fairly quickly. I received a telephone call one evening at my home in Steinenbronn.

TRIAL

A *New York Times* reporter called to tell me he was writing a story on the Clyde Lee Conrad arrest. He asked if I objected to his using my name. When I tried to refer him to the U.S. Army public affairs office, he said, "I was given your name by U.S. Army counterintelligence. I don't need your permission to use your name, but I wanted to give you an opportunity to express your preference."

I stated that I preferred he didn't because the Germans, who were prosecuting the case, had not released my name. He was surprised. He said, "I appreciate your position. I will decide later whether or not to include your name in my story."

Because of his tone, I was not surprised later when the *New York Times* story did not include my name, but I was grateful. When I called Roland the morning after the reporter's call and repeated our conversation, Roland's only comment was, "You did good, Danny."

Later, USAI arranged for me to meet with the German investigators for my deposition. For nearly eighty hours, I provided a complete account of more than forty-five meetings I'd had with Clyde, involving at least five hundred hours of conversation. I developed a genuine friendship with Inspectors Mueller and Rippar, the two lead investigators.

They provided lodging and took me to lunch and dinner every day for two weeks. Mueller, along with a translator and stenographer, questioned me most of the time, while Rippar usually was busy investigating.

I reported my conversations with Clyde the way I had with USAI, but I couldn't always be certain they had translated everything the way I said it. I would explain that Clyde was purposely ambiguous, but his meaning was clear to me from the context of our conversations.

DAMIAN and MONGOOSE

They kept wanting to simplify by quoting Clyde, when he hadn't actually used the words they wanted to attribute to him. I insisted on quoting exactly what Clyde said, when I could, then explaining how I knew what he meant. It took them a while to understand that.

For the first few days, I detected some reservation in their questioning. I discovered they were having difficulty understanding U.S. military concepts and procedures, especially the security practices that Clyde had exploited to gain access to so many classified documents. They were sure their German military security system wouldn't have allowed such a thing.

Finally, Mueller explained the other reason for their reservation. They were under the impression I'd been directed not to tell them everything. I explained that I'd been told by USAI to tell them everything I knew about Clyde and any documents given to Clyde. They thanked me and informed me that they would try not to reveal anything they were learning from their own investigation that might corrupt my testimony. In their enthusiasm, they managed to break that rule a few times.

Mueller had asked me to provide chronologically all the information I had learned from Clyde. But often at the beginning of the day or when he had just returned from a special meeting, he would ask me to address specific information about Clyde and his activity. Several times after being called away from the deposition, Mueller would return and excitedly report information that had been found in Clyde's computers or gained from other sources, which verified what I had been giving them.

Mueller and Rippar both seemed especially pleased each time my information could be confirmed. Mueller, whose English was very good, finally told me one reason for their desire to inform me of those verifications.

"Danny, after we had gone to Sweden to get the transcripts from the Kercsiks' trial, a meeting was held here at the headquarters. Because we were waiting for a translation of the transcripts, we were a little late getting to the meeting.

"Experts from all our counterespionage branches, Russian, Hungarian, Czech, East German, everybody, attended the meeting. Your people were there too. Everyone had read the information you and your people provided.

"When we arrived, all the experts were saying this was all impossible. None of the intelligence services worked like this. No one could make the kind of money you said Clyde made, and no one would be allowed to do the things you said he did. Some people even said, 'The Americans must really hate this guy to make up all these lies about him.'

"We just sat there quietly. I really felt sorry for our director. Your guys didn't say a word. When everyone finished, our director's head was hanging, but he asked us if we had anything to add. I stood up and read the transcripts.

"Danny, you could have heard a pin drop. The Kercsiks verified everything you've been telling us. When I finished, our director was smiling, and everyone was patting him on the back.

By the way, I have a message for you. The Swedish inspector we were supposed to meet had to leave on another investigation, so he left the transcript in the safe. When it was handed to us, the inspector had left a note on top. It said, 'Imre Kercsik said to tell Danny, congratulations.'"

"I appreciate you telling me all this. Is this why you seem so happy to get verification from other sources?"

"It helps, Danny."

"Yes. I'm sure it does. I'm glad you're getting it."

USAIs computer expert was busy in a room down the hall retrieving all the pertinent data he could from Clyde's computers and disks. He completed his work before I finished mine, and he was invited to join us for dinner that evening.

I had met the expert once when Grant asked me to loan him my computer for a short time during the investigation, but I didn't really know him. After we had ordered our meals, he looked me straight in the eyes and asked me a question that unfortunately didn't surprise me.

"Danny, be truthful. If you had it all to do over again, wouldn't you have done it different?"

"Well there is always room for improvement, especially with hindsight. But no, I don't think I could have done it any differently. I think Clyde determined the direction I had to take."

"Well, I'll tell you this, Danny. If I'd been in charge of this operation, I'd have closed down your part long ago."

"I see. And why is that?"

"You were completely out of control, Danny."

"Oh, I see."

Mueller and Rippar looked at each other without comment. They spoke fairly good English, but I couldn't tell if either of them understood the exchange they had just heard. I decided to change the subject, but they seemed a little cold toward the computer expert the rest of the evening.

The next evening, they invited me to one of their favorite

restaurants. As soon as the meals were ordered, Mueller caught Rippar's attention with a glance, and Rippar nodded as if they had reached some silent agreement. Mueller asked me, "Danny, we were a little confused about that conversation you had with the computer guy last night. Was he saying you didn't do a good job?"

"Sort of."

"Danny, we talked this over after we left you last night. We have never seen it done better by anyone. What more could he possibly have expected from you?"

"Well, it wasn't as much the information I got as the way I got it. It's true my supervisors didn't believe most of what Clyde was telling me. You can understand that. So they wanted to direct me, tell me what to ask, and tell me how to act, to force Clyde into the mold they believed he should fit.

"But they especially didn't like the fact that I'm a talker. They made it clear the Justice Department expected Clyde to incriminate himself on tape and provide them a smoking gun. So they wanted me to shut up and let Clyde do all the talking. I tried to convince them Clyde knew me well and would expect me to be the same talker I always was. I believed if I wasn't, he'd know he had good reason to suspect I'd been sent by CI.

"I also told them I knew Clyde, and he would only tell me as much as he thought he could get by with, unless I interrupted him and challenged him or even changed the subject when one of my questions worried him.

"I sometimes even accused him of lying to me so he would have to prove some of the things he was saying, but they still were never impressed with my methods, possibly because they didn't believe him in the first place."

Mueller nodded and Rippar voiced his agreement. "We get the same thing in our investigations. You're right about knowing Clyde, Danny. That electronic diary of his was right by his head, next to his bed." Rippar followed with a complete description of the arrest, emphasizing Clyde's arrogant, cocky attitude during the entire episode.

Mueller commented that he had recently let Clyde's arrogance get to him. "He's been arrogant every time we've seen him. Anytime his family wants to visit him in the Koblenz prison, they have to arrange it with us. We accompany them and stand where we can watch them and hear everything they say.

"For weeks now he's been coming in all smiles and cocky. He hasn't cooperated with the federal prosecutor's office at all. We don't want him to cooperate. We don't want to see him get a lighter sentence.

"The other day, I just couldn't take any more of it. I said, 'If you're trying to protect your friend, Danny, you may think he's your friend, he is your friend, but he's not on your side.' All of a sudden his head went down and he slumped over. He hasn't smiled once since that day."

My vision of that scene saddened me, and I think Mueller and Rippar knew it. Mueller actually apologized for letting Clyde's arrogance get to him.

They continued to reveal things now and then, sometimes accidently or by the questions they asked, but there were some things they thought they should tell me. For one, they wanted me to understand the differences between the United States and German justice systems. A few in particular were enlightening.

There was no such thing as a speedy trial. As long as the

prosecution continued their investigation, Clyde could be kept in prison. His court-appointed defense attorneys would not be given access to evidence until the investigation was completed. Also, once the case came to trial, the verdict would be determined by a panel of judges, not a jury. Important too were differences in the rules of evidence and conduct of the court, which Mueller explained.

"The judges will want to hear anything you can tell them about Clyde, even if you heard it from someone else or it was just a rumor and you don't know where you heard it. They will want to know anything he said and what you thought it meant.

They will ask your opinion, Danny. The attorneys will ask very few questions, and they won't be able to stand in your face and badger you. Germany doesn't have an adversarial court system. The head judge will ask most of the questions.

"The way they decide if a person is guilty, Danny— The judges will study the testimony and evidence presented. Then the head judge will ask the other judges, 'Does he seem guilty to you?' If they say, 'He seems guilty,' he's guilty."

I received a little information from other sources as well. During my second week, Mueller introduced me to two visiting Swedish investigators who had asked to interview me. They thanked me for my services and told me a few of the details of their case against the Kercsiks.

In the Kercsiks' homes they found spying paraphernalia, notes, accounts of the money they had earned, and records chronicling all their activities with the Hungarians and Clyde. The Swedish prosecutor agreed not to prosecute other members of the Kercsiks' families in exchange for the brothers' complete cooperation.

Alexander said he had been recruited by the Hungarians in 1967, and Imre said he had been recruited in 1980.

Although the Swedish prosecutor had asked for twelve months in prison for both Kercsiks, the judge gave them eighteen months. The Swedish inspectors also asked me if I had received Imre's message of congratulations.

They informed me that Imre had been allowed to join his wife at the hospital when she gave birth to their new child. They were generally convinced that the Kercsiks were not the ruthless characters that Clyde thought they were. They believed the Kercsiks had conned Clyde as much as he had conned them. I couldn't help wondering if they knew Imre's definition of cooperation in the event of an arrest.

Mueller had told me the Kercsiks were reluctant to provide the Germans any information about Clyde until they told them what I had learned about Clyde's indoctrination of Jeurgen. They were indignant, as I was, at the pressure Clyde had put on Jeurgen all his life.

Mueller told me later that the Swedes had also confirmed through the Kercsiks that Szabo had recruited Clyde in 1974 and that Clyde had been paid at least one million two hundred thousand dollars by the Hungarians, one hundred thousand dollars by the Czechoslovakians, and more than one hundred thousand dollars by the Americans.

The Germans had found several of Clyde's safety deposit box keys, but they hadn't located his money. They were getting no help from the Swiss banking officials, whom they invited to their headquarters and pointed out to me in their headquarters dining hall.

They were also having trouble getting the cooperation they would have liked from the Austrians and the Italians. They believed these agencies resented the U.S. Army's lack of coordination with them during the investigation. That resentment also seemed evident in the news reports of arrests these countries made.

On 29 September 1988, the Austrians gave Zolton Szabo a ten-month suspended sentence for gathering military intelligence for a foreign power. In December 1988, the Italians convicted former U.S. Sergeant Tommaso Martati of selling information about a U.S. Army facility in Vicenza, Italy, and sentenced him to twenty months of house arrest. The Italians made a particular point that the arrest was based on information from Szabo and had no connection to any U.S. investigation. The Germans continued their investigation of Clyde, and by August 1989, they had expanded his charge to treason, which carried a possible life sentence.

In the mean time, I received a visit at my home in Steinenbronn by an investigative reporter from *ABC News*. The reporter told me he had just received the transcripts from the Kercsiks' trial and had visited Clyde's family.

He also informed me that Clyde's stepdaughter, Hanelore, really hated me, quoting her as saying, "It's that scheisse religion of his." I told him I couldn't give him any information about the investigation or about Clyde, and he said he was on his way to Austria to interview Szabo.

Since it was a weekend, I decided to wait until Monday to inform Grant of the reporter's visit, but the next day the reporter called me to say he had already returned from Austria and wanted to know if I would agree to have my picture taken just standing outside by my car. I declined, and he said, "Then let me buy your dinner. I found out some things from Szabo that I believe would interest you." I agreed to meet him for dinner to hear what he had to say as long as he took no pictures and understood I couldn't tell him anything.

At dinner, the reporter explained that he had learned from the Austrians and from German investigators that the U.S. Army CI conducted an illegal investigation. I suggested he talk to the German prosecutor's office about that, because that wasn't their attitude.

I assumed he was referring to our use of a recording device during the investigation, but I didn't mention it, and he didn't elaborate. He attempted to elicit information from me concerning the extent of my involvement in Clyde's activities.

I suspected from his questions that he had concluded from information given to him by Clyde's family and Szabo that I had been working with Clyde in espionage, then decided to cooperate with CI when Clyde was arrested. I had already read newspaper articles suggesting the same thing. I made no attempt to negate his impression.

I was anxious for Grant and Roland to know the Austrian's attitude toward CI, though I doubted the reporter's account about the Germans. When I reported my two encounters with *ABC News* to CI, Roland informed me that I had disobeyed a direct order not to talk to reporters. That angered me, because I knew no such order had been given to me. I argued that, while I hadn't told the reporter anything, I thought I had learned something from him that USAI would want to know.

USAI stayed unhappy with me, but I didn't know how unhappy

until LTC Sharp, my new battalion commander, paid a visit to my B Company commander, who called me into his office. When I reported to my commander's office, my battalion commander put me at ease, then he explained to me his reason for being there.

"The CI branch you worked with on the Conrad case has brought charges against you before the brigade commander. He directed me to issue a letter of reprimand to be placed in your personnel file. It has to do with you talking to that reporter. I've refused to do that, Danny. I've told them as far as I'm concerned this is between you and them. I don't know what they plan to do, but I wanted to warn you."

"I certainly appreciate that, Colonel. I'll take care of that myself. Right now, I think I'll just wait and see what happens."

"That's what I recommend, Danny."

I heard nothing further concerning charges against me, but I received a subpoena to testify in Clyde's trial in January 1990. I met in Koblenz with Grant and an INSCOM attorney, who gave me instructions on how to conduct myself as a witness. As we sat in a restaurant, the attorney started his speech.

"Danny, you will have to be sure not to exaggerate or elaborate on anything. You can't say something in a way that makes him look bad if you don't know for sure it's true."

Grant didn't have to look at me to know how infuriated I was at having someone tell me how to be honest under oath. He interjected in a low voice. "Sir, I don't think you have to tell him that."

The attorney didn't like being interrupted and continued. "Well, I just want him to know he should only say what he knows to be a fact."

"Yes, I think he knows that, Sir." Grant turned to me. "Danny, you don't want to volunteer any information. The judge is not going to ask you to tell everything that happened during the whole fifteen months. He's just going to ask you specific questions about a few areas they need to clarify. And it's okay to say, 'I don't remember.' In fact, it would be better if you don't come across like you remember everything, because that looks like you have some kind of vendetta against Clyde."

Fortunately, I had a night in my hotel room to think over Grant's and the attorney's instructions before my testimony. Based on what I'd learned from Mueller and Rippar, I decided not to take any chances. Before falling asleep with Shirley beside me, I raced over in my mind everything I could remember from my first meeting with Clyde to my last.

Shirley and I entered the courtroom the next morning. She sat with the spectators, and I sat in a chair about six feet in front of the entry. I introduced myself to the female interpreter who sat directly behind me.

Our backs were to the closed entry door. We were facing the chief prosecutor, who sat behind a table fifteen feet in front of us on the opposite side of the courtroom. To my right about eight feet, four judges sat on a raised platform behind a long table extending almost completely across the room. In front of the judges stood a long row of three-ring binders.

About four feet to my left and on my level, Clyde, with an attorney on each side of him, sat behind another long table facing the judges. Behind Clyde and his attorneys were four or five rows of spectators, including Shirley. Head Judge Ferdinand Schuth asked me to introduce myself, then asked me his first question, which the lady behind me translated into English.

TRIAL

"Mr. Williams, I would like you to start at the beginning and tell us everything that happened, your previous association with Mr. Conrad, how you became involved with the investigation, and everything you learned about Mr. Conrad's activities."

I gave him an abbreviated summary, but I elaborated when questioned. My testimony took two days. Judge Schuth asked most of the questions. He eventually asked me a question I wasn't expecting. "Mr. Williams, when did you actually become involved in Clyde Conrad's activities?"

"As I said before, I became involved around April 1987, when CI sent me to Bad Kreuznach."

Judge Schuth raised his eyebrows and said, "But you said in your deposition that Clyde hired you when you were working with him at eighth infantry division."

"Your honor, I can't tell you how it was translated, but what I said was, 'Clyde told me he was going to tell the Hungarians that he had hired me when I worked with him in eighth infantry division because they were concerned about his association with a CI agent. I don't know for sure that he told them that, only that he said he did."

Judge Schuth reached for one of the binders in front of him and opened it at one of several markers. After reading for a few seconds, he turned to each of the other judges and smiled as he nodded his approval of my answer.

Clyde talked periodically to his attorney sitting on his right. He never even acknowledged the one sitting two seats away on his left, until that attorney asked me a question.

"Mr. Williams, how could you even believe him when he told you things like, 'I met with defense ministers of foreign countries?'"

"Sir, actually, at first I didn't believe most of the things he told me, and I told him so several times to get him to offer proof of some of the claims he was making. And he did prove most of his claims. That's why I met the Kercsiks. The fact is I think Clyde made a logical assumption that the man he met was the Hungarian defense minister when everyone in the room, including the head of Hungarian intelligence, stood up as he entered."

As soon as I finished my answer, Clyde stood up from his chair, walked over to the attorney, and whispered in his ear, and then he returned to his chair. The attorney never asked me another question. The chief prosecutor asked the last question.

"Mr. Williams, how did you feel when you learned your friend was a traitor to his country?"

"I felt the way I would feel if my best friend raped my wife." I had anticipated his question. I had decided that no one would understand that I hadn't taken it as a personal affront that Clyde had decided to betray my country and that he didn't even consider it his country. They certainly wouldn't understand that I was still his friend. They would only understand righteous indignation.

To me, Clyde was a friend who had made some incredibly bad decisions that carried serious consequences. I was his friend who never once considered compromising my principles or shunning my sworn duty. I knew Clyde understood that, but I didn't know how to convey it to those who kept expecting an emotional response.

As Clyde's trial proceeded, newspapers in several countries picked up the story. Eventually *ABC News* did a segment on it on Peter Jennings' television show. I heard about the show the following day when the commander of one of my detachments called me to say, "Danny, you've been vindicated," and to assure me he would send me a tape of the show. I wasn't sure what he meant, but I hoped he meant USAI wasn't mad at me any longer about talking to the reporter. I was wrong.

Grant called me later and instructed me to come to his office in Munich. He and Crocker, who had started accompanying him at my last debriefings, were waiting for me. Grant started challenging my claim that, except for Szabo, I had never met any of Clyde's espionage associates before my involvement in the operation.

He told me I had said in court that I had met them much earlier. I suggested that someone probably misheard me. He insisted I had said it, and he wanted to know if I could produce documents to show that I wasn't in Germany at the time in question.

I said I could do that, but they could read that off my military forms 2 and 2-1. When he said he didn't have those, I reminded him they were the personnel documents he had approved for me to give to Clyde and he surely kept copies of them. He finally said, "Danny, your meeting with that reporter has come back to haunt you."

I decided that was the last straw. "So that's what this is all about? Some reporter has repeated what Szabo said Clyde told him about me, and now, after all we've been through, you would believe the reporter's story before you would believe mine? You even want me to do your investigating for you, and you haven't even read me my rights? I have a better solution."

"What's that?"

"I volunteered for this job, didn't I?"

"Yes, you did."

"Good. Then I'm quitting. You can do your own investigating. Don't call me. I'll call you." As I stood to leave, Grant offered a retort.

"You would sign a statement to that effect, Danny?"

351

DAMIAN and MONGOOSE

"Absolutely." I signed a statement dissociating myself from them and left.

No one contacted me about the case until I received a telephone call from a USAEUR attorney stationed in Heidelberg. "First Sergeant Williams, this is Major Pickett. I have a complaint concerning your illegal tapping of the telephone and tape recording of retired Sergeant Conrad. I'm obliged to inform you that I will be conducting an investigation and will prosecute you if the allegations prove true."

I quickly responded. "Major Pickett, I can give you the number of the office that conducted that investigation, but my only involvement was at their direction and in accordance with duly executed warrants issued by a U.S. judge."

"First Sergeant, your name is on the complaint, and you're the one I have to investigate. I can assure you USAEUR won't take this accusation lightly."

"Major, you have to do what you have to do, but you might want to check with the German prosecutor's office in Koblenz. They have the same complaint, and they have rejected it."

"Really? What's this about?"

"Retired Sergeant Conrad is being tried for treason. He has no defense. U.S. counterintelligence investigated the case according to U.S. laws, but the Germans are trying him because he has been living here since his retirement. Their court doesn't accept tape recordings I made of our conversations as evidence, so they haven't used them. I assure you, I did not tap anyone's phone. Sergeant Conrad is trying everything he can think of to discredit the case against him, but no one is buying it. What you do with it is up to you, Sir."

"If that's what this is, I say forget it. Have a nice day, First Sergeant."

"Sounds right to me, Sir. Thank you."

A short time later I received a call from Grant. He said I would be getting another subpoena to testify in Clyde's trial. Clyde had requested me. Grant explained that Szabo's deposition had been admitted into evidence, and Clyde wanted me to help him discredit Szabo. Obviously Clyde knew I would be truthful on the stand.

Shirley sat with the spectators again as I testified. Clyde questioned me personally. He brought up my altercation with Szabo in the field when we were all in the infantry. He asked me to explain what had happened, apparently wanting to paint Szabo as brutal and vindictive. I explained the incident but admitted that I had been out of line when I challenged Szabo's authority, and Szabo had walked away without resorting to violence.

Clyde recalled another incident concerning Szabo, which he believed demonstrated that Szabo had compromised highly classified radio encryption devices. I acknowledged that Clyde had told me that story several months earlier, and I explained that I had not actually been present during the incident in the field several years before.

Judge Schuth asked Clyde what was the purpose of this line of questioning. When Clyde replied, "I just wanted to check his memory," Judge Schuth asked, "You wanted to test *his* memory?"

Clyde's whole line of questioning backfired, because the Judge asked me, "Mr. Williams, what can you tell us to help us decide whether we should believe Mr. Szabo's statements, which we have before us?"

"Your honor, I know nothing about Mr. Szabo's statements. The

353

only thing I can tell you about his truthfulness is what Clyde told me."

"Please do, Mr. Williams."

"When Szabo came to see Clyde at his home, asking for help, he admitted to Clyde that he had told the Hungarians about Clyde's schemes against them. Clyde was surprised that Szabo told him the truth, and Clyde knew exactly what Szabo had told the Hungarians, because Clyde had a friend at the meeting.

"I could also tell you about a similar situation in which Szabo told the truth."

"We'd like to hear it."

"When Szabo was arrested for stealing gas coupons and selling them, he told the investigators exactly what he did and how he had done it, and he seemed ready to accept whatever punishment he received."

Thank you, Mr. Williams. I believe that will be very helpful to us." The other judges nodded in agreement, and I was dismissed and asked to remain in the courthouse.

While other testimony was given, I waited in the lobby outside the courtroom. At lunch break, I stood in the middle of the lobby. Clyde left the courtroom first and passed within two feet of me, shackled hand and foot and accompanied by two guards as he walked toward the men's room. He had his head down as he passed me. I asked him quietly, compassionately, "How are things going for you, Clyde?"

His guards stopped when he stopped. He looked up with a smile and answered, "Things couldn't be better." I nodded, and he proceeded until he disappeared into the men's room at the end of the corridor.

TRIAL

Other people had begun to enter the lobby, and Clyde's attorney, the one he had been ignoring, walked up to me and asked, "What did you ask him?"

"I asked how things were going for him."

"What did he say?"

"He said, 'Things couldn't be better.'"

As the chief prosecutor walked up beside him, Clyde's attorney looked at me, and with some compassion of his own, he said, "And you know, I think he believes that."

I replied sadly, "Oh, he does."

We were joined by others, and I was invited by the German prosecutors and a few U.S. investigators from the States to join them in the court lunchroom. Shirley knew we might be talking shop, so she volunteered to eat lunch in a Gasthaus outside the courthouse. The investigators were eager to inform me of the latest development in the ongoing Conrad investigation.

I learned that Roderick Ramsay, an ex-U.S. Army sergeant and former co-worker of Clyde's, had been in custody for some time. He had recently helped investigators tie down the final loose end in Clyde's case. Ramsay, cooperating to avoid life in prison, had been to Clyde's apartment on the side but couldn't remember how to get there.

Investigators had flown him over the general neighborhood in a helicopter, and he had identified the apartment from the air. They said, "We didn't find anything in the apartment, because Clyde had given it up some time ago, but it was the last thing you told us that needed to be verified."

When everyone had cleared the lunchroom, I found the

lobby outside the courtroom empty except for Clyde, who was standing alone at the end of the wall opposite the courtroom. He was smoking a cigarette and looking out the corner window. He wasn't shackled, and his guards were standing about twenty feet behind me in the corridor. I walked up behind Clyde and engaged him in conversation as if we were still friends.

"I wouldn't jump if I were you, Clyde. It's too far down. You'll break both legs."

He turned around and smiled and said, "You're probably right." He had lost considerable weight, and his hair was almost completely white. I expressed a genuine concern for his health, asking, "Are they treating you well, Clyde?"

"They're treating me all right." Still smiling he said, "I'm not sure we should be talking, Danny."

"You may be right, Clyde. I just wanted to make sure you're okay. Good luck, young man." I offered my hand, which he shook as he responded to my concern for him. "Thanks."

I walked away, believing we were still friends. We both knew Clyde had been true to his nature, I had been true to my principles, and neither of us could escape his destiny. Clyde returned to the courtroom, and I remained until the end of the day, which was the last of his trial.

Before Shirley and I left Koblenz the next morning, I received a call from my battalion commander telling me to start packing for a permanent change of duty station (PCS) as soon as I returned to Stuttgart.

He explained that I would be going TDY to Washington DC en route to my PCS. He didn't say where my PCS would be, and he wouldn't say what I would be doing in DC, only that he would provide TDY orders and USAI would inform me later of my assignment. When Shirley and I returned to Stuttgart, we learned of Clyde's conviction.

Clyde Lee Conrad was convicted of high treason on 6 June 1990 for spying for the Hungarians. He was sentenced to life in prison. He also received a four-year sentence for spying for Czechoslovakia and was fined two million Marks.

In sentencing him, Chief Judge Ferdinand Schuth emphasized Clyde's deadly act of treason saying, "He was willing to kill and torture for money." Judge Schuth said Clyde had "turned over all the classified U.S. and NATO documents, everything, including top secret and cosmic top secret documents, that could have led to a breakdown in the defenses of the Western Alliance and to capitulation and the use of nuclear weapons on German territory."

Shirley and I managed to be ready to leave Germany in less than two weeks. I received TDY orders to DC, and Grant told me I would be met at the DC airport by someone from the Justice Department, who would explain my temporary assignment. I arranged my airline ticket, put our household goods in storage, and bought a ticket for Shirley to visit her parents in Louisiana.

B Company arranged a great farewell party for us, and I said goodbye to some excellent soldiers and agents. My jobs as operations NCO and first sergeant had been as rewarding to me as the undercover assignment had been. Clyde had been right about me. I enjoyed life, especially difficult challenges.

Shirley and I joked about the pettiness, demonstrated by the fact that no further mention had been made of my Legion of Merit supposedly sitting in the brigade commander's desk drawer. The day Shirley and I were to depart, we received an urgent message from my company commander, ordering us to change our airline tickets to two days later.

The USAEUR commander had just learned that I had not received my award. He arranged to personally present my Legion of Merit at the Kaiserslautern Army Theater, with most of 527th MI battalion in attendance. I saw no one from the operation in attendance.

A few members of the operation never conceded any value in my part of the operation, and some continued to suspect me of collusion. Some feeble, almost comical reminders of their discontent came to my attention for several years.

Shortly after my promotion to sergeant major in 1990, I received a call from an INSCOM legal officer while I was assigned as assistant commandant of the Fort Huachuca NCO Academy but continued my duties with the U.S. Justice Department.

The legal officer informed me that he had a request from the German prosecutors office in Koblenz for INSCOM to determine whether it would be appropriate to launch an investigation of Danny Williams for illegally tapping the phone of a civilian in Germany and illegally recording his conversations.

Either he didn't know or he didn't care that the chief prosecutor had already told me that the motion for such an investigation was part of Clyde's appeal and it didn't stand a chance in hell. The INSCOM attorney warned me, "Sergeant Major, the INSCOM commander still has the letter on his desk. He's on leave, and I don't know what he plans to do with it."

I could only speculate as to why he had called me. Because I wasn't intimidated, I asked the attorney to fax me a copy of the letter. When I read it, I realized it was clearly what I thought it was: the German prosecutor's office was following appeal procedure with a courtesy letter to INSCOM.

The second reminder of USAIs continued discontent came a few years later from my friend and former operations officer, Greg Zientek, then the head of CI instruction at Fort Huachuca. Greg informed me of his conversation with a current member of the unit that had run the operation. Not realizing Greg was a friend of mine, the agent commented at the mention of my name, "Everyone knows Williams is dirty."

Though there remains considerable resistance to the value of an undercover insertion of a trained CI agent into an espionage investigation, the merit of that approach was not lost on everyone. An observation was made by the former U.S. assistant chief of staff for intelligence and, more recently, the former director of the National Security Agency (NSA), when he was interviewed by the *Army Times*.

"The Intelligence and Security Command has just done a spectacular job. They proved to have better trade craft than the other side. It's a spectacular success in going after [a spy] rather than waiting until he goes to you or someone turns him in."

In addition to the earlier revelation in Houston that at least one agency actually had changed the way they conduct espionage investigations, I was most gratified by a comment from one agent who had supported the operation, now a retired sergeant major.

"Even if we had never been able to arrest Clyde Conrad, everything you taught us, Danny, would have made the whole operation worthwhile."

The operation also produced what every counterespionage agent wants to see. Extensive investigation by the FBI over the next eight years led to the conviction of more of Clyde's former associates and other spies. Including Clyde, Szabo, the Kercsik brothers, and the Italian, Mortati, nine espionage agents in five countries were convicted as a result of this operation. In some cases, I was called to testify concerning the conspiracy.

Roderick James Ramsay was convicted of espionage in August 1992 and sentenced to thirty-six years in prison by a Florida court. He had delivered hundreds of highly classified documents to Clyde Conrad from 1983 to 1985.

Staff Sergeant Jeffrey Stephen Rondeau, a U.S. Army recruiter stationed in Bangor, Maine, and Staff Sergeant Jeffrey E. Gregory, stationed at Fort Richardson, Alaska, were convicted of espionage in June 1994 for selling military secrets to Hungary and Czechoslovakia through Roderick Ramsay and Clyde Conrad in 1985. Each was sentenced to eighteen years in prison.

Kelly Teresa Warren, former U.S. Army soldier, was convicted in 1998 of conspiracy to commit espionage as part of Clyde Conrad's espionage ring while stationed at 8th infantry division in Bad Kreuznach, West Germany, from 1986 to 1988. She was sentenced to twenty-five years in prison.

Clyde Lee Conrad died in prison of a heart attack on 8 January 1998. When the German prosecutor's office informed USAI that Clyde had died, they provided additional information. During his eight years in prison, Clyde had developed his own little mafia. Interviews by German investigators of some of his prison associates revealed a general skepticism concerning Clyde's reported death. Some explained their doubts with the statement, "Clyde always said he would find a way out of this prison."

9 781604 945164